A

GENEALOGICAL REGISTER

OF THE

DESCENDANTS IN THE MALE LINE

OF

ROBERT DAY,

OF

HARTFORD, CONN.,

WHO DIED IN THE YEAR 1648.

Second Edition.

NORTHAMPTON:
PRINTED BY J. & L. METCALF.
1848.

WITH A SUPPLEMENT GIVING DESCENDANTS OF
CAPTAIN JOHN DAY,
NUMBER 194, WHO MOVED TO SHEFFIELD,
OHIO, IN 1816.

Notice

In many older books, foxing (or discoloration) occurs and, in some instances, print lightens with wear and age. Reprinted books, such as this, often duplicate these flaws, notwithstanding efforts to reduce or eliminate them. The pages of this reprint have been digitally enhanced and, where possible, the flaws eliminated in order to provide clarity of content and a pleasant reading experience.

Originally published:
Northampton:
1848

Reprinted:
Janaway Publishing, Inc.
2011

Janaway Publishing, Inc.
732 Kelsey Ct.
Santa Maria, California 93454
(805) 925-1038
www.janawaygenealogy.com

ISBN: 978-1-59641-244-6

Made in the United States of America

PREFACE

It is now *two hundred years* since ROBERT DAY, one of the early settlers of Hartford, and the ancestor of those whose names are recorded in the following pages, was gathered to his fathers. In presenting therefore to his numerous living descendants, on the second centennial anniversary of his death, this enlarged edition of their Family Register, the intention has been to render it a *commemorative offering*. Scattered as they already are, and every year becoming more widely separated, it has been the hope of the compiler in laboring to preserve the memory of their Puritan lineage, that this Register, borne with them as they leave their fathers' sepulchres, will ever remind them of the obligation they are under, as descendants of the early settlers of New England, to cherish the virtues of their Pilgrim ancestors, and in testimony of their descent to uphold and support wherever they may dwell, *freedom, law, learning* and *religion*.

The small edition of this Register, printed at New Haven in 1840, was not only soon exhausted, but was found to contain, what indeed with the information then had it was impossible to avoid, some serious errors. These, with a considerable number of smaller mistakes, have been corrected and important additions made, by which the number of names is nearly doubled. Still, it is not expected that the present edition will be found entirely free from error. In consequence of the great variety of sources from which information of the kind is gathered, and the defective accuracy of many informants, perfect correctness is probably out of the question. No means, however, have been left unemployed to approximate to it as nearly as possible.

Where the genealogy of any branch has not been followed out, or where dates are wanting, no further information could be obtained. There are some families of whom their nearest surviving relatives have wholly lost sight. The compiler would respectfully request the aid of the family in *supplying the deficiencies which exist*. Although he does not expect to issue another edition of the Register, it is not impossible that a *supplement* containing additions and corrections may hereafter be printed.

The two most prominent changes in the *plan* of the Register consist in denominating what was called the Colchester branch in the former edition the *Hartford* branch, and in reckoning the generations in the running title according to the *parents* instead of the children. The reason of the first mentioned change is that so many of the descendants of John Day (son of Robert) have been traced — and among others the entire Northampton branch — whose ancestors never resided in Colchester, as to render the former designation obviously inappropriate.

A sufficient explanation of the delay which will be experienced before the members of the family will receive their copies, will be found in the necessity of sending proof-sheets to different and distant parts of the country. A few copies extra will be struck off and left at the book store of Mr. Horace Day in New Haven, Conn., and also with Mr. Aaron Day in West Springfield, of either of whom they may be ordered by members of the family who are not supplied, on inclosing (post paid) one dollar, for which one copy will be sent.

In addition to the gentlemen who aided him in the preparation of the first edition, the compiler desires to express his acknowledgements to Mr. Horace H. Day of New York, Mr. James I. Day of New Orleans, and Mr. Thomas D. Day of St. Louis, for their liberal pecuniary aid; also to Mrs. Charles Day and Mr. Guy B. Day of Colchester, to whom the members of that branch are indebted for the careful examination of the Colchester records and tomb-stones; and to Rev. Hiram Day of South Cornwall, Conn., and Mr. Gideon Day of Monson, Mass.

For the valuable additions to the notices of the early settlers of New England of the name of Day, which will be found in the introduction, the family are under obligation to Hon. James Savage, by whose liberality the entire article under that name as it now stands in the manuscript copy of the forthcoming edition of Farmer's Genealogical Register, on which he is now engaged, has been placed in the hands of the compiler. It has certainly been no small privilege, also, in preparing this edition, to be able to refer in cases of difficulty to Sylvester Judd, Esq., of this town, whose wide acquaintance with the history of the Connecticut river valley, and accurate knowledge of the genealogy of the families inhabiting it, have rendered the present Register much more perfect than it would otherwise have been.

GEORGE E. DAY.

NORTHAMPTON, DEC. 25, 1848.

INTRODUCTION

It has been handed down by tradition that the family of Day originally came from Wales. This tradition is undoubtedly correct. In a book of Heraldry, containing the arms of William Day, B.D., Provost of Eton College and Dean of Windsor, confirmed by William Flower, Norroy, on the 21st of October, 1582, in the twenty-fourth year of the reign of Queen Elizabeth, he is said to be "descended from the Dees of Wales, viz. being younger son of Richard Day, who was the son of Nicholas Day, the son of John Dee, (called by the English, Daye.) He was son of Morgan Dee, younger brother to Richard Dee, Welshman."

Dee, signifying, it is said, *dark* or *dingy*, is the name of a small river in Wales, and was probably applied to some ancestor of the family, dwelling upon its banks, in order to distinguish him from others — just as Wickliffe took his name from the village in which he was born — and in time, the word Dee came to be written, according to its apparent sound, Daye or Day. This name, moreover, still prevails in Wales, and is there pronounced as in England and this country.*

Within the first thirty years after the settlement of New England, eight persons of the name of Day are found upon record, viz.:—

1. *Robert*, first of Cambridge, then of Hartford, Conn., who arrived in 1634, and was the ancestor of those whose names are given in the following pages.

2. *Robert* of Ipswich, came over in 1635, in the Hopewell, Capt. Bundock, from London, aged 30: made freeman June 2, 1641, and was living in 1681.

3. *Nathaniel* of Ipswich, in 1637. (Kimball's Eccl. Sermon.)

4. *Stephen* of Cambridge, who is considered by Thomas, in his history of printing, as the first printer in this country. He was brought over by Rev. Mr. Glover, who died on the passage; and begun business in March, 1639. He had probably a wife and family, as the death of a *Stephen* is on the record Dec. 1, 1639, and of *Rebecca* Oct. 17, 1658, presumed to be his son and wife. He died Dec. 22, 1668, aged 58. Thomas, vol. 1, pp. 227-234, gives a

---

* MS letter from Rev. Warren Day of Richmond, N. Y.

catalogue of the books supposed to be printed by him. He was, perhaps, unthrifty, for the press passed into the hands of Green twenty years before Day's death, and Day wrought as a journeyman. Yet he was engaged in the settlement of Lancaster, in 1643, and had received a grant of 300 acres in 1641, for his enterprise.

5. *Wentworth* of Boston, received into the Church Sept. 12, 1640, with prefix of respect, though a single man: member of the Artillery Company in 1640. He was perhaps the surgeon of Cambridge in 1652, who saved a woman accused as a witch: (Hale's Witchcraft, 65.) had *Elizabeth* bapt. Sept. 26, 1641, who died eight days after birth, and a son *Wentworth*, bapt. Aug. 13, 1643.

6. *Ralph* of Dedham, made freeman in 1645, and died Oct. 28, 1677, naming in his will, Sept. 12, his wife *Abigail*, and children *John*, *Ralph*, *Mary* (wife of John Payne,) and *Abigail;* also his son in law John Ruggles. His wife was daughter of Daniel Pond; but his first wife *Susan*, by whom he had four children, was daughter of Jonathan Fairbanks, who in his will, 1668, speaks of her four children, and in the records of Dedham, are found *Elizabeth*, bapt. July 3, 1648, *Mary*, b. Nov. 9, 1649, *Susan*, b. in 1652, and *John*, b. April 15, 1654; followed by *Abigail*, daughter of Ralph and Abigail, b. April 6, 1661. From him are descended the Days in Wrentham, and also it is supposed in Attleborough, Ms. and Killingly, Ct.

7. *Matthew* of Cambridge, a printer, whose name is found in the imprint of Danforth's Almanac for 1647: was steward of Harvard College in 1645: freeman in 1646: died in May, 1649. It is inferred from his will that he had neither wife nor child, because he gave most of his property to his mother, and to elder Frost, £4.

8. *Anthony* of Gloucester, in 1645, had a wife *Susanna* and several children born after 1656. He died April 23, 1707, aged 91; his widow died Dec. 10, 1717, aged 94.

Besides these, there were at a later period, (1.) *John* of Boston, in 1677, a merchant, who died that year. By his will, dated Sept. 4, he gives all his property to his brother Robert of Frome Woodlands, near Warminster in Wilts, close to Somersetshire, and describes himself of the same: (2.) *William* of Boston, in 1669, a mariner.

From these have descended, it is supposed, the greater part of those bearing the name in the United States. There are however a few of the name in Virginia, descended from one or more of the early settlers of that State. There are some also in Newark, N. J. who trace their descent from *George Day*, one of the first settlers of that place. Within the last few years, also, a considerable number have been found, especially in the larger cities, who were born in Great Britain.

GENEALOGY

THE first knowledge we possess of our ancestor, **Robert Day,** commences with his emigration to America, in April, 1634. He was at that time thirty years of age, and was accompanied by his wife *Mary,* aged twenty-eight, as is gathered from the list of passengers of the bark, *Elizabeth,* in which he took passage from Ipswich in England to Boston in New England. He was born therefore about the year 1604. The efforts to trace him beyond this have been unsuccessful, and it is now probable that his parentage and the place of his birth must be to his descendants forever unknown.

On his arrival in this country, he first settled in Newtown, now Cambridge. His wife Mary probably died soon after. He was made freeman May 6, 1635, which shows him to have belonged to some church in the jurisdiction. In 1639, we find him a resident of Hartford, Conn., of which place he was one of the first settlers. As such his name is found on the monument erected to their memory in that city. He was probably in the company of one hundred persons who, with their pastor, Rev. Mr. Hooker, penetrated through the wilderness in 1636.

For his second wife, he married *Editha Stebbins,* sister of Dea. Edward Stebbins (or Stebbing) of Hartford, and had four children, two sons and two daughters, viz:

1. *Thomas:* the ancestor of the Springfield branch.
2. *John:* the ancestor of the Hartford branch.
3. *Sarah:* who married Nathaniel Gunn of Hartford, Sept. 1658; 2d husband, Samuel Kellogg of Hatfield, Nov. 24, 1664. She was slain with her son Joseph, by the Indians, Sept. 19, 1677.
4. *Mary:* who married Samuel Ely of Springfield, Oct. 28, 1659: 2d husband, Thomas Stebbins, April 12, 1694: 3d husband, Dea. John Coleman of Hatfield, Dec. 11, 1696. She died at Hatfield, in 1725, quite aged.

Robert died in Hartford, in 1648, aged 44. From a comparison of the dates of his will,* and of the inventory of his estate, it is evident that his death occurred between May and the middle of October in that year. His widow then married Dea. John Maynard of Hartford, who died without issue shortly after, leaving all his property, which was considerable, to his wife's children, "provided they carried themselves well towards their mother."* For her third husband, she married in 1658, Elizur Holyoke of Springfield,

---

*[*Copy of the Will and Inventory of* ROBERT DAY.—*Colony Records, vol.* 1. *pp.* 255, 6.]

MAY 20th, 1648.

The will of Robert Day hee being sick and weake, yet in perfect memory: doth order and dispose of his estate to his wife and children, in the manner following:

Impr'mis I give vnto my beloued wife Edatha Day my now dwelling howse and howsing thereto adioyning, howse Lott, Allso all my Land whereof I stand possessed, or that of right doth belong vnto mee, lying in Hartford, during the tarme of her naturall life: And at the end of her life, my will is that the said howse and land shall bee deuided in an equall proportion: my will allso is that all my howsehold stuff, and Cattle and other moueable goods shall bee my wiues to bring vp my children: And in case my wife should bee married to another man, then my surviers of my will shall haue power if they thinke good to take security for the bringing vp of the chidren, and for so much estate as shall bee thought meete by them, and to this my last Will and Testament I make my wife my Executrix, and I doe desire my Deare Brethren Mr. Tailecoate, Wilerton, and Stebbing, to take care of and Assist my wife in the ordering her selfe and my children, and I give them power to doe what in their Judgments may bee for the best, to bring vp my Children and dispose of them, and that I leaue, for theire good And to this my will I sett to my hand the day aboue written.

EDWARD STEBBING,   ROBERT DAY.
WALLTER GAYLERD.

14th OCTOBER, 1648.

An Inventory of the Goods of Robert Day deceased.

	£	s.	d.
In the Chamber. Impr. one Bedstead; one feather bed and feather Boulster and flock boulster: 2 pillowes, & bedcase & Curtaines.	07	00	00
Item: 2 blankitts, one red & yellow Couerlitt			
Item: 1 chest 10s: 1 Box 3s: 1 desck box 3s:	00	16	00
Item: 1 table 5s: 1 Cubberd 5s and Chaiers	00	16	00
Item: 3 paier of sheetes	02	00	00
Item: 6 table napkins 12s: 1 table cloth 5s.	00	17	00
Item: 6 pillow beeres	01	10	00
Item: the wearing Clothes with 3 skinns	05	00	00
Item: in Linnen yearne and Cotton wool yearne	01	10	00
Item: 2 Cushins 6s: 1 paire of Bellowes 3s.	00	09	00
Item: 1 Little Baskitt 12d: 1 warming pann 6s.	00	07	00
Item: in working tooles	01	08	00

Mass. grandfather of President Holyoke of Harvard College. To that town she removed with a part of her family, and died there Oct. 24, 1688, having survived her last husband, who died Feb. 6, 1676.

In the Hall. Item: 1 Brass Kettle	02 10 00
Item: 1 Little kettle 12s: 1 little brass kettle	00 15 00
Item: 1 brass possnett (†) 4s: 1 brass pott 16s: 1 Iron pott 14s.	01 14 00
Item: 1 brass Chafin dish 3s: one skimer	00 05 06
Item: 7 pewter dishes, and some broken pewter: 1 saser: 2 pewter potts: 1 Candlestick: 1 salte: 1 small bottle: 6 ockumy (‡) spoons, 2 porringers and 4 old spoones.	01 10 00
Item: I Lattin(§) dripping pann: 1 spitt, 1 pistoll: 1 smoothing Iron	00 10 00
Item: in earthern ware, and wooden ware	00 10 00
Item: 1 muskitt Bandleers(‖) and sword	01 00 00
Item: 1 table and 2 Chaires	00 05 00
In the sellar, Item: in tubbs and Tables and formes	01 00 00
In ye little chamber: It: one flockbed, 2 blankitts: 1 Couerlitt, 1 feather boulster, 2 feather pillows, 2 bedsteads	04 12 00
Item: 3 hogsheads, 2 Linnen wheeles, 1 woolen wheele, one Barrill	00 19 00
Item: 1 table, 1 wheele, 1 hatchett	00 05 00
Item: 1 Leather Bottle 2s: VId: 1 paire of tongs: fier pann, grid Iron: frying pann, one trammell	00 15 00
Item: in Bookes, and Sackes, and Ladders	01 00 00
Item: one Cow: 1 3 yeare ould heifer: one 2 yeare old heifer, with some hay to winter them	14 10 00
Item: 2 hoggs 3£.	03 00 00
Item: in seuerall sortes of Corne with some hemp and flax	15 00 00
Item: the dwelling howse and out howsing, howse lott and Garden.	45 00 00
Item: about 6 Akers of meadow, in severall parcells with vpland	26 00 00
Summa: Totalis	142:13:06

JOHN TAILECOATE
GREGORY WILLTERTON
EDWARD STEBBING:

(†) **Posnet,** a little basin or skillet.
(‡) **Ochimy,** (alchemy) a mixed base metal.
(§) **Latten,** tin, iron plate covered with tin.
(‖) **Bandoleers,** a large leathern belt, thrown over the right shoulder, and hanging under the left arm; worn by ancient musketeers for sustaining their fire arms, and their musket charges, which being put into little wooden cases, and coated with leather, were hung to the number of twelve to each bandoleer.—**Webster.**

In the following register, the descendants of Thomas, the ancestor of the Springfield branch, will first be given, and then of John, the ancestor of the Hartford branch.

To each name a number is attached which it retains under all circumstances and by which it may always be distinguished from every other. For the sake of adding new names not at present known, and also of making it easy to tell at a glance how many children there were in a family, the numbering in each family ordinarily begins with a decimal. In some cases there are still wider gaps. Those known to have died are designated by a star. It is scarcely necessary to mention that b. signifies born; bapt., baptized; d., died, and m., married.

---

*MS letter from Hon. Thomas Day of Hartford.

SPRINGFIELD BRANCH

DESCENDANTS OF THOMAS, SON OF ROBERT

SECOND GENERATION.

1. *Thomas Day, of Springfield, son of Robert, m. Sarah Cooper, daughter of Lieutenant Thomas Cooper, (who was killed when the town was burnt by the Indians,) Oct. 27, 1659, and d. Dec. 27, 1711.† His widow died Nov. 21, 1726. Their children were—

---

†[*Copy of the Will of* THOMAS DAY *of Springfield, proved March* 25, 1712: *Probate Records of the County of Hampshire, vol.* III. *pp.* 269—70.]

1, THOMAS DAY of Springfield, in the County of Hampshire within her Majesty's province of the Massachusetts Bay in New England having by God's good hand of providence unto me attained to old age and being in daily expectation of my dissolution; yet through God's mercy towards me in ye enjoyment of a competent measure of health and in perfect memory, have thought good to make, appoint and constitute, this my last will and testament; hereby abrogating and nulling all other wills and testaments. And first I do give and bequeath my soul to God,, my most merciful Father in Jesus Christ, hoping by ye merit of his Son my Saviour that I shall obtain eternal redemption and the forgiveness of my sins for his sake; and that my departing soul shall be received into the arms of his everlasting mercy, being pardoned by the blood of my most dear Redeemer and Saviour, and sanctified by his Holy Spirit, to enjoy everlasting happiness in the kingdom of glory, forevermore. And my body I do commit to the earth, there to rest till the resurrection at which time I firmly believe I shall obtain resurrection of my dead body and reunion of my immortal soul and so to live with Christ to all eternity.

And as to that portion of outward estate which God hath been pleased to bless me withal, I do hereby dispose of in manner following:

1st. I do give unto Sarah my well-beloved wife, in case she survive and outlive me, the improvement of all my whole estate both lands and movables to be for her comfort and maintainance so long as she shall continue in the estate of widowhood and bear my name, together alsoe with all the income of my estate in my son Jonathan's hand, that so she may be comfortably provided for. And further I do give unto my beloved wife aforesaid one third part of the moveable estate to be at her own dispose, according as she shall see convenient.

2dly. I do give unto my son Thomas Day all my woolen wearing Clothes after my decease together with my best Hatt.

3dly. I do give unto my son Samuel Day my lower lot in the Neck over the Great River, containing two acres more or less and

10. *Thomas* 2d, b. March 23, 1662.
11. *Sarah*, b. June 14, 1664; m. John Burt, Feb. 21, 1683.

---

alsoe one third part of my land in the piece called Ashquenunseck Neck over the Great River aforesaid: moreover one fourth part of the Meadow called the World's End, the whole being ten acres.

4thly. I do give to my son John Day my upper lot in ye Neck containing two acres more or less and one third part of my land in Asquenunseck aforesaid, the whole being twenty three acres and also one fourth part of my land at the place called the World's End aforesaid.

5thly. I do give unto my son Ebenezer Day three acres and a half of land in the plain above End Brook, being the whole of my land in that place: and alsoe four acres of land lying upon the hill lying between the lands of James Warriner, Jun. and William Warriner; only provided that if my son Jonathan Day see cause to pay unto my son Ebenezer Day nine pounds cash within the space of two years after the decease of myself or wife which shall last happen that then the aboves'd four acres of land on the hill shall be his. Further, I do give unto my son Ebenezer one third part of my land in Asquenunseck Neck, he having his choice which side of the lot to take the land; and also one fourth part of my land at the World's End Meadow.

6thly. I do give to my son Jonathan Day six acres of land lying on the back side of my pasture on Garden Brook and one fourth part of my land at ye World's End, he having his choice which side of the land to take it, and alsoe all my rights in the Outward Commons.

7thly. I do give unto my three daughters, Sarah Burt, Mary Mirick and Abigail Warriner, that is to say to each daughter particularly the sum of nine pounds apiece as money to be paid out of the moveables if it hold out so much and what overplus there may happen to be in the moveables more than to pay the daughters their respective portions, to be equally divided among all my children. It is to be understood that all the improveable lands in my estate be improved by my son Jonathan according to covenant and agreement with him so long as either myself or wife shall continue and then the will to take place. And further what moneys shall happen to be in the house at my decease, I give unto my well-beloved wife for her supply and maintenance, if God so order that shee survive and that my funeral charges and what other debts may happen, to be paid out of the estate. And whereas I have twenty six acres of land granted to me on the south side of Agawam River, I do give the same to my two sons Samuel and John Day.

I being very desirous to maintain love and unanimity among my children, if any of them shall go about to break my will, they shall forfeit their respective portions. And I do hereby order and appoint my well-beloved wife executrix and my two sons John Day and John Mirick executors to this my last will and testament. And to the confirmation of these presents I have hereto set my hand and seal this 29th day of May, 1711.

THOMAS DAY.

SPRINGFIELD BRANCH—THIRD GENERATION. 13

12. *Mary, b. Dec. 15, 1666; m. John Merrick, Feb. 11, 1687.
13. *John, b. Feb. 20, 1669; d. Aug. 6, 1670.
14. *Samuel, b. May 20, 1671.
15. *John, b. Sept. 20, 1673.
16. *Ebenezer, b. Feb. 18, 1676; d. June 12, 1676.
17. *Ebenezer, b. Sept. 5, 1677.
18. *Jonathan, b. Aug. 8, 1680.
19. *Abigail, m. Samuel Warriner, Feb. 18, 1703; 2d husband Thomas Miller in 1726, & d. Oct. 6, 1747.

THIRD GENERATION.

10. *Thomas II. m. Elizabeth Merrick of Springfield, Jan. 28, 1685. Children—
20. *Elizabeth, b. Feb. 28, 1687.
21. *Thomas 3d, b. Oct. 23, 1689.
22. *Sarah, b. Sept. 30, 1691.
23. *Ebenezer, b. Aug. 1, 1694.
24. *Jonathan, b. May 20, 1697; d. at East Windsor, Conn. Sept. 21, 1721, aged 25.
25. *Deborah, b. Sept. 14, 1699.
26. *Nathan, b. Nov. 6, 1701.
27. *Samuel, b. 1704.

After the birth of these children, except perhaps the last, he removed from Springfield to Colchester, Conn. and there died Jan. 14, 1729, aged 67. His widow d. Dec. 28, 1743.

14. *Samuel, of West Springfield, son of Thomas I., m. Mary Dumbleton, July 22, 1697, and d. Oct. 19, 1729, aged 58. His widow d. May 17, 1759. Children—

30. *Samuel 2d, b. Oct. 8, 1698.
31. *Josiah, b. March 10, 1701.
32. *Mary, b. Sept. 10, 1703; d. Oct. 24, 1703.
33. *Lydia b. Aug. 2, 1706; m. Miles Morgan, April 0, 1735.
34. *Thomas, b. Aug. 19, 1708.
35. *Mary, b. March 29, 1711; m. Hezekiah Day, (41) Dec. 29, 1744.
36. *Abigail, b. March 17, 1713; m. Timothy Woodbridge of Housatonic, Nov. 23, 1736.
37. *Aaron, b. Aug. 11, 1715.

15. *John, of West Springfield, son of Thomas I. m. Mary Smith of Hadley, March 10, 1697, who d. Feb. 28, 1742, aged 65. They had the following children—

40. *John 2d, b. July 5, 1698.

14   DESCENDANTS OF ROBERT DAY.

41. *Hezekiah, b. Oct. 15, 1700.
42. *Joseph, b. June 24, 1703.
43. *Mary, b. Jan. 20, 1706; m. Benjamin Stebbins of Belchertown, Dec. 17, 1724.
44. *Sarah, b. May 14, 1708; m. Aaron Ashley of Sheffield.
45. *Benjamin, b. Oct. 27, 1710.
46. *Rebecca, b. May 12, 1713; m. Benjamin Stebbins of Northampton, Sept. 26, 1733.
47. *William, b. Oct. 23, 1715.
48. *Elizabeth, b. Jan. 19, 1718; m. —— Hall of Wallingford, Conn.
49. *Thankful, b. Jan. 19, 1721; m. Eldad Taylor of Westfield, Nov. 21, 1742.

For his second wife, he m. Hannah Kent of Hadley, August 27, 1743, and d. Nov. 20, 1752, aged 79.

17. *Ebenezer, of West Springfield, son of Thomas I. m. Mercy Hitchcock, April 18, 1700, and d. Sept. 1, 1763, aged 88. His wife d. Sept. 29, 1761, aged 80. Children—

50. *Ebenezer 2d, b. Oct. 23, 1701.
51. *Mercy, b. Nov. 4, 1703; m. James Ashley. Dec. 30, 1725.
52. *Luke, b. July 2, 1706.
53. *Sarah, b. Nov. 3, 1709; m. Josiah Leonard,† Feb. 25, 1730.
54. *Thankful, b. Dec. 24, 1711.
55. *Timothy, b. June 15, 1714; d. June 24, 1714.
56. *Editha, b. Aug. 20, 1715; m. Caleb Bliss.
57. *Miriam, b. March 4, 1718; m. Reuben Leonard.†
58. *Timothy, b. Sept. 5, 1720.
59. *Caleb, b. Sept. 15, 1723.
60. *Elinor, b. Dec. 10, 1725: m. Jonathan Leonard,† Feb. 24, 1746.

18. *Jonathan, of Springfield, son of Thomas I. m. Mercy Burt, Dec. 2, 1709, and d. July 10, 1712, aged 32. His widow m. John Kilborn, Sept. 26, 1720. Children—

61. *Mercy, b. Dec. 4, 1710; m. John Moore of Kingstown, Sept. 11, 1730.
62. *Jonathan 2d, b. March 3, 1712.

FOURTH GENERATION.

21. *Thomas III. first of Colchester, Conn. and then of Sharon, Conn. to which place he removed, about the year 1755, m. Sarah Barnes, June, 1722, who d. March 29, 1726. For his second wife,

† These three Leonards were brothers.

he m. Mary Wells of Colchester, Feb. 2, 1727, who was b. Jan. 22, 1702. He died in Sharon, Feb. 28, 1772, aged 82. Children—

70. *Tamar, b. Nov. 29, 1727; m. Jonathan Gillett of Sharon, Oct. 18, 1750, and d. June 17, 1807.
71. *Jonathan, b. Aug. 7, 1729; d. Jan. 8, 1763, aged 33.
72. *Abel, b. July 26, 1734; died Dec. 23, 1726.
73. *Jeremiah, b. Jan. 25, 1737.
74. *Israel, b. Jan. 25, 1739; died July 10, 1740.
75. *Sarah, b. June 24, 1742; m. David Downs of Sharon, and d. Dec. 14, 1808.

23. *Ebenezer, of Colchester, Conn. son of Thomas II. m. Sarah ——— who died Oct. 1, 1775. He d. 1751, aged 57. Children—

80. *Silence, b.   m. Isaac Jones, Feb. 28, 1752.
81. *Deborah, b.   m. David Adams.
82. *Samuel, b.
83. *Elizabeth, b.
84. *Sarah, b.   m. John Chamberlain.
85. *Mercy, b.
86. *Miriam, b.

26. *Nathan, of East Windsor, Conn. son of Thomas II. m. Deborah ——— who d. Nov. 11, 1774, aged 72. He d. Dec. 28, 1779, aged 78. Children—

100. *Oliver, b.
101. *Justus. b.
102. *Mary, b.

27. *Samuel, of Colchester, Conn. son of Thomas II. m. Mary ——— who d. Dec. 2, 1773. He d. Aug. 24, 1780, aged 76. Children—
105. *Samuel 2d, b.

30. *Samuel II. of West Springfield, m. Martha Stebbins, Nov. 21, 1728; was deacon of the Congregational church 'in that place, and died in 1773, aged 75. Children—

110. *Martha, b. Oct. 1, 1729; m. Jonathan Kilborn, July 30, 1761.
111. *Lydia, b. Feb. 16, 1732; m.† Joseph Bedortha, May 25, 1750.
112. *Orpha, b. May 21, 1734; m. ——— of Amherst.
113. *Tabitha, b. April 20, 1737; m. Ebenezer Cadwell, Nov. 27, 1764.

---

† The letter m in italics indicates the intention of marriage. In such cases the exact date of the marriage has not been ascertained.

114. *Esther, b. June 13, 1740; d. Aug. 3, 1811, aged 71.
115. *Samuel 3d, b. July 23, 1743.

31. *Josiah, of West Springfield, son of Samuel, m. Elizabeth Bliss, Feb. 25, 1731, who d. Aug. 25, 1739, aged 35. Children—
120. *Moses, b. Jan. 7, 1732; d. Jan. 27, 1742.
121. *Gideon, b. Sept. 17, 1733.
122. *Elizabeth, b. Jan. 31, 1736; m. Seth S. Coburn of Springfield, Nov. 12, 1775.
123. *Aaron, b. June 2, 1738.

For his second wife, he m. Hannah Ingraham, Dec. 24, 1748, and d. Jan. 15, 1770, aged 69.

34 *Thomas, of West Springfield, m. Abigail ——, who d. July 5, 1736. Thomas d. June 15, 1739, aged 31. One child—
125. *Enos, b. May 25, 1736; d. Aug. 19, 1736.

37. *Aaron, son of Samuel, was graduated at Yale College in 1738; m. Sybil Munson of New Haven, Sept. 13, 1741, who d. Oct. 31, 1742. He then m. Susannah Stanley, daughter of Nathaniel Stanley, Esq. of Hartford, Sept. 18, 1745. Children—
130. *Mary Ann, b. Aug. 1746; m. Samuel Curtiss of Southington, and d. about the year 1826.
131. *William, b. May 25, 1748.
132. *Thomas Stanley, b. May 19, 1751.
133. *Horace, b. April, 1754.
134. *Abigail, b. April, 1756; m. in 1778 or 9, Whiting Stanley of Cheshire, and d. Jan. 23, 1827.
135. *Susannah, b. Sept. 1756; d. Sept. 10, 1799.

After the birth of these children, he removed from New Haven to North Haven, and finally to Southington, Conn. where he died, Sept. 9, 1778, aged 63. His widow d. Apr. 1, 1805, aged 88.

40. *John II. of West Springfield, (Ireland Parish,) m. Abigail Bagg, Jan. 2, 1724, and d. March 30, 1751, aged 52. Children—
140. *Abigail, b. Sept. 2, 1724; m. Ebenezer Jones.
141. *Mary, b. Aug. 7, 1726; m. Joseph Ely 3d, Feb. 3, 1749.
142. *John 3d, b. April 23, 1728.
143. *Joel, b. April 6, 1730.
144 *David, b. Jan. 24, 1732.
145. *Jael, b.   d. Aug. 27, 1787, aged 55.
146. *Eunice, b. March 4, 1734; m. Benjamin Eastman.
147. *Sarah, b. March 25, 1736; d. April 15, 1813.
148. *Mercy, b. May 26, 1738; m. William Kendall, Sept. 5, 1765.

CAPT. WILLIAM DAY (47).

(FROM A PAINTING BY COPLEY.)

Given him by the Admiralty of England in honor of his bravery in capturing four French frigates and bringing them into Plymouth Harbor during the French and Indian War.

SPRINGFIELD BRANCH—FOURTH GENERATION. 17

41. *Hezekiah, of West Springfield, (Ireland Parish,) son of John, m. Mary Day, (35) Dec. 29, 1744, and d. Oct. 11, 1778, aged 78. His widow d. Aug. 7, 1780, aged 69. Children—
150. *Mary, b. Aug. 18, 1746; d. Sept. 23, 1763.
151. *Thankful, b. Dec. 30, 1751; m. David Mason.
152. *Elijah, b. June 6, 1754.

42. *Joseph, of West Springfield, (Ireland Parish,) son of John, lived some years at Northfield, Mass. where his three elder children were born; m. Elizabeth Mattoon of Northfield, and d. at Fort Edward, Aug. 14, 1758, aged 55. His widow d. Oct. 13, 1776, aged 58. Children—
160. *Eunice, b. 1733; m. Joel Day, (143) May 17, 1751.
161. *Silence, b. 1736; m. David Day, (144) Feb. 4, 1756.
162. *Lucy, b. 1738; m. Samuel Ely, March 15, 1759.
163. *Eleazer, b. Feb. 22, 1741.
164. *Elizabeth, b. Sept. 22, 1743; m. John Cooley.
165. *Joseph 2d, b. Nov. 20, 1745.
166. *Giles, b. May 24, 1748.
167. *Hannah, b. Nov. 14, 1750; m. Oliver Leonard, Oct. 10, 1771.
168. *Jacob, b. Aug. 4, 1753.
169. *Asa, b. Dec. 14, 1755; died young.
170. *Zebulon, b. June 17, 1757; died young.

45. *Col. Benjamin, of West Springfield, son of John, m. Eunice Morgan, Oct. 9, 1742, who d. Jan. 25, 1765, aged 49. Children—
180. *Eunice, b. July 16, 1743; m. Elijah White of Bolton, Nov. 7, 1770.
181. *Benjamin, b. Feb. 23, 1746; d. Sept. 25, 1746.
182. *Benjamin 2d, b. April 23, 1747.
183. *Daniel, b. July 8, 1749.
184. *Robert, b. Aug. 16, 1751; d. Aug. 29, 1751.
185. *Mahala, b. July 31, 1752; d. Sept. 18, 1754.
186. *Heman, b. Jan. 27, 1755.
187. *Mahala, b. June 30, 1757; m. Solomon Stebbins, Dec. 20, 1785.
188. Lydia, b. Nov. 1, 1759; m. Henry Dwight, Sept. 12, 1791.
189. *Clarissa, b. June 18, 1764; m. David Smith of South Hadley, Dec. 23, 1788.

He m. for his second wife Lucy Sheldon of Deerfield, who d. April 28, 1808, aged 82. He died May 10, 1808, aged 97.

47. *William, of Sheffield, Mass., son of John, was for many years engaged in the sea-faring business and had the command of various vessels. He was married three times: first to Polly, daughter of Col. John Day of Boston, about 1746 or 7, who d. in

Jamaica. about 1755: next to widow Eunice Ingersoll of Westfield, by whom he had no issue: and for his third wife to Rhoda Hubbell of Litchfield, Conn. who d. July 25, 1795. He died at Sheffield, March 22, 1797, aged 83. Children—

190. *William, b. about 1730.
191. *William Junius, b. 1748.
192. *Polly, b. about 1749; and d. in Liverpool, aged 8.
193. Mary, b. April 26, 1772; m. Henry Root of Sheffield, Ohio, Sept. 10, 1800.
194. *John, b. Feb. 3, 1774.
195. Ithamar H., b. Aug. 14, 1776.
196. James, b. June 7, 1780.
197. *William, b. March 8, 1787.

50. *Ebenezer II. of West Springfield, m. Mary Smith, April 23, 1724, who d. Dec. 6, 1748, aged 47. Children—
199. *Ruth, b. March 4, 1725; m. Joseph Taylor of Springfield, Nov. 12, 1746.
200. *Mary, b. Nov. 24, 1726; m. Nathan Morgan, June 14, 1759.
201. *Ebenezer 3d, b. Sept. 9, 1728
202. *Margaret, b. April 10, 1730; m. David Smith.
203. *Ezekiel, b. May 9, 1732.
204. *Esther, b. Feb. 20, 1734; m. Eldad Taylor of Westfield, Aug. 15, 1754.
205. *Asaph, b. Jan. 22, 1736; died young.
206. *Asaph, b. Oct. 18, 1739; d. Sept. 24, 1751.
207. *Submit, b. Aug. 28, 1743; died young.
208. *Submit, b. June 6, 1745; died young.

For his second wife, he m. Rachel Morgan, who d. Nov. 11, 1773. He d. Sept. 1, 1763, aged 62.

52. *Luke, of West Springfield, son of Ebenezer I. m. Jerusha Skinner of Windsor, Nov. 9, 1734, & d. in 1791 or 2. Children—
210. *Jerusha, b. Feb. 8, 1736; m. Aaron Smith, Jan. 1, 1755.
211. *Lucy, b. Feb. 3, 1737; m. Isaac Morgan, Feb. 23, 1757.
212. *Luke 2d, b. July 21, 1743.
213. *Thomas, b. Oct. 27, 1745.
214. *Naomi, b. Feb. 4, 1747; m. Nathaniel Gaylord, Nov. 29, 1770.
215. *Martha, b. April 24, 1753; m. Justin Morgan, Oct. 29, 1774.
216. *Simon, b. Oct. 4, 1759; d. Oct. 23, 1759.

For his second wife, he m. Mercy Dewey of Westfield, Dec. 5, 1776.

58. *Timothy, of West Springfield, son of Ebenezer I. m. Sarah Mun of Deerfield, Feb. 6, 1747, and d. Sept. 29, 1797, aged 77. His widow d. Oct. 4, 1800, aged 76. Children—

SPRINGFIELD BRANCH—FIFTH GENERATION. 19

220. *Sarah, b. June 24, 1748; m. Giles Day, (166) Sept. 25, 1774.
221. *Timothy, b. March 13, 1750.
222. *Roswell, b. Sept. 2, 1752; lived in Granby, Conn.; m. Lucy Atchinson, July 2, 1776; no children.
223. *Lewis, b. July 19, 1754.
224. *Thankful, b. Aug. 10, 1756; m. Elisha Farnam, June 23, 1783.
225. *Asa, b. Nov. 19, 1759; slain by the Indians in an ambush, at Stone Arabia, (Johnstown) on the Mohawk, in the Revolutionary war, Oct. 19, 1780, aged 21.
226. *Rebecca, b. Aug. 20, 1761; m. Henry Rogers, June 12, 1788.
227. *Edmund, b. Jan. 17, 1767.

59. *Caleb, of West Springfield, (Agawam Parish,) son of Ebenezer I. m. Mary Jones, Feb. 13, 1744. One child—

229. *Mary, b. Dec. 23, 1744; d. Feb. 20, 1745.

For his second wife he m. Rebecca Ward of Southwick, June 16, 1782; and died in the winter of 1798-9, aged 75.

62. *Jonathan II. of Springfield, m. Hannah Bliss, Jan. 8, 1732, and d. of the small pox, Dec. 3, 1760, aged 63. His widow d. July 2, 1800, aged 86. Children—

230. *Hannah, b. March 13, 1733; m. Ebenezer Stebbins, June 13, 1754.
231. *Mercy, b. Feb. 4, 1735; m. John Fox of Wethersfield, Oct. 13, 1757.
232. *Jonathan, b. April 22, 1737.
233. *Mary, b. Oct. 23, 1739.
234. *Sarah, b. March 6, 1742; d. of small pox, Dec. 5, 1760.
235. *Joel, b. July 16, 1747.
236. *Abner, b. Oct. 17, 1749.
237. *Lovisa, b. March 15, 1752.
238. *Nancy, b. Aug. 9, 1754.
239. *Lois, b. July 2, 1759.

FIFTH GENERATION.

73. *Rev. Jeremiah Day, of New Preston, Conn. son of Thomas 3d, was graduated at Yale College, in 1756; m. Sarah Mills of Kent, who d. August, 1767; settled in Sharon, Conn. which town he represented in the General Assembly, Oct. 1766 and May 1767; was ordained Pastor of the Congregational Church in New Preston, Jan. 31, 1770. In the autumn of 1770, he m. Lucy Wood of Danbury, who d. Aug. 1771. For his third wife he m. Abigail, widow of Rev. Sylvanus Osborn of East Greenwich, (now Warren,) and daughter of Stephen Noble of New Milford, Oct. 7, 1772. who d.

June, 1810. He d. Sept. 12, 1806, aged 69.† Children—
240. *Mills, b. Aug. 13, 1767; d. Nov. 9, 1770.
241. Jeremiah, b. Aug. 3, 1773.
242. Thomas, b. July 6, 1777.
243. Noble, b. May 20, 1779.
244. *Sarah, b. Dec. 9, 1781; d. Dec. 31, 1782.
245. *Mills, b. Sept. 30, 1783; was graduated at Yale College, in 1803; and d. while Tutor there, June 20, 1812.

101. *Justus, of East Windsor, Conn. son of Nathan, m. Mary Wells of Colchester, who was b. Oct. 29, 1746. After the birth of one child, he died.

105. Samuel II. of Colchester, m. Elizabeth ——— of Hebron. Children—
260. Charles Whiting, bapt. April 20, 1779.
261. ——— ———, a son bapt.   1780.

115. *Samuel III. first of Wilbraham, Mass. then of Adams, Mass. and afterwards of ———, N. Y.; m. Lois Merrick of Wilbraham. Children—
270. Samuel 4th, b. Feb. 22, 1764.
271. Roxanna, b.   m. Jason Parker of Utica.
272. *Winston, b.
273. Liberty, b. Jan. 16, 1775.
274. Lois, b.
275. Martha, b.

121. *Gideon, son of Josiah, resided several years in West Springfield, but afterwards removed to Westfield, Mass.; m. Elizabeth Duncan, Dec. 9, 1762. Children—
280. *Moses, b. Oct. 25, 1763.
281. Jemina, b. Sept. 24, 1765; m. Peter Rose of Granville.
282. Ambrose, b. July 7, 1767.
283. Asenath, b. Feb. 24, 1771.
284. Electa, b. July 13, 1773; m. Gaius Searls.
285. *Martin, b. March 22, 1777.
286. Calvin, b. March 19, 1779.
287. *Gideon Bliss, b. Feb. 8, 1781; died young.

123. *Aaron, of West Springfield, son of Josiah, m. Eunice Bliss of Longmeadow, Feb. 22, 1775, who d. Dec. 6, 1818, aged 79. He d. Jan. 17, 1827, aged 89. Children—

† For obituary notice, see Conn. Evangelical Magazine, vol. 7, pp. 217—216.

SPRINGFIELD BRANCH—FIFTH GENERATION.

290. *Eunice*, b. Jan. 15, 1776; m. Gad Bliss of Longmeadow, Sept. 8, 1817.
291. *Aaron, b. Oct. 23, 1777; d. Sept. 25, 1779.
292. *Aaron* 2d, b. Sept. 14, 1780.
293. *Gad*, b. April 21, 1784.

131. William, son of Aaron, lived first in North Haven, Conn. where he m. Lois Ives; then in Great Barrington, Mass. and removed about the year 1810 to——, Chenango Co. N. Y. Children—
300. *Joseph*, b. Dec. 29, 1777.
301. *William*, b. March 27, 1784.
302. *Mary*, b. m. —— Pixley.
303. *Aaron*, b.
304. *Nancy*, b.
305. *Clarissa*, b.

132. *Thomas Stanley, of Avon, Conn. son of Aaron, m. Ruth Newell of Southington, Dec. 1774, who d. Oct. 12, 1840, aged 85. He d. Oct. 12, 1837, aged 86. Children—
310. *Erastus*, b. Oct. 1, 1775.
311. *Newell*, b. Jan. 3, 1778.
312. *Ruth, b. Feb. 3, 1781; d. Feb. 27. 1782.
313. *Julia*, b. Aug. 6, 1783; m. Roger Woodford of Avon.
314. *Marcus*, of Avon, b. March 21, 1787; m. Almira Hart of that place.
315. *Wareham*, b. March 19, 1790.
316. *Stanley, b. Aug. 25, 1792.

133. *Horace, son of Aaron, m. Mary Ferguson, Dec. 26, 1781; lived first in Southington, then in Berlin, (Kensington Parish,) Conn. where he died in the autumn of 1812. His wife died in less than a week after her husband. Children—
320. *Horace* 2d, b. Oct. 19, 1782.
321. *Curtiss, b. April 6, 1785.
322. *Sophia*, b. April 29, 1787.
323. *Murray, b. Sept. 7, 1790; d. April 8, 1793.
324. *Pamela*, b. April 22, 1792.
325. *Samuel Murray, b. Feb. 26, 1798; d.
326. *William, b. April 30, 1800; d.

142. *John III. of West Springfield, (Ireland Parish,) m. Rhoda Chapin, June 1, 1758, and d. Nov. 21, 1810, aged 82. His widow d. Aug. 9, 1817, aged 80. Children—
340. *Rhoda*, b. Feb. 10, 1759; m. Justin Day, (370) Feb. 16, 1788.
341. *Thankful*, b. April 14, 1761; m. Ithamar Jones, Feb. 21, 1787. .

342. *Abigail*, b. Aug. 24, 1763; m. Samuel White of Granby, March 12, 1801.
343. *Chloe*, b. Jan. 27, 1766; m. Moses Ely, March 9, 1787.
344. *John* 4th, b. Dec. 20, 1767; drowned, Oct. 15, 1787.
345. *Sarah*, b. Feb. 2, 1770; m. Daniel White, Jr. Dec. 17, 1801.
346. *Catharine*, b. June 14, 1772; m. ———— Pomeroy.
347. *Mary*, b. Oct. 22, 1774.
348. *Asenath*, b. Oct. 2, 1777; d. Oct. 17, 1796.

143. *Joel, of West Springfield, (Ireland Parish,) son of John 2d, m. Eunice Day, (160) May 17, 1751, and d. Feb. 14, 1803, aged 73. His widow d. Dec. 29, 1815, aged 81. Children—
350. *Joel* 2d, b. 1751.
351. *Tryphena*, b. Feb. 14, 1753; m. Oliver Bagg, Aug. 12, 1783.
352. *Jedediah*, b. March 7, 1755.
353. *Zervia*, b. March 19, 1757; died young.
354. *Edward*, b. Jan. 6, 1759; d. at Troy, Oct. 25, 1777, while serving in the Revolutionary army, aged 20.
355. *Eli*, b. April 12, 1761.
356. *Zervia*, b. Jan. 19, 1763; died young.
357. *Robert*, b. 1764; d. Aug. 27, 1777, aged 13.
358. *James*.
359. *Alexander*, b. Oct. 5, 1769.
360. *Eunice*, m. Abraham Ives, Jan. 22, 1795.
361. *Lucy*, m. Jube Ely, Dec. 1808.

144. *David, son of John 2d, m. Silence Day (161) Feb. 4, 1756, and after the birth of the following children, removed from West Springfield, (Ireland Parish,) to Essex, Vt. where he died, June, 1795, aged 63.—His widow died in Louisville, N. Y. in 1807, aged 51. Children—
370. *Justin*, b. Jan. 10, 1757.
371. *David* 2d, b. May 2, 1758.
372. *Asa*, b. 1760.
373. *Nathaniel*, b. 1762; drowned in Lake Champlain in 1785.
374. *Roderic*, b. 1764; m. Esther Patterill, in 1792; lived in Essex, Vt. till about 1834 or 5, then removed to Cambridge and died there without issue, Jan. 15, 1842.
375. *Horace*, b. 1766; d. unmarried in 1810.
376. *Hezekiah*, b. 1768.
377. *Edward*, b. 1772; of Louisville.

152. *Elijah, of West Springfield, son of Hezekiah, m. Polly Leonard; was a Lieutenant in the Revolutionary Army, and d. in Delaware Co. N. Y. in 1799, aged 45. Children—
380. *Polly*, b.
381. *Sidney*, b.

SPRINGFIELD BRANCH—FIFTH GENERATION.   23

163. *Eleazer, of West Springfield, (Ireland Parish,) son of Joseph, m. Martha Snow, Dec. 10, 1765, and d. June 9, 1825, aged 84 His wife d. June 7, 1809, aged 65. Children—
400. *Brigham, b. May 20, 1767.
401. *Zebulon, b. April 18, 1769; d. Nov. 30, 1769.
402. Patty, b. Nov. 1, 1770; m. Oliver Ely of Warren, N. Y.
403. Elizabeth, b. July 2, 1773; m. Jacob Bradley of Warren, N. Y, Oct. 11, 1791.
404. *Eleazer Mattoon, b. Nov. 1, 1777.
405. Hosea, b. June 20, 1779.
406. Charlotte, b. April 26, 1781; m. John D. Ely, Dec. 4, 1813.

165. *Joseph II. of West Springfield, (Ireland Parish,) m. Azubah Adams, Nov. 20, 1771, who d. Dec. 11, 1786, aged 37. For his second wife, he m. Lois Lyman of Northampton, Nov. 21, 1788, and d. March 19, 1813, aged 77. Children—
410. Azubah, b.   m. Julius Morgan of Hinsdale, Ms.
411. *Joseph 3d, b. Feb.   1773.
412. *Hannah, b. Nov. 2, 1777; m. Hosea Day, (405) July 4, 1805.
413. *Sylvester, b. Nov. 10, 1779.
414. Keziah, b.

166. *Giles, of Marlborough, Vt. to which place he removed from West Springfield, in 1781, m. Sarah Day, (220) Sept. 25, 1774, who d. Nov. 12, 1825, aged 77. He d. Aug. 31, 1795, aged 47. Children—
420. Aribut, b. Jan. 31, 1775.
421. *Solomon, b. Dec. 20, 1776; d. July 24, 1778.
422. *Sarah, b. June 12, 1778.
423. Solomon, b. June 3, 1780.
424. Roswell, b. Nov. 10, 1781.
425. Sarah, b. June 12, 1782; m. Erastus Thomas of Canada.
426. Giles 2d, b. Feb. 13, 1784.
427. Meroy, b. May 20, 1785; m. Moses Ely, Jr. Feb. 28, 1825.
428. Zebulon, b. Jan. 19, 1787.
429. Phebe, b. Jan. 20, 1789; m. Jedediah Day, (372) March 4, 1824.
430. Lucy, b. Aug. 13, 1791; m. Nicholas Groesbeck of Searsborough, Vt.

168. *Jacob, son of Joseph, m. Abigail Leonard, Aug. 20, 1778; about the year 1803, removed from West Springfield to Chester, Mass. and afterwards to Moravia, N. Y. where he died Sept. 5, 1816, aged 63. His wife, who was born Aug. 3, 1755, died in Chester, March 5, 1814. Children—

440. *Rowland*, b. March 6, 1779.
441. *Lucy Ely*, b. Nov. 6, 1780; d. May 1, 1786.
442. *Hervey*, b. July 3, 1783.
443. *Lucy Ely*, b. June 25, 1786; m. John Leonard, April 4, 1814.
444. *Jacob 2d*, b. May 6, 1791.
445. *Abigail*, b. Aug. 13, 1793; m. Charles Shepherd of Canandaigua, N. Y.
446. *John Franklin*, b. July 27, 1795.
447. *Samuel Ely*, b. March 5, 1798.
448. *Anna Noble*, b. April 22, 1803.

182. *Benjamin II.* of West Springfield, was graduated at Yale College in 1768; m. Sarah Dwight of Springfield, July 16, 1772, and d. March 24, 1794, aged 47. His wife d. June 11, 1785, aged 33. Children—
450. *Henry*, b. March 23, 1773.
451. *Sarah*, b. 1778; d. in infancy.

183.*Daniel*, of West Springfield, son of Col. Benjamin, m. Anna Vanhorne, March 3, 1773, who d. Jan. 27, 1787. Children—
460. *Erastus*, b. 1773.
461. *Harriet*, b. May 1776; m. Mather Shepherd.
462. *Daniel 2d*, b. March 30, 1779.
463. *Alfred*, b. June 26, 1783.

For his second wife, he m. Abi Granger, May 18, 1788, and d. Aug. 9, 1825, aged 74. Children—
464. *Anna*, b. June 15, 1789; m. Sylvanus G. Morley of Westfield, Dec. 1814.
465. *Abi*, b. July 15, 1792; m. Horace Osborn, Dec. 9, 1817.
466. *Lucy*, b. Aug. 22, 1794; m. Thomas Taylor of Pittsfield.
467. *David*, b. Oct. 27, 1797.
468. *Alfred*, first of Pittsfield, now of Leyden, N. Y., b. Sept. 22, 1802, m. Margaret Gaylord, Dec. 1826; without issue.

186. *Heman*, of West Springfield, son of Col. Benjamin, m. Lois Ely, and d. Jan. 9, 1837, aged 82. His wife d. July 29, 1819, aged 60. Children—
470. *Henry*, b. Dec. 22, 1779.
471. *Laura*, b. Aug. 15, 1781; d. March 18, 1842.
472. *Rodney*, b. Feb. 23, 1783.
473. *Robert*, b. July 29, 1785; d. Dec. 13, 1839.
474. *Sarah*, b. Aug. 12, 1788.
475. *Benjamin*, b. Nov. 9, 1790.
476. Twins. { *Heman*, b. May 5, 1793.
477. { *Lydia*, b. May 5, 1793; m. Julius White of Bolton, Conn.; d. June 12, 1839.

ITHAMAR H. DAY (195).

478. *Harriet*, b. Oct. 30, 1797; m. Daniel G. White, March, 1830.
479. *Frances*, b. June 8, 1800.

190. *William, of West Springfield, son of Capt. William, m. Lucretia Sackett, Oct. 25, 1759. Children—
480. *Lucretia*, b. 1760; m. Joel Day, (370)
481. **Richard*, b. Feb. 1, 1762; removed to Canada and left a family there.
482. **William*, b. Feb. 10, 1764.
483. **Frederick*, b. Dec. 6, 1766; d. in the West Indies.
484. *Cynthia*, b. May 4, 1769; m. George Hunt, May 17, 1786, and afterwards, ——— Thayer.

191. *Willam Junius, son of Capt. William, m. Susanna Cother of Boston, where he d. about 1785, leaving a wife and three children, viz.:
490. **William*, b. 1780; supposed to have died in Maine, in 1804 or 5.
491. *Susan*, b.
492. **Elijah*, b. d. in childhood.

194. *John, son of Capt. William, removed in 1816 to Sheffield, Ohio; m. Lydia Austin of Sheffield, Mass. in 1794, and d. Oct. 8, 1827. Children—
500. **Rhoda*, b. Nov. 26, 1794; d. Nov. 24, 1795.
501. *William*, b. Dec. 15, 1796.
502. *Rhoda Maria*, b. March 29, 1799; d. Oct. 10, 1825.
503. *John* 2d, b. March 23, 1801.
504. *Norman*, b. Jan. 24, 1803.
505. *Fanny*, b. April 3, 1805; m. William H. Root of Sheffield, O. April 15, 1834.
506. *James*, b. Aug. 27, 1807.
507. *Lydia*, b. March 5, 1810; m. Kendrick K. Kinney of Oberlin, Sept. 17, 1840.
508. *Kellogg*, b. Jan. 23, 1813.
509. **Frederick*, b. Feb. 12, 1815.
510. *Edmund*, b. Feb. 24, 1818.
511. *Eleanor*, b. July 13, 1820; m. James Austin of Sheffield, April 3, 1840.

195. Ithamar H. of Hull, Canada, East, son of Capt. William, m. Laura Dewey of Sheffield, Mass. in 1792, who d. Sept. 15, 1844.
515. *Charles Dewey*, b. May 6, 1806.
516. *Camilla Catharine*, b.
517. *Sophia Eleanor*, b.

196. James, of New London, Conn., son of Capt. William, m. Hannah Hinman of that place, May 10, 1811. Children—

520. *James Ingersoll*, b. March 5, 1812.
521. *Abigail Hinman*, b. June 9, 1813; m. John P. Brown of Medway, S. C.
522. *Mary Sherwood,* } Twins, b. Nov. 28, 1814. d. Aug. 1815.
523. *William,*
524. *Thomas Davis*, of St. Louis, Mo., b. June 27, 1820.

197. *William, son of Capt. William, m. widow Sally Curtis of Sheffield, Mass. who d. in 1820. After his wife's death, he removed to New Orleans and died there, April 6, 1821. Children—
530. *Robert, b. Sept. 17, 1808; of Bayou Mason, La.; d. Aug. 1847, leaving three children.
531. *Charles*, b. about 1814; of Springfield, Ill.; has three children.
532. *Sophia*, b. about 1817; m. Dr. S. G. Cloud of Bayou Mason, La.

201. *Ebenezer III. of West Springfield, m. Martha Ingraham of Springfield, Dec. 21, 1758, and d. Nov. 3, 1805, aged 77. His wife d. Sept. 13, 1791, aged 54. Children—
540. *Asaph*, b. April 14, 1760; d. Nov. 21, 1768.
541. *Hannah*, b. May 25, 1761; m. Samuel Alvord, May 13, 1784.
542. *Ebenezer* 4th, b. July 9, 1764; d. Nov. 26, 1768.
543. *Martha*, b. May 4, 1766; m. George Chapin of Springfield, Feb. 22, 1792.
544. *Anne*, b. May 31, 1770; m. John Stiles of Westfield, Nov. 6, 1806.
545. *Eunice*, b. Oct. 4, 1775; died young.
546. *Sylvia*, b. March 6, 1777; m. Jonathan Bedortha, Feb. 22, 1796.

203. *Ezekiel, of West Springfield, son of Ebenezer 2d, m. Catharine Gaylord of South Hadley, Dec. 22, 1762, and d. April 28, 1805, aged 73. His widow d. Sept. 28, 1824, aged 88. Children—
550. *Submit*, b. Nov. 25, 1763; m. Moses Ashley, Jan. 28, 1799.
551. *Catharine*, b. Oct. 19, 1765; m. Joseph Ashley, May 28, 1789.
552. *Mercy*, b. Feb. 21, 1769; d. Oct. 8, 1769.
553. *Ezekiel* 2d, b. Jan. 25, 1771.
554. *Mercy*, b. Aug. 27, 1776; m. Ezekiel Porter of Westfield, Jan. 31, 1810.
555. *Justin*, b. July 21, 1780.
556. *Amanda*, b. March 20, 1783; m. Isaac Carter of Louville, N. Y. March 6, 1820.

212. *Luke II. of West Springfield, m. Lydia Kelsey of Westfield, Aug. 20, 1762, and d. June 1, 1801, aged 58. Children—
560. *Luke*, b. May 19, 1763; d. June 7, 1763.
561. *Luke*, b. July 3, 1764; died young.
562. *Stephen*, b. April 6, 1766.

CAPT. JAMES DAY (196).

Who wrecked his ship off Point Judith to escape a British frigate during the War of 1812. Taken from a historical painting by Daniel Huntington of New York City.

SPRINGFIELD BRANCH—FIFTH GENERATION.

563. *Simon, b. March 26, 1768; d. May 5, 1768.
564. Lydia, b. April 15, 1769; m. Alexander Cooley, Dec. 21, 1786.
565. *Horace, b. May 11, 1772.
566. *Kelsey, b. Sept. 12, 1776.
567. Luke 3d, b. April 5, 1779.

213. *Thomas, of West Springfield, son of Luke I., m. Johanna Noble of Westfield, Sept. 12, 1767. Children—
570. Johanna, b. Jan. 14, 1769; m. David Ely, Oct. 15, 1788.
571. Sophia, b. Feb. 1771; m. Israel Williston, Dec. 17, 1788.
572. Thomas 2d, b. Oct. 22, 1772; resides in Hopkinton, St. Lawrence Co. N. Y., and has several children.
573. *Electa, b. Nov. 13, 1774; died young.
574. *Jerusha, b. Aug. 27, 1776; m. Solomon Ely, Feb. 1796, and died soon after.
575. Roxanna, b. Aug. 17, 1780; m. Solomon Ely, March 1, 1799.
576. *Noble, b. June 7, 1782.

221. *Timothy II. first of Granby, and then of Otis, Mass.; m. Eunice Hale of Longmeadow, Jan. 29, 1778, who d. Aug. 9, 1811. For his second wife, he m. ——— ———, Feb. 1812, and d. June 22, 1829, aged 79. Children—
580. Linus, b. Nov. 13, 1778.
581. Asa, b. Jan. 20, 1781.
582. *Noah Hale, b. April 26, 1783; d. unmarried, at Deerfield, O., June 12, 1810.
583. *Flavia, b. Aug. 14, 1785; died young.
584. Flavia, b. Oct. 2, 1789; m. Linus Gillett, Nov. 24, 1808.
585. *Timothy III, b. Apr. 26, 1791.
586. *Bliss, b. March 21, 1793.

223. *Lewis, son of Timothy, removed to Deerfield, Portage Co. Ohio, in the year 1800; m. Sebra Ward, Nov. 28, 1778, who died almost instantly from the sting of a wasp, Sept. 25, 1823, aged 68. He d. Feb. 17, 1847, aged 92 years and 7 months.
590. Horatio, b. June 19, 1779.
591. Alva, b. Feb. 7, 1781.
592. Mun, b. Sept. 9, 1783.
593. *Seth, b. Sept. 27, 1785.
594. *Lewis 2d, b. Sept. 21, 1787.
595. Solomon, b. Feb. 12, 1790.
596. *Sebra, b. Nov. 17, 1791; d. Sept. 5, 1793.
597. Sebra, b. July 1, 1794; m. Peter Mason, Dec. 24, 1810.

227. *Edmund, of West Springfield, son of Timothy, m. Bede Hitchcock, Jan. 16, 1794, and d. Sept. 2, 1831, aged 64. Children—
600. Adah, b. Nov. 10, 1794; m. Orrin Loomis, Jan. 1, 1817.

601. *Bede,* b.   m. Cyrus Leonard, Dec. 4, 1817.
602. *Julius,* b. May 10, 1797.
603. *Harriet,* b. March 23, 1799; m. Leonard Parmelee, April, 1818.
604. *Sarah Mun,* b. Dec. 17, 1800; m. Justus Bagg, June, 1826.
605. *Edmund* 2d, b. Oct. 27, 1802.
606. *Maria,* b. June 28, 1804; d. Aug. 25, 1828.
607. *Diadema,* b. March 22, 1806; m. Daniel Ashley, Jan. 1830.
608. *Ralph,* b. Feb. 21, 1808; m. Sophronia Yeomans, resides in Springfield; has no children.
609. *Julia Ann,* b. Feb. 24, 1811; d. Jan. 15, 1830.
610. *Lucy,* b. 1812; d. Aug. 28, 1814.
611. *Henry Lewis,* b. Dec. 22, 1814.

235. *Joel, of Springfield, son of Jonathan 2d, m. Mercy Chapin, May 10, 1775, and d. Oct. 8, 1797, aged 50. His widow d. April 9, 1814, aged 64. Children—
620. *Aminta,* b. Dec. 7, 1775; m. Daniel Holmes of Kingston, March 21, 1801; d. Jan. 12, 1811.
621. *Jonathan,* b. Dec. 24, 1777; d. Sept. 6, 1799, aged 21.
622. *Joel* 2d, b. Dec. 20, 1779; d. Sept. 4, 1802.
623. *Isaac Chapin,* b. July 31, 1782; d. Aug. 4, 1782.
624. *Mercy,* b. Sept. 28, 1783; died young.
625. *Lucy,* b. Aug. 24, 1785; m. William Chapin of Springfield, April 12, 1804.
626. *Isaac Chapin,* b. June 27, 1788; d. May 5, 1817.
627. *Mercy,* b. April 7, 1791; m. Daniel Holmes, Aug. 26, 1816.
628. *Norman,* b. May 20, 1795; d. Sept. 6, 1796.

236. *Abner, of Springfield, son of Jonathan 2d, m. Tryphena Steele, Sept. 21, 1777, and d. June 3, 1804, aged 56. Children—
630. *Abner* 2d, b. May 4, 1778.
631. *Sarah,* b. April 7, 1780.
632. *Deodatus,* b. May 20, 1782.
633. *Hannah,* b. Aug. 25, 1784.
634. *Lovina,* b. Nov. 14, 1786.
635. *Tryphena,* b. April 14, 1788.
636. *Squire,* b. June 9, 1792.

SIXTH GENERATION.

241. Rev. Jeremiah Day, D.D., LL.D., of New Haven, Conn., son of Rev. Jeremiah, was graduated at Yale College in 1795; in 1796, elected Tutor in Williams College, and in 1798, in Yale College; in 1801, Professor of Mathematics and Natural Philosophy, Y. C.; from 1817 to 1846, President of Yale College; m. Martha Sher-

man, daughter of Hon. Roger Sherman of New Haven, Jan. 1805, who d. April 4, 1806, aged 26. For his second wife, he m. Olivia Jones of Hartford, Sept. 24, 1811. Children—

640. *Sherman*, b. Feb. 13, 1806.
641. *Martha*, b. Feb. 15, 1813; d. Dec. 2, 1833, aged 21.
642. *Jeremiah*, b. July 1, 1815; d. Sept. 4, 1816.
643. *Henry*, b. Nov. 4, 1817; d. Feb. 17, 1840, aged 22.
644. *Elizabeth*, b. Dec. 24, 1820; m. Thomas A. Thatcher, Professor of the Latin Language in Yale College, Sept. 16, 1846. They have one child, *James Kingsley*, b. Oct. 19, 1847.
645. *Mary*, b. Nov. 5, 1823; d. March 28, 1829.
646. *Olivia*, b. Sept. 24, 1826.

242. **Hon. Thomas Day, LL.D.**, of Hartford, Conn., son of Rev. Jeremiah, was graduated at Yale College in 1797; in 1798-9, Tutor in Williams College; admitted to the bar in Dec. 1799; from 1810 to 1835, Secretary of the State of Conn.; President of Conn. Hist. Society, &c. m. Sarah Coit of Preston, now Griswold, Conn. March 18, 1813. Children—

650. *Sarah Coit*, b. Sept. 23, 1814.
651. *Elizabeth*, b. Feb. 16, 1816; m. Nathan Perkins Seymour, Professor of Languages in the Western Reserve College, Hudson, Ohio. Sept. 7, 1841. They have three children: *Charles*, b. Dec. 20, 1843: *Sarah Day*, b. Nov. 30, 1845: *Thomas Day*, b. April 1, 1848.
652. *Thomas Mills*, b. Nov. 21, 1817: graduated at Yale College in 1837; admitted to the bar in Hartford Co. Aug. 1840; now residing in Hartford, Conn.
653. *Catharine Augusta*, b. Aug. 6, 1819.
654. *Harriet*, b. Nov. 26, 1821; m. John Phelps Putnam, a lawyer in Boston, Sept. 21, 1842. They have two children, *Catharine Day*, b. May 24, 1844: *Anne*, b. Feb. 1847.
655. *Robert*, b. Feb. 28, 1824; d. June 22, 1824.
656. *Mary Frances*, b. May 7, 1826.
657. *Ellen*, b. Sept. 7, 1820.

243. **Noble**, of New Preston, Conn., son of Rev. Jeremiah, m. Elizabeth Jones of Hartford, April, 1805. Children—

660. *Daniel Jones*, b. July 15, 1806; of Apalachicola, Fa.
661. *Henry Noble*, b. Aug. 4, 1808.
662. *Jeremiah*, b. Oct. 4, 1810.
663. *Mills*, b. April 15, 1813; d. March 31, 1834, aged 21.
664. *Thomas*, b. June 1816; graduated at Yale College in 1839: now a lawyer in Cleveland, O.
665. *Charles*, b. Aug. 18, 1818; graduated at Yale College in 1840: now of Apalachicola, Fa.

666. *Elizabeth, b. Nov. 18, 1821; m. Rev. Samuel T. Seeley of Wolcotville, Conn., Sept. 1846, and d. Nov. 25, 1846.
667. *Sarah, b. April, 1823; died young.

270. **Samuel IV.** of Armada, Mich., m. Sarah Parker of Adams, Mass., who was b. May 10, 1769. Children—
670. *Daniel Merrick, b. Nov. 3, 1791.
671. Loring Parker, b. Oct. 4, 1794.
672. *Hiram Tuttle, b. Aug. 16, 1796; d. Aug. 16, 1826, at Lyons, N. Y.
673. Mary, b. Aug. 19, 1798; m. Willey Bancroft of Armada.
674. Cynthia, b. Nov. 6, 1800; m. James Leslie of Bruce, Mich.
675. Martha, b. Oct. 8, 1802; m. Ira Phillips of Armada.
676. *Benjamin Franklin, b. Nov. 1, 1806; d. Aug. 5, 1831, at Canandaigua, N. Y.
677. *Lois, b. July 4, 1808; d. April 27, 1837.
678. *Isaac N., died young.

272. *Winston, son of Samuel 3d, m. Thankful Clark, and d. at Skaneateles, N. Y. Children—
680. Cornelia, b.   m. Alexis Phillips. Phelps
681. *Ann, b.
682. Richard, b.   m. Anna Thomas.

273. **Liberty**, of Canandaigua, N. Y., son of Samuel 3d, m. Sarah Hovey of Clarendon, Vt., who d. Oct. 3, 1847. Children—
690. Lois, b. Jan. 20, 1809.
691. Horatio Nelson, b. Aug. 4, 1811.
692. Samuel Harrison, b. Oct. 29, 1813.
693. Julia Ann, b. Aug. 11, 1817.
694. Sarah Ann, b. Nov. 16, 1820.
695. Emily Eliza, b. Nov. 17, 1822.

280. *Moses, of West Springfield, son of Gideon, m. Polly Carew. May 27, 1793, and d. Oct. 2, 1828, aged 65. Children—
700. Betsey, b. Feb. 22, 1794; m. Isaac Eggleston.
701. Mahala, b. May 30, 1797; m. Francis Rockwell.
702. *Polly, b. March 8, 1799; d. Sept. 4, 1800.
703. Polly, b. Nov. 3, 1800; m. Joseph Winship, May 14, 1819.
704. Moses 2d, b. Aug. 20, 1802.
705. Francis, b. Aug. 17, 1804.
706. Lyman, b. Nov. 2, 1806.
707. Lester, b. June 19, 1809.

282. **Ambrose**, of Westfield, Mass., son of Gideon, m. Polly Ely, May 5, 1791, who d. Feb. 27, 1839, aged 69. Children—
710. Ambrose 2d, b. Feb. 9, 1792.

711. *Robert*, b. Dec. 18, 1794; of Arkansas.
712. *Albert*, b. Nov. 29, 1797.
713. *Mary*, b. Oct. 26, 1801; m. Alford Topliff.
714. *Calvin*, b. Feb. 2, 1803.
715. *Horatio E.*, b. June 18, 1814.

285. *Martin, of Westfield, Mass., son of Gideon, m. Polly Noble of Pittsfield, Mass., March, 1799, and d. Dec. 19, 1833, aged 56. She d. Nov. 17, 1825. Children—

720. *Martin* 2d, b. April 2, 1801.
721. *Emily, b. May 24, 1802; m. Hezekiah Bush; d. Nov. 1841.
722. *Jairus, b. Oct. 5, 1804; d. unmarried in Peoria, Ill., Sept. 1839.
723. *Sarah A.*, b. Jan. 19, 1806.
724. *David Noble*, b. Aug. 4, 1808.
725. *Samuel Duncan*, b. Feb. 4, 1810.
726. *William Taylor*, b. March 3, 1812.
727. *Mary Elizabeth, b. Oct. 5, 1813.
728. *Julia, b. April 20, 1817; d. Jan. 16, 1818.
729. *James Root*, b. Aug. 10, 1819.
730. *Edward Bliss*, b. Nov. 10, 1820.

286. Calvin, of Boston, Ms., m. Polly Farnham. Children—
740. *Louisa*, b.　　　　　　　　　　m. Lester H. Treat of West Granville, Mass.
741. *Frances*, b.　　　　　　　　　m. William Carter.

292. Aaron II. of West Springfield, m. Anne Ely of Wilbraham, Jan. 22, 1810. Children—
750. *Lucinda*, b. Nov. 5, 1810.
751. *Amanda*, b. Sept. 9, 1812; m. Guy C. Munsell of Greenfield, Mass., Dec. 28, 1836.
752. *Anne, b. July 28, 1815; d. July 7, 1843, aged 28.
753. *Lydia*, b. Aug. 8, 1817.
754. *Eunice*, b. July 22, 1823; m. Rev. Isaac G. Bliss, Missionary of the A. B. C. F. M. to the Nestorians in Persia, May 9, 1847.
755. *Josiah*, b. Sept. 2, 1826.

293. Gad, son of Aaron, removed first to Pittsfield, Mass., and in 1822 to New Haven, Conn.; m. Roxanna Rice, (b. July 2, 1788) of Southington, Conn., May 29, 1814. Children—
760. *George Edward*, b. March 19, 1815.
761. *Horace*, b. Nov. 5, 1816.

310. Erastus, of Durham, N. Y., son of Thomas S., m. Amelia Doty of that town, Nov. 15, 1804. Children—

770. *Thomas Stanley*, b. Sept. 26, 1805.
771. *Erastus W.*, b. April 9, 1807.
772. *Carlos C.*, b. June 14, 1809.
773. *Philo*, b. Aug. 10, 1811; d. Oct. 27, 1812.
774. *Newell*, b. April 15, 1814.
775. *Philo*, b. July 1, 1816; d. Sept. 11, 1818.
776. *Almira*, b. Oct. 26, 1818; m. James Jewell, July 25, 1844.
777. *Julia*, b. Dec. 30, 1820; m. Ebenezer L. Ingersoll, March 11, 1844.
778. *Elizur*, b. July 27, 1823; d. Nov. 22, 1843.
779. *Caroline*, b. Sept. 7, 1826; d. Dec. 2, 1843.

311. Newell, of Shalersville, O., son of Thomas S., m. Nancy Wright of Southington, Conn. Children—

780. *Julia*, b. Sept. 15, 1801; m. Oliver Tillotson.
781. *Ruth*, b. June 28, 1804; m. Cyrus Foster, March 17, 1825.
782. *Dennis C.*, b. Nov. 4, 1807.
783. *Louisa M.*, b. May 8, 1810; m. George Woodford, June 26, 1837.
784. *Charlotte*, b. April 26, 1812; m. John Hoskins, April 14, 1843.
785. *Andrew J.*, b. May 26, 1817.
786. *Harriet*, b. March 18, 1821; m. Harrison Cooley, March 1, 1843.

315. Wareham, son of Thomas S., m. Lucretia Hoadley of Branford, Conn.; after her death, he removed from Avon, Conn. to Canaan, Wayne Co., Pa., and m. Olive Samson, Nov. 19, 1819. Children—

790. *Sophia*, b. Sept. 20, 1820; m. Stacy B. Clark, Jan. 14, 1841.
791. *Marcus*, b. July 7, 1822.
792. *Thomas*, b. May 31, 1824.
793. *William*, b. Aug. 26, 1827.
794. *Stanley*, b. July 27, 1829.
795. *Dan Newell*, b. Jan. 27, 1833.

316. *Stanley, of Avon, Conn., son of Thomas S., m. Anna Thompson of Avon, Nov. 1, 1815, and d. at Claysville, Ky., Aug. 1, 1828. Children—

800. *Rollin*, b. May 5, 1817.
801. *Henry*, b. Oct. 15, 1818.
802. *John*, b. Feb. 19, 1823.

SPRINGFIELD BRANCH—SIXTH GENERATION. 33

320. **Horace II.** first of Litchfield, Conn., afterwards of ———, Genessee Co., N. Y.; m. Mercy Hills of Farmington, (Plainville) Conn. Children—
810. *Jane*, b.
811. *Henry*, b.
812. *Augustus*, b.

350. *Joel II. of West Springfield, (Ireland Parish) m. Lucretia Day, daughter of William, (190) Aug. 19, 1782, who d. Feb. 1, 1802, aged 42. For his second wife, he m. Eunice Bedortha, Feb. 10, 1803, and d. March 13, 1830, aged 79. Children—
820. *Chester*, b. Dec. 8, 1782.
821. *Sophia*, b. May 25, 1784.
822. *Edward*, b. March 1, 1786.
823. *Lucretia*, b. Sept. 5, 1787; m. Rufus Colton of Hartford, Conn., Feb. 23, 1809.
824. *Joel* 3d, b. Sept. 10, 1789; m. Chloe Ely: no children.
825. *Francis*, b. Sept. 25, 1791.
826. *Amelia*, b.   1792; d. July 1, 1793.
827. *Laura*, b. Aug. 8, 1794; m. Daniel Merrick, Jan. 21, 1818.
828. *Harriet*, b. Feb. 21, 1799; m. Lucius Ely, 1825.
829. *Lucy*, b. Dec. 30, 1803; m. Russell Ely, Jr.. Nov. 1828.
830. *Newton*, b. March 4, 1806.

352. *Jedediah, of West Springfield, (Ireland Parish), son of Joel I., m. Hepziba Chapin Miller, Aug. 6, 1782. For his second wife, he m. Phebe Day, (429) March 4, 1824, and d. Dec. 26, 1839, aged 85. Children—
840. *Isaac Newton*, b. Feb. 8, 1826.
841. *Jedediah* 2d, b. March 3, 1828.
842. *Sarah Hepziba*, b. July 15, 1830.

355. *Eli, of Northampton, (South Farms,) Mass., son of Joel I., m. Lydia Judd of South Hadley, and d. in 1833, aged 72. Children—
850. *Electa*, b. June 26, 1785; m. James Proser.
851. *Silence*, b. Jan. 1, 1787; m. Samuel Alvord of Northampton.
852. *Eli* 2d, b. Dec. 9, 1789.
853. *Lydia*, b.   m. Simeon Judd of South Hadley.
854. *Jedediah*, b.
855. *Allethe*, b.
856. *Eunice*, b. ——— ———, m. ——— Booth of Windsor.
857. *Tryphena*, b.   died young.
858. *Julia*, b.   died young.

358. *James, of Gill, Mass., son of Joel I., m. Asenath Ely, May 20, 1790, who d. Nov. 8, 1827, aged 59. He d. Jan. 5, 1841, aged 72. Children—

860. *Clarissa*, b. July 22, 1791; m. Rowley Leonard; d. July 20, 1845.
861. *Lora*, b. Dec. 1, 1792; m. Alfred Goodrich.
862. *James*, b. Aug. 18, 1795; d. Feb. 11, 1802.
863. *Robert*, b. Aug. 18, 1800.
864. *James* 2d, b. Aug. 19, 1805.
865. *Asenath*, b. Feb. 21, 1807; m. John Horsley, May, 1825.

359. Alexander, of West Springfield, (Ireland Parish,) son of Joel I., m. Phebe Atkins, June 2, 1802, who was born Oct. 10, 1778. Children—

870. *Linus*, b. June 22, 1803.
871. *Pattison*, b. June 4, 1805.
872. *Ruth*, b. April 22, 1807.
873. *Samantha*, b. June 5, 1809; m. Edward Kneeland, Nov. 9, 1835.
874. *Newbury*, b. Feb. 12, 1812.
875. *Alexander* 2d, b. April 18, 1817.
876. *Olive Louisa*, b. Aug. 28, 1821.

370. *Justin, son of David I., m. Abigail Morgan, Feb. 11, 1785. For his second wife he m. Rhoda Day, (340) Feb. 16, 1788, who d. Dec. 3, 1840; lived some years in West Springfield, (Ireland Parish,) then removed to Essex, Vt., and finally to Chateaugay. Franklin Co., N. Y., where he d. March 9, 1829, aged 72. Children—

880. *Nathaniel*, b. May 6, 1786.
881. *John*, b. Dec. 25, 1788.
882. *Justin* 2d, b. July 10, 1790.
883. *Oreda*, b. Nov. 15, 1791.
884. *Abigail*, b. Aug. 1, 1794; d. June 15, 1835.
885. *Asenath*, b. Sept. 11, 1796; d. Feb. 15, 1814.
886. *Rhoda*, b. March 18, 1799; d. Oct. 17, 1822.
887. *Sarah*, b. April 6, 1802; m. John Pixley, Oct. 14, 1840.

371. *David 2d, Essex, Vt., m. Asenath Childs, May 1, 1788, and d. Aug. 6, 1845, aged 87. Children—

890. *Pamela*, b. June 4, 1789.
891. *Horatio*, b. Oct. 21, 1790.
892. *Rodney*, b. Jan. 9, 1792; d. March 13, 1792.
893. *Childs*, b. March 29, 1794.
894. *Sophia*, b. Aug. 10, 1796; m. Reville Noble of Rockingham, Iowa, in 1826.
895. *Hannah*, b. July 7, 1798; m. Ava Woodruff of Westford, 1820; d. Feb. 1846.
896. *David 3d, b. Oct. 2, 1800.

SPRINGFIELD BRANCH—SIXTH GENERATION.

897. *Sabrina, b. Jan. 11, 1803; d. Nov. 1808.
898. Irad, b. Jan. 11, 1805.
899. Asenath, b. Sept. 14, 1813; m. Giles Pettibone of Bloomington, Iowa, 1841.

372. **Asa**, of Massena, N. Y., son of David I., m. Esther Chapin of Chicopee, Mass., Jan. 25, 1788. Children—
900. *Octavius, b. Aug. 28, 1790; d. July 30, 1817.
901. *Jube C., b. May 7, 1792.
902. Marinda, b. Oct. 7, 1793; m. Chester Day (820).
903. Elizabeth, b. March 29, 1798; m. Hiram Wilson, June 4, 1832.
904. Robert, b. April 12, 1800.
905. Mattoon, b. Aug. 7, 1803; of Lockport, N. Y.

376. **Hezekiah**, of Essex, Vt., son of David I., m. Elizabeth Wickham in 1796. Children—
910. Silence, b. Jan. 5, 1799; m. Abel Gilson, May, 1826.
911. Hezekiah 2d, b. Oct. 13, 1800.
912. Zilpha, b. July 23, 1802; m. ——— Corbit, April, 1845.
913. Samuel, b. May 22, 1808.
914. Chester, b. July 9, 1809.
915. Artentia, b. Oct. 28, 1811; m. Archibald Crosby, June 9, 1834.
916. Dorothy, b. Oct. 18, 1814; m. Lyman Damon, Oct. 7, 1841.
917. Jonathan, b. May 21, 1817.
918. Benjamin, b. Aug. 8, 1822.

400. ***Brigham**, of West Springfield, (Ireland Parish,) son of Eleazer, m. Silence Pitt of Westfield, Mass., Jan. 30, 1796; and d. Jan. 29, 1849, aged 82. Children—
920. Alden, b. Dec. 28, 1796; m. Chloe Roberts, April 13, 1822, and has no children; resides in Greene, N. Y.
921. *Lucius, b. Nov. 27, 1798; d. about 1820.
922. Quartus, b. Aug. 10, 1800; resides in Ohio, and has three or four children.
923. Parma, b. Oct. 11, 1802; m. Miletus Pendleton of Springfield, Nov. 25, 1826.
924. Sophronia, b. Dec. 17, 1804.
925. Emily, b. Nov. 7, 1806; m. ——— Torrey of Ludlow, 1838.
926. Brigham 2d, b. Aug. 9, 1809.
927. Martha, b.   1814; m. Charles Gunn of Ohio.
928. Jenette, b. Aug. 28, 1816; m. Henry Meller of South Hadley.

404. ***Eleazer Mattoon**, of West Springfield, (Ireland Parish,) son of Eleazer, m. Mary Chapin, March 17, 1803, and d. May 9, 1846, aged 69. Children—

930. *Eleazer*, b. Dec. 14, 1804.
931. *Sophia*, b. Aug. 16, 1807; m. Nathan Clapp, May 7, 1831.
932. *Alonzo, b. Oct. 10, 1809; d. June 19, 1825.
933. *Elijah, b. Nov. 19, 1811; d. Oct. 28, 1836.
934. *Jube C.*, b. Oct. 6, 1814.
935. *Eveline*, b. Oct. 30, 1817; m. Calvin Andrews of Burlington, Ill., Oct. 30, 1843.
936. *Sullivan M.*, b. Dec. 12, 1820.

405. Hosea, of West Springfield, son of Eleazer, m. Hannah Day, (412) July 4, 1805, who d. April 2, 1813, aged 35. Children—
940. *Sullivan, b. Jan. 1, 1806; d. May 15, 1807.
941. *Sylvester*, b. Sept. 23, 1807.
942. *Elbridge*, b. July 12, 1809.
943. *Hannah*, b. April 29, 1812.

411. *Joseph III. of Winchester, N. H., m. Sarah Morgan, Jan. 14, 1802, who d. May 22, 1842, aged 63. He d. May 24, 1842, aged 69. Children—
950. *Maria Kingsbury, b. Nov. 1803; d. May 12, 1844.
951. *Caroline Louisa, b. Dec. 1805; d. Aug. 15, 1831.
952. *Chloe*, b. June 1, 1807; m. John Smith of Winchester.
953. *Delia Calista*, b. Oct. 31, 1809; m. Charles Cook of Hadley.
954. *Sarah Ann*, b. Sept. 14, 1811.
955. *William Harrison*, b. Nov. 22, 1814.
956. *Joseph Morgan*, b. Sept. 7, 1817; of Worcester, Mass.
957. *Laura Amelia*, b. March 25, 1820.

413. *Sylvester, of Chicopee, son of Joseph 2d, m. Ruba Frink, Feb. 6, 1817; and d. Sept. 3, 1827, aged 48. Children—
960. *Angeline, b. Feb. 18, 1818; d. Nov. 25, 1829.
961. *Morris*, b. Dec. 23, 1819.
962. *Norman*, b. Dec. 4, 1821.
963. *Wealthy Frink, b. May 10, 1824; d. July 28, 1845.
964. *Chloe Ann*, b. Oct. 1, 1826.

420. Aribut, son of Giles, supposed to live in Cooperstown, N. Y., m. Esther May of Marlborough, Vt.; for his second wife, m. Sally Lassals. Children—
970. *Joel*, b.
971. *Giles*, b.
972. *Esther*, b.

423. Solomon, of Marlborough, Vt., son of Giles, m. Polly Randall of Bennington, Vt. Children—
980. *Roswell*, b. Aug. 6, 1804.

SPRINGFIELD BRANCH—SIXTH GENERATION. 37

981. *Henry Burrell*, b. Feb. 7, 1807.
982. *Harriet Maria*, b. Sept. 8, 1810.
983. *Lyman*, b. Dec. 8, 1811.

424. **Roswell**, of Granby, Conn., son of Giles, m. Hilpah Goddard, One child—
985. *Newton*, of Granby; has three children.

426. **Giles II.** of Johnston, Trumbull Co., Ohio, m. Hannah Cutler (b. March 28, 1788) of Marlborough, Vt., March 10, 1808. Children—

990. *Flavia*, b. Nov. 20, 1808; m. Salmon Bunnell of Jefferson, Ohio, Dec. 10, 1829.
991. *Diana*, b. Aug. 9, 1811; m. Sherman Cooley of Johnston, Oct. 3, 1830.
992. *Giles Lewis*, b. Oct. 30, 1815.
993. *Willard*, b. July 30, 1817.
994. *Edward Newton*, b. April 17, 1819.
995. *Betsey Cutler*, b. April 30, 1821; m. Sherman Skinner, (deafmute) Jan. 1, 1842, and d. Dec. 5, 1842.
996. *Leicester*, b. April 4, 1823.
997. *Sybil*, b. Dec. 28, 1824; m. Sherman Skinner, June 11, 1843.
998. *Julia Maria*, b. July 15, 1828; d. Sept. 16, 1828.
999. *William Butler*, b. April 8, 1831.
1000. *Lovina*, b. May 28, 1833.

428. **Zebulon**, of Deerfield, Ohio, son of Giles, m. ——— ———, Jan. 15, 1815. Children—

1010. *Lydia*, b. Oct. 15, 1815; m. ——— ———, May 28, 1835; d. Dec. 8, 1837, aged 22.
1011. *Sarah*, b. May 2, 1817; m. ——— ———, Oct. 7, 1838.
1012. *Laura*, b. Aug. 11, 1823.
1013. *Sebra W.*, b. Dec. 27, 1826.
1014. *Hinman F.*, b. Nov. 15, 1829.
1015. *George F.*, b. May 6, 1832.
1016. *Phebe C.*, b. Dec. 11, 1834.
1017. *Sophronia M.*, b. July 14, 1837.

440. **Hon. Rowland**, son of Jacob, removed from Chester, Mass. to Skaneatales, N. Y. in 1805, and in 1810 to Moravia, N. Y.; in 1816, elected a member of the State Legislature; in 1821, a member of the Convention to revise the Constitution; in 1822, and again in 1832, a member of Congress; m. Nancy Ely of West Springfield, Feb. 21, 1811. One child—

1020. *William H.*, b. Jan. 14, 1812.

442. **Hervey,** of Moravia, N. Y., son of Jacob, m. Amanda Hitchcock of Springfield, Sept. 1812. Children—
1030. *Horatio,* b. May 4, 1813.
1031. *Oscar,* b. Aug. 6, 1815.
1032. *Dwight,* b. Feb. 5, 1817.
1033. *Delia,* b. Dec. 9, 1818.
1034. *Charles,* b. Aug. 3, 1820.
1035. *Julia,* b. April 14, 1822; d. Aug. 11, 1823.
1036. *Dudley,* b. July 4, 1825.
1037. *Jacob,* b. July 8, 1827; d. March 4, 1835.
1038. *George,* b. July 18, 1829.

444. **Jacob II.** of Franklin, Portage Co., Ohio, m. Mary Spears, Feb. 15, 1820. Children—
1040. *Mary E.,* b. Jan. 26, 1823; m. William Reed of Franklin Mills, O.
1041. *Samuel F.,* b. May 30, 1827.
1042. *Lucy E.,* b. July 16, 1829.
1043. *Rowland H.,* b. Nov. 21, 1831.
1044. *Robert J.,* b. Dec. 14, 1833.

446. *****John F.** of Buffalo, N. Y., son of Jacob, m. Phebe Root of New Berlin, N. Y.; and d. July 25, 1837, aged 42. Children—
1050. *Aurelia L.,* b. Aug. 11, 1823; m. John Boyden, Oct. 25, 1848.
1051. *Ralph R.,* b. April 25, 1825; d. March 27, 1827.
1052. *Franklin H.,* b. Jan. 5, 1827.
1053. *Ralph R.,* b. Sept. 4, 1828.
1054. *Caroline W.,* b. Oct. 4, 1830.
1055. *Charles W.,* b. Oct. 13, 1833.
1056. *Samuel E.,* b. March 28, 1837.

447. **Samuel E.** of Moravia, N. Y., son of Jacob, m. Nancy Jane Aiken, Feb. 1, 1836. Children—
1060. *William Franklin,* b. Dec. 14, 1837.
1061. *Samuel Edwin,* b. Jan. 20, 1840.

450. *****Henry,** of West Springeld, son of Benjamin 2d, m. Mary Ely, May 25, 1794; d. Oct. 10, 1811, aged 38. Children—
1070. *Sarah Dwight,* b. March 20, 1796; m. George Dutton, now of Utica, N. Y., Jan. 1, 1817.
1071. *Drusilla Brewster,* b. Jan. 24, 1798; m. Henry Morse, March 20, 1818; d. Sept. 28, 1833.
1072. *Alfred Ely,* b. April 15, 1800; d. Oct. 15, 1811.
1073. *Nancy,* b. July 9, 1802; m. Moses Y. Beach of New York, Nov. 10, 1819.
1074. *Mary,* b. Dec. 10, 1806; m. Joseph Perkins of New York.
1075. *Benjamin Henry,* b. April 10, 1810.

460. **Erastus**, of Fort Ann, N. Y., son of Daniel, m. Mariba Clark. For his second wife, he m. Olive Dewey. Children—
1080. *Erastus D.*, b.
1081. *Thaddeus D.*, b.
1082. *Daniel*, b.
1083. *Andrew Jackson*, b.
1084. *George*, b.
1085. *Alfred*, b.

462. **Daniel II.** of West Springfield, m. Elizabeth Cooley, Dec. 30, 1802. Children—
1090. *Norman*, b. Oct. 11, 1803; m. Aurelia Ely, Nov. 1828.
1091. *Erastus*, b. Aug. 15, 1805.
1092. **Elizabeth Cooley*, b. Sept. 6, 1807; m. Frederic Palmer, Jan. 1829; d. May 21, 1829, aged 22.
1093. *Anne Van Horne*, b. Jan. 13, 1810.
1094. **Harriet*, b. Dec. 4, 1813; d. May 26, 1829.
1095. *Daniel 3d*, b. Jan. 23, 1821.
1096. *Eveline Maria*, b. 1827.

467. ***David**, son of Daniel, removed to Franklin, Portage Co, Ohio; m. Mary Farnham of Westfield, June 1, 1820; d. May 10, 1838, aged 40. Children—
1100. *William F.*, b. Nov. 11, 1821.
1101. **Harriet A.*, b. Sept. 22, 1823; d. Feb. 1839.
1102. *David Edward*, b. Aug. 26, 1829.
1103. **Francis A.*, b. Nov. 14, 1828; d. March 7, 1832.
1104. *Mary L.*, b. Aug. 31, 1831.
1105. *Francis A.*, b. Dec. 8, 1833.
1106. *Lucy A.*, b. Feb. 14, 1836.
1107. *Alfred H.*, b. June 31, 1838.

472. **Rodney**, of West Springfield, son of Heman, m. Lovisa Bagg, Jan. 1, 1806. Children—
1110. **Charles*, b. Oct. 19, 1806; d. Feb. 27, 1809.
1111. **Caroline*, b. Sept. 13, 1809; d. Dec. 7, 1826.
1112. **Charles*, b. Aug. 25, 1811; d. Sept. 2, 1835.
1113. **John*, b. June 15, 1813; d. April 12, 1814.
1114. **Sarah*, b. Jan. 17, 1815; d. May 12, 1824.
1115. **Lydia*, b. Dec. 27, 1817; d. June 2, 1837.

475. **Benjamin**, for some years of New York City, now of Springfield, Mass., son of Heman, graduated at Yale College in 1812; m. Frances Dwight of Springfield, Dec. 3, 1820. Children—
1120. *Mary Sanford*, b. Sept. 4, 1821; m. Rev. Thomas H. Skinner, Jr. of New York City, Nov. 1843.

1121. *Benjamin, b. Feb. 21, 1823; d. Sept. 10, 1831.
1122. *Elizabeth Dwight, b. March 17, 1825; d. July 10, 1839.
1123. Frances, b. Aug. 25, 1833.

476. *Heman II. of West Springfield, m. Susan Rising, Dec. 6, 1835, and d. Dec. 24, 1847, aged 54. Children—
1130. Sarah, b. May 12, 1837.
1131. Benjamin, b. Sept. 16, 1839.
1132. Charles, b. Aug. 3, 1842.
1133. Lydia, b. Sept. 16, 1844.
1134. Lois, b. July 24, 1847.

482. *William, of Marcellus, N. Y.; m. Lucretia McIntire in 1786, and d. Dec. 11, 1813, aged 49. Children—
1150. *Frederic, b. Aug. 29, 1786.
1151. Henry, b. July 22, 1788.
1152. *William, } d. in childhood, on the same day, of Canker Rash,
1153. *Orpha, } and were buried in the same coffin.
1154. Calista, b. Nov. 19, 1794; m. Benjamin Ellsworth of East Windsor, Conn., Nov. 17, 1825.
1155. *Cynthia, d. in childhood.
1156. *Harriet, b. April 16, 1799; m. David C. Spear of Ellington, Conn.; d. Sept. 1, 1844.
1157. *William, b. Feb. 1, 1801.
1158. *Mahala, d. in infancy.
1159. *Eliza, b. Feb. 6, 1808; m. Milton Bush; d. June 19, 1838.

501. William, of Sheffield, Ohio, son of John I.; m. Augusta Burrell of that town, May 6, 1832. Children—
1160. Huldah Maria, b. March 5, 1833.
1161. William Augustus, b. June 14, 1835.
1162. Henry Kellogg, b. Aug. 22, 1837.
1163. Mariette, b. Sept. 30, 1839.
1164. Sumner Burrell, b. April 19, 1842.
1165. Eugene, b. April 12, 1847.

503. John II. of Sheffield, Ohio, m. Cornelia Ann Sackett of Avon, Ohio, March 24, 1831. Children—
1170. *John Ingersoll, b. Sept. 4, 1832; d. Oct. 15, 1838.
1171. *Sophia Ann, b. May 21, 1834; d. Oct. 1, 1838.
1172. *Harriet Cornelia, b. May 2, 1836; d. Oct. 26, 1837.
1173. Alfred, b. July 28, 1837.
1174. John Ingersoll, b. Nov. 27, 1838.
1175. Robert Ithamar, b. Nov. 16, 1842.
1176. Hubert, b. Aug. 11, 1844.

SPRINGFIELD BRANCH—SIXTH GENERATION.   41

504. Norman, of Sheffield, Ohio, son of John I., m. Julia Ann Root of Sheffield, Aug. 10, 1830. Children—
1180. *Delia Maria*, b. July 3, 1831.
1181. *Richard William*, b. March 26, 1833.
1182. *Laura Jane*, b. July 20, 1835.
1183. *Eliza Florentine*, b. March 10, 1839.
1184. *Lydia Amelia,* } Twins, b. Dec. 9, 1841
1185. *Mary Cornelia,* }
1186. *Charles Norman*, b. Feb. 8, 1847.

506. James, of Sheffield, Ohio, son of John I., m. Ann Eliza Austin of that town, Sept. 18, 1835. Children—
1190. *Charles Eugene*, b. Dec. 24, 1836; d. April 13, 1837.
1191. *Oscar*, b. Nov. 1, 1838; d. Jan. 16, 1846.
1192. *Franklin*, b. March 20, 1841.
1193. *George W.*, b. Aug. 25, 1843.
1194. *Cerelia*, b. Nov. 19, 1845.

508. Kellogg, son of John I., belonging to the mission of the A. B. C. F. M. to the Cherokee Indians, and residing at Dwight, m. Mary L. Ingalls of Napoli, N. Y., Aug. 11, 1841. Children—
1200. *Mary Ermina*, b. Oct. 10, 1843.
1201. *Laura Ellen*, b. Sept. 5, 1845.
1202. *Harriet Caroline*, b. Dec. 29, 1847.

509. *Frederic, of Sheffield, Ohio, son of John I., m. Mary A. Sackett of Avon, Ohio, Aug. 18, 1835, and d. Aug. 11, 1840, aged 25. Children—
1210. *Helen Amelia*, b. May 5, 1836.
1211. *Frederic 2d*, b. March 2, 1840.

510. Edmund, of Gross Lake, Mich., son of John I., m. Camilla Austin of Sheffield, Ohio, Sept. 2, 1846.

515. Hon. Charles D. of Montreal, Canada, son of Ithamar, late of Her Majesty's Executive Council for the province of Canada: Solicitor General: member of the Provincial parliament: since June 20, 1842, one of the Judges of the Court of Queen's Bench at Montreal; m. Barbara Lyon of Dublin, Ireland, Oct. 9, 1830. Children—

1220. *Mary*, b.
1221. *Laura*, b.

520. James I. of New Orleans, son of James, m. Sarah Eliza Armitage of Baltimore, Jan. 5, 1836.

1230. *Abby Hannah*, b. Oct. 5, 1836.
1231. *Helen Amelia*, b. Sept. 24, 1840.
1232. *Sarah Eliza*, b. July 18, 1843.
1233. *Jennie Whiting*, b. Sept. 20, 1846.
1234. *James Armitage*, b. Oct. 26, 1848.

553. *Ezekiel II. of West Springfield, m. Climena Chapin of South Hadley, Mass., Jan. 21, 1797, who d. Feb. 15, 1842, aged 72. He d. Oct. 25, 1843, aged 73. Children—
1240. *Almon*, b. June 3, 1798.
1241. *Elihu*, b.   d. 1800.
1242. *Elihu*, b. Sept. 14, 1801.
1243. *Emma*, b. Aug. 4, 1803; m. Hiram Carter, May 7, 1833.
1244. *Climena*, b. Sept. 3, 1807.
1245. *Harriet*, b. Dec. 7, 1808.
1246. *Ezekiel* 3d, b. Nov. 20, 1811.

555. Justin, of Martinsburg, N. Y., son of Ezekiel I., m. Lydia Noble of West Springfield, Mass., Nov. 26, 1801, who d. Aug. 16, 1826. For his second wife, he m. ——— ———, July 3, 1828. Children—
1250. *Ann*, b. Dec. 15, 1803; m. Allen Babcock in 1833.
1251. *Charles N.*, b. Jan. 7, 1806; d. Aug. 26, 1830: left a son, *Charles*, b. about 1829, residing in Waterloo, N. Y.
1252. *Lyman*, b. March 8, 1808; of Westfield, Mass.
1253. *Sylvester*, b. June 9, 1810.
1254. *Justin* 2d, b. June 30, 1812.
1255. *Harvey*, b. May 3, 1814.
1256. *Arætus*, b. Nov. 3, 1816; d. Feb. 14, 1822.
1257. *Mary*, b. Oct. 22, 1821; m. James Allen of Lowville; d. Sept. 29, 1848.

562. *Stephen, son of Luke II., m. Sophia Bagg, July 12, 1787; removed to Randolph, and then to Buffalo, N. Y., where he died. Children—
1260. *Rodney*, b. Aug. 25, 1787; of Buffalo, N. Y. Has several children.
1261. *Russell*, b. Feb. 25, 1789.
1262. *Gordon*, b. Aug. 25, 1791.
1263. *Phelps*, b.   died young.
1264. *Sophia*, b.   died, aged 12.

565. *Horace, of West Springfield, son of Luke II., m. Theodosia Ely, and d. Jan. 6, 1816, aged 44. Children—

SPRINGFIELD BRANCH—SIXTH GENERATION.

1270. *Horace 2d*, b. May 29, 1795.
1271. *Luke*, b. Feb. 17, 1805.

566. *Kelsey, of West Springfield, son of Luke II., m. Jerusha Hamlin, May 25, 1803, and d. May 15, 1843. Children—
1280. *Lydia*, b. March 20, 1805.
1281. *Eliza*, b. Jan. 17, 1807.
1282. *Asher H.*, b. March 25, 1809.
1283. *Lora Ann*, b. March 16, 1811; d. July 9, 1814.
1284. *Selden*, b. Aug. 16, 1815; d. Oct. 25, 1848.
1285. *Loren*, b. Oct. 20, 1816.

567. Luke III. of New York City, m. Phebe Stillwell of Huntington, L. I., May 5, 1803. Children—
1290. *Thomas S.*, b. July 8, 1805.
1291. *Lydia*, b. June 10, 1808; m. John Reed.
1292. *Wheeler*, b. Feb. 21, 1810; d. Aug. 1823.
1293. *Henry*, b. March 20, 1812.
1294. *Andrew*, b. May 19, 1815.
1295. *Betsey*, b. June 5, 1817.

576. *Noble, of West Springfied, son of Thomas, m. Polly Dewey, Nov. 25, 1802, and d. Dec. 13, 1841. Children—
1320. *Frederic*, b. Sept. 2, 1803.
1321. *Mary*, b. Aug. 4, 1805; m. Norman Ashley, Dec. 25, 1827.
1322. *Henry*, b.
1323. *Robert*, b.
1324. *Electa*, b. April 27, 1812; m. Jeremiah Plummer of Biddeford, Me.
1325. *Alfred*, b. Dec. 7, 1814.
1326. *Noah Dewey*, b. Nov. 21, 1816.
1327. *Franklin*, b. July 27, 1819; d. Aug. 11, 1822.
1328. *Caroline Sophia*, b. April 14, 1821; m. Joseph Cady.
1329. *Elizabeth Hamlin*, b. Feb. 20, 1823.
1330. *Franklin*, b. June 21, 1825; of Biddeford, Me.

580. Linus, of Bennington, N. Y., son of Timothy II., m. ———, Oct. 4, 1808. Children—
1340. *Volney*, b. Aug. 13, 1809.
1341. *Eunice O.*, b. April 14, 1811; m. ——— Feb. 11, 1835.

581. Asa, of Bennington, N. Y., son of Timothy, II., m. ——— ———. Children—
1350. *Asa 2d*, b. Nov. 20, 1800.
1351. *Almon*, b. Feb. 7, 1803.

1352. *Lucy*, b. Aug. 13, 1805; m. ———— ————, Oct. 27, 1824.
1353. *Flavia*, b. Sept. 13, 1808; m. ———— ————, Aug. 15, 1842.
1354. *John D.*, b. June 20, 1814.
1355. *Johnson L.*, b. Sept. 10, 1818; d. May 11, 1838.
1356. *Francis H.*, b. Aug. 10, 1821.
1357. *Wealthy M.*, b. July 26, 1826.

585. *Timothy III. of Bennington, N. Y., m. ———— ————, Feb. 11, 1820; and d. May 7, 1824. His widow d. Jan. 1840. Children—
1360. *Charles B.*, b. July 21, 1821.
1361. *Henry B.*, b. Jan. 26, 1823; resides at Lockport, Illinois.

586. *Bliss, of Murray, N. Y., son of Timothy II., m. ———— ————, 1815, and d. Sept. 11, 1819. Children—
1365. *Catharine*, b.

590. Horatio, of Deerfield, Portage Co., O., son of Lewis, m. Hannah Hinman, Jan. 28, 1802. Children—
1370. *Judson Hinman*, b. Sept. 2, 1804.
1371. *Julia Ann*, b. Aug. 4, 1807; m. William Endley, May 20, 1828.
1372. *Malvina S.*, b. Dec. 27, 1809.
1373. *Almira S.*, b. July 26, 1812; m. Peter Gee, May, 1835.
1374. *Anson H.*, b. Nov. 13, 1816.
1375. *Solon F.*, b. July 11, 1824.

591. Alva, of Deerfield, O., son of Lewis, m. Sarah Beach, Jan. 28, 1800, who d. June 11, 1838. Children—
1380. *Polly P.*, b. Aug. 22, 1800; m. Jeduthan Farnham, Sept. 21, 1824.
1381. *Ralph*, b. July 1, 1803.

592. Mun, of Deerfield, Ohio, son of Lewis, m. Lucy Ely, Jan. 2, 1804. Children—
1390. *Heman E.*, b. Nov. 23, 1804.
1391. *Harriet*, b. Nov. 6, 1806, m. Aribut Tibbals.
1392. *Mortimer L.*, b. Feb. 12, 1810.
1393. *Julius H.*, b. May 2, 1813.
1394. *Maria L.*, b. Oct. 4, 1815; m. Sylvester Card, May 9, 1833.
1395. *Roswell Merrick*, b. Feb. 26, 1818.
1396. *Frances Laura*, b. Feb. 26, 1818; d. June 26, 1847.
1397. *Lucy Ann*, b. March 19, 1828; d. Sept. 11, 1834.

593. *Seth, of Ravenna, Portage Co., Ohio, son of Lewis, m. Matilda Martin, Jan. 14, 1821, who d. Nov. 21, 1829, aged 27. For his second wife, he m. Mary Clark, Nov. 3, 1831, and d. Children—

SPRINGFIELD BRANCH—SIXTH GENERATION. 45

1400. *Julia Ann, b. Nov. 12, 1821; d. Oct. 16, 1824.
1401. Julius, b. June 7, 1823.
1402. Frances Louisa, b. Aug. 18, 1825.
1403. Helen Maria, b. April 15, 1827.
1404. *Augustus, b. Jan. 23, 1829; d. Dec. 31, 1831.
1405. Mellville A., b. Oct. 27, 1833.
594. *Lewis II. of Deerfield, O., m. Peny Deming, May 13, 1810; d. at Malden, U. C., Aug. 26, 1812, aged 25. Children—
1410. Alva O., b. May 5, 1811.
1411. Lewis A., b. Nov. 23, 1812.

595. Solomon, of Deerfield, Ohio, son of Lewis, m. Chloe Cook, in 1815. Children—
1420. *Diantha, b. Jan. 3, 1816; d. Feb. 2, 1816.
1421. Edmund, b. Oct. 1, 1817.
1422. Augusta, b. June 28, 1820.
1423. Lavina, b. May 26, 1822.
1424. Frances, b. Aug. 15, 1833.

602. Julius, of West Springfield, son of Edmund I., m. Lois Goodyear, Jan. 15, 1824. Children—
1430. Austin Goodyear, b. Nov. 24, 1824.
1431. Henry Perdy, b. March 12, 1829.
1432. Edmund, b. Dec. 12, 1831.
1433. Lois Ann, b. March 27, 1834.

605. Edmund II. of Fredonia, N. Y., m. Maria Drake of that place April 6, 1829, who d. March 5, 1847. For his second wife, he m. Mary Ann Drake, Oct. 5, 1847. Children—
1440. Ralph Bliss, b. March 10, 1831.
1441. Ann Maria, b. Nov. 26, 1833.
1442. Juliette, b. May 5, 1836.
1443. *Edmund Lewis, b. Aug. 16, 1838; d. Oct. 21, 1840.
1444. Harriet Austin, b. Dec. 6, 1840.
1445. Saruh Mun, b. June 4, 1843.

611. Henry L. of Ravenna, O., son of Edmund I., m. Winnfred Gelston Coffin of Nantucket, Mass., May 1, 1838.
1450. Henrietta Gelston, b. July 8, 1839.
1451. Henry Lewis, b. May 6, 1841.
1452. Roland Gelston, b. May 13, 1843.

SEVENTH GENERATION.

640. Sherman, of Brooklyn, N. Y., son of Rev. Jeremiah, was graduated at Yale College in 1826; m. Elizabeth Ann King of Westfield, Mass., in 1832. Children—
1500. *Henry, b. and d. Feb. 1, 1835.
1501. Harriet King, b. March 6, 1836.
1502. Roger Sherman, b. July 6, 1838.
1503. Martha Elizabeth, b. April 19, 1842.
1504. Jane Olivia, b. Nov. 6, 1844.
1505. Clinton, b. March 17, 1847.
1506. Mary, b. Dec. 12, 1848.

661. Rev. Henry N. of Hudson, Ohio, son of Noble, was graduated at Yale College in 1828: in 1831-4, Tutor in Yale College: in 1837, ordained Pastor of the Congregational Church in Waterbury, Conn.; in 1840, elected Professor of Sacred Rhetoric in the Theological Department of the Western Reserve College; m. Jane L. Marble of New Haven, Conn., April 27, 1836. Children—
1510. Henry Mills, b. Oct. 20, 1838.
1511. *Edwin Marble, b. Feb. 16, 1841; d. March 23, 1841.
1512. Mary Elizabeth, b. Nov. 9, 1845.

662. Jeremiah, of New York City, son of Noble, m. Emily C. Day, daughter of Orrin Day of Catskill, N. Y., Nov. 10, 1846. Children—
1520. Alice, b. Sept. 1847.

670. David M. son of Samuel 4th, m. Nancy Stevens, Oct. 8, 1816, and d. at Buffalo, N. Y., Dec. 12, 1839, aged 48. Children—
1530. John S., b. Aug. 5, 1817.
1531. Harriet, b. Sept. 1819; m. ——— ———, 1840.
1532. Charles Henry, b. Dec. 3, 1821; of Buffalo?
1533. Maria Loisa, b. Nov. 1824.
1534. David Merrick 2d, b. May 3, 1830; of Buffalo?

671. Loring P. of Lockport, N. Y., son of Samuel 4th, m. Amanda M. Leet, Sept. 25, 1828. Children—
1540. Charles Leet, b. July 20, 1831.
1541. Myron, b. May 1834.
1542. George, b. July 22, 1846.

691. Horatio N. of ———, Wisconsin, son of Liberty, m. Jane Ameaman, Children—
1550. Charles C., b.
1551. Julia Ann, b.
1552. Cornelia Malvina, b
1553. Louisa, b.

SPRINGFIELD BRANCH—SEVENTH GENERATION. 47

1554. *Addison Warner*, b.
1555. *Francis Miriam*, b.

692. Samuel H. of Canandaigua, N. Y., son of Liberty, m. Sophia Lincoln. Children—
1560. *Ann Averett*, b.
1561. *Liberty*, b.
1562. *Francis Marion*, b.
1563. *James Byron*, b.

704. Moses II. of Otis, Mass., m. Henrietta McKean of Otis, Dec. 31, 1832. Children—
1570. *Edward Latimer*, b. April 30, 1834.
1571. *George De Witt*, b. April 4, 1837; d. Sept. 5, 1837.
1572. *Henry Albert*, b. Feb. 25, 1839.

705. Francis, of Springfield, son of Moses I., m. Ann S. Bates, April 10, 1842. Children—
1580. *Henry Francis*, b. Jan. 17, 1843.
1581. *Mary L. Sanderson*, b. Oct. 9, 1846.

706. Lyman, of Waterloo, N. Y., son of Moses I., m. Frances Clemens, Dec. 14, 1835. Children—
1590. *Maria*, b. May 12, 1839.
1591. *Charles Lyman*, b. Sept. 16, 1840.
1592. *Julia*, b. Oct. 15, 1842.
1593. *William Henry*, b. March 28, 1844.
1594. *Francis*, b. Oct. 28, 1845.
1595. *Mary Ellen*, b. Sept. 6, 1848.

707. Lester, of Colebrook, Conn., son of Moses I., m. Caroline Goss of Schagticoke, N. Y., Nov. 21, 1829, who d. Dec. 7, 1846. Children—
1600. *Charles L.*, b. Aug. 15, 1830.
1601. *James W.*, b. Feb. 3, 1832; d. Aug. 3, 1835.
1602. *Mary E.*, b. July 6, 1833.
1603. *James H.*, b. Sept. 2, 1835.
1604. *Eunice S.*, b. Feb. 11, 1837.
1605. *Lydia C.*, b. Feb. 4, 1839.
1606. *Adelphia A.*, b. July 27, 1842; d. Oct. 8, 1843.
1607. *Joseph C.*, b. July 8, 1844.

710. Rev. Ambrose, of Westfield, Mass., m. Sarah Spencer, May 31, 1815; ordained as an Evangelist, August 19, 1830. Children—
1610. *Harriet*, b. March 31, 1816; m. Rev. Otis Fisher of Illinois, Oct. 13, 1844.

1611. *Henry,* b. May 14, 1818; was graduated at Brown University in 1843; in 1846, Professor of Mathematics in Georgetown College, Ky., and in 1848, of Natural Sciences.
1612. *Spencer,* b. June 27, 1820.
1613. *Nathan,* b. Aug. 11, 1822.
1614. *Sarah Jane,* b. Dec. 22, 1824; d. Feb. 21, 1842, aged 17.
1615. *Wealthy Frances,* b. April 15, 1827.
1616. *Adoniram Judson,* b. Dec. 2, 1829.
1617. *Milton,* b. April 7, 1832.
1618. *Samuel Calvin,* b. Sept. 2, 1834.
1619. *Ellen Augusta,* b. Aug. 28, 1837.

712. **Albert,** of Hartford, Conn., son of Ambrose I., m. Harriet Chapin of Springfield, Nov. 11, 1819. Children—
1620. *Harriet Louisa,* b. Feb. 2, 1821; m. Lucius Barbour, 1840.
1621. *Albert Frederic,* b. July 19, 1824.
1622. *Charles Gustavus,* b. April 19, 1829.

714. **Calvin,** of Hartford, Conn., son of Ambrose I., m. Catharine Seymour of that city, Dec. 5, 1827. Children—
1630. *Julia Seymour,* b. July 7, 1829.
1631. *Caroline Elizabeth,* b. Oct. 19, 1833.
1632. *John Calvin,* b. Nov. 3, 1835.
1633. *Catharine Perkins,* b. Feb. 24, 1837.

715. **Horatio E.** of Hartford, Conn., son of Ambrose I., m. Adelia Burt of that city, Nov. 19, 1839. Children—
1640. *James Raymond,* b. Nov. 19, 1842.
1641. *Mary Adelia,* b. Nov. 14, 1844.

720. **Martin II.** of Westfield, Mass., m. Almira Weller of that town, Nov. 16, 1827. Children—
1650. *Sarah Ann,* b. March 24, 1830.

724. **David N.** of Westfield, Mass., son of Martin I., m. Eliza L. Johnson of Bristol, Conn., April 4, 1833. Children—
1660. *Helen Rosalie,* b. June 2, 1834.
1661. *Martin N.,* b. Jan. 8, 1836.

725. **Samuel D.** of Fredericksburgh, O., son of Martin I., m. Angelica Brower, Feb. 1835. Children—
1670. *Andrew V. P.,* b. Nov. 1835.
1671. *Gertrude,* b. 1837.
1672. *Samuel,* b. 1845.

728. **William T.** of Fredericksburgh, O., son of Martin I., m. Catharine Gillett, Dec. 17, 1833. Children—
1680. *Virginia P.*, b. May 1837.
1681. *Harrison*, b. 1840.

729. **James R.** of Northampton, Mass., son of Martin I., m. Sarah J. Hart of that town, Oct. 22, 1843. Children—
1690. *Mary Elizabeth*, b. July 20, 1844; d. Sept. 10, 1845.
1691. *Charles Noble*, b. June 8, 1846.

730. **Edward B.** of Westfield, Mass., son of Martin I., m. Almira Atkins of that town, Dec. 1844. Children—
1700. *Louisa B.*, b. Nov. 7, 1845.
1701. *Elizabeth M.*, b. Sept. 17, 1847.

760. **Rev. George E.** of Northampton, Mass., son of Gad, was graduated at Yale College in 1833, and in the Theological Department in 1838: ordained Pastor of the Union Congregational Church in Marlborough, Mass., Dec. 2, 1840; dismissed Dec. 21, 1847: installed Pastor of the Edwards Church in Northampton, Jan. 12, 1848; m. Amelia H. Oaks (b. June 30, 1821) of New Haven, Conn., Aug. 24, 1843.

761. **Horace**, of New Haven, Conn., son of Gad, was graduated at Yale College in 1836: m. Sarah R. Seaver, daughter of Heman Seaver of Montreal, Nov. 20, 1844. Children—
1710. *Robert Ellsley*, b. Oct. 2, 1845.
1711. *George Edward*, b. Aug. 1, 1847.

770. **Thomas S.** of ———, N. Y., son of Erastus, m. Lucy A. Gilbert, July 5, 1834.
1720. *Elizur C.*, b. May 5, 1835.
1721. *Margaret L.*, b. Aug. 29, 1839; d. June 10, 1840.

771. *Erastus W. of ———, N. Y., son of Erastus, m. Indiana Toles, Jan. 13, 1831, and d. Oct. 18, 1843, aged 36. Children—
1730. *Carlos M.*, b. Aug. 1833.
1731. *Philemon R.*, b. Jan. 1838.
1732. *Sylvia S.*, b. Oct. 1842.

772. **Carlos C.** of Avon, Conn., son of Erastus, m. Lavilla Woodruff of Avon, Sept. 20, 1834. Children—
1740. *Roger Stanley*, b. June 9, 1842.
1741. *Julia L.*, b. Aug. 5, 1843.
1742. *Carlos E.*, b. April 14, 1847.

774. **Newell,** of Durham, N. Y., son of Erastus, m. Mary Ann Scoville, Nov. 5, 1835. Children—
1750. *Adaline Bathsheda,* b. Dec. 9, 1837.
1751. *Caroline Amelia,* b. Aug. 6, 1845.

782. **Dennis C.** of ———, son of Newell, m. Matilda Spencer, Sept. 2, 1830.

785. **Andrew J.** of ———, son of Newell, m. Minerva P. Nichols, Feb. 15, 1841. Children—
1760. *Lucella,* b. Dec. 12, 1843.

791. **Marcus,** of Canaan, Pa., son of Wareham, m. Hannah Spangenberg, March 10, 1843. Children—
1770. *Olive,* b. Sept. 1, 1844.

800. **Rollin,** of West Candor, Tioga Co., N. Y., son of Stanley, m. Sarah E. Hart, Sept. 3, 1840. Children—
1780. *Mary Emily,* b. Jan. 11, 1843; d. Feb. 16, 1847.
1781. *Elizabeth Ann,* b. Oct. 4, 1845.

801. **Henry,** of Candor, N. Y., son of Stanley, m. Almira E. Munroe of that town, Nov. 10, 1842. Children—
1790. *Henry Stanley,* b. Nov. 2, 1848.

802. **John,** of Spencer, N. Y., son of Stanley, m. Sarah Shepherd of that town, Feb. 25, 1847.

820. *****Chester,** of Louisville, N. Y., son of Joel 2d, m. Marinda Day, (902) Feb. 12, 1812, and was drowned Nov. 18, 1824. Children—
1800. *Lucretia,* b. Aug. 24, 1814; m. Harvey Church, April 5, 1835.
1801. *Francis,* b. May 28, 1817.
1802. *Asa,* b. Feb. 24, 1820; of Michigan.

822. **Edward,** of Massena, N. Y., son of Joel 2d, m. Aurelia Miller, Aug. 30, 1814. Children—
1810. *Dwight,* b. Jan. 4, 1815.
1811. *Joseph,* b. Dec. 1, 1818.
1812. *Cyrus,* b. May 27, 1820; of Norwich, Conn.
1813. *Laura,* b. Aug. 27, 1825; m. Silas Felton, Jan. 14, 1849.
1814. *Joel H.,* b. May 27, 1830.

830. **Newton,** of West Springfield, (Ireland Parish,) son of Joel 2d, m. Laura Morgan, May 30, 1830. Children—

SPRINGFIELD BRANCH—SEVENTH GENERATION. 51

1820. *Laura, b. Jan. 27, 1831; d. Dec. 7, 1832.
1821. *Amanda, b. Nov. 26, 1833; d. Aug. 7, 1838.
1822. Martha, b. June 19, 1837.
1823. Eunice Amelia, b. Sept. 12, 1839.
1824. Laura Sophia, b. March 14, 1845.

852. Eli II. of Northampton, (South Farms,) m. Hannah Waite of Northampton, June 9, 1812. Children—
1830. *Caroline, b. Nov. 8, 1813; d. Jan. 28, 1840, aged 27.
1831. Harriet, b. Nov. 6, 1815; m. (1st) Lorenzo K. Strong; (2d) Mason Butts of Napier, Mich.
1832. Tryphena, b. Jan. 27, 1817; m. Elisha Parsons of Easthampton, Mass.
1833. Ebenezer Waite, b. Dec. 5, 1819.

854. Jedediah, of West Springfield, (Ireland Parish,) son of Eli I., m. Mehitable Wolcott, Children—
1840. *Jedediah, b.
1841. Emerson, b.

863. Robert, of Irving, Mass., son of James, m. Adaline Pomeroy of Gill, Nov. 13, 1823. Children—
1850. *Ellen Clayton, b. April 14, 1826; d. Jan. 7, 1827.
1851. Ellen Clayton, b. July 1, 1829.
1852. Frances Pomeroy, b. Nov. 1, 1832.
1853. Josephine Field, b. May 22, 1835.
1854. James Pomeroy, b. Aug. 4, 1837
1855. *Robert Newton, b. Sept. 20, 1840; d. Jan. 13, 1843.
1856. Susan Ferry, b. Oct. 16, 1843.

864. James II. of Gill, Mass., m. Merceline Sprague of that town, Nov. 14, 1824. Children—
1860. Edwin Ely, b. Sept. 3, 1825.
1861. Joseph Sprague, b. Jan. 30, 1827.
1862. Robert, b. Oct. 1, 1828.
1863. Ann Maria, b. Nov. 10, 1830.
1864. Charles Wright, b. Feb. 19, 1833.
1865. Cornelia Merceline, b. April 14, 1839.
1866. James Perkins, b. April 27, 1842.
1867. Sarah Jane, b. Oct. 17, 1845.
1868. Clarissa, b. April 12, 1848.

871. Pattison, of Greene, Chenango Co., N. Y., son of Alexander, m. Carlisle Caniff, May 1, 1832. Children—
1870. Luman, b.

1871. *Eliza*, b.
1872. *Dwight*, b.

880. **Nathaniel**, of Burke, Franklin Co., N. Y., son of Justin, m. Eunice Cole (b. April 22, 1782) of Amherst, Mass., Dec. 29, 1818. Children—

1880. *Joseph Eastman*, b. Oct. 17, 1821.

881. **John**, of Chateaugay, N. Y., son of Justin, m. Cynthia Newton of that town, Jan. 25, 1823, who was b. Oct. 8, 1804. Children—

1890. *Henry S.*, b. April 23, 1826.
1891. *John W.*, b. Nov. 30, 1829.

882. **Justin II.** of Chateaugay, N. Y., m. Diadema Bateman, Feb. 10, 1818, who was b. Aug. 25, 1792. Children—

1900. *Laura*, b. Dec. 6, 1819; d. Dec. 25, 1831.
1901. *Angeline A.*, b. March 6, 1821; m. James M. Wilder, Aug. 6, 1843.
1902. *Delia A.*, b. May 30, 1824; m. Moses C. Willis, May 27, 1847.
1903. *Celinda A.*, b. Sept. 25, 1826.
1904. *Andrew J.*, b. July 10, 1828.
1905. *John W.*, b. Aug. 8, 1829.
1906. *George W.*, b. March 6, 1831.

883. **Oreda**, of Bombay, N. Y., son of Justin I., m. Eliza Allen, Dec. 30, 1818, who d. Jan. 13, 1841. Children—

1910. *Louisa*, b. Dec. 20, 1820; m. Almanzo Robinson, Sept. 9, 1845.
1911. *Orrin*, b. Dec. 15, 1822; d. Oct. 26, 1844.
1912. *Rodney E.*, b. Sept. 23, 1826; of Bernardston, Mass.
1913. *Anna M.*, b. Dec. 5, 1824.
1914. *James A.*, b. July 3, 1828; of Bernardston, Mass.
1915. *Rhoda*, b. Aug. 13, 1830; m. Thomas J. Waite of Southport, Wis.
1916. *Phebe M.*, b. June 11, 1832.
1917. *Cynthia*, b. Feb. 22, 1834.
1918. *Charles D.*, b. Jan. 10, 1836.
1919. *De Witt A.*, b. May 5, 1838.

891. **Horatio**, of Essex, Vt., son of David 2d, m. (1st) Huldah Richardson, Feb. 14, 1819, who d. Sept. 2, 1827; (2d) Esther Richardson, Jan. 23, 1828. Children—

1920. *Charles E.*, b. Feb. 17, 1820.
1921. *Pamela V.*, b. May 3, 1821; m. Lewis Whitney of Petersham, N. Y., Oct. 17, 1848.

1922. *Seth R.*, b. May 31, 1823; of Jay, Essex Co., N. Y.
1923. *William C.*, b. June 13, 1825.
1924. *Elizabeth H.*, b. March 11, 1827.
1925. *Laura Ann*, b. Nov. 1, 1832.

893. Childs, of Essex, Vt., son of David 2d, m. Mahala Collins, Feb. 24, 1822. Children—
1930. *Edwin*, b. Dec. 25, 1823; of Buffalo, N. Y.
1931. *Angeline*, b. July 11, 1825.
1932. *Oscar*, b. March 27, 1827.
1933. *Thaddeus*, b. Feb. 14, 1829; of Buffalo, N. Y.
1934. *Frances*, b. July 5, 1830.
1935. *Cornelius*, b. Aug. 20, 1832.
1936. *Henry*, b. May 15, 1834.
1937. *Lucius*, b. March 5, 1836.
1938. *Marquis*, b. Nov. 28, 1837.
1939. *Mary*, b. Oct. 25, 1841.
1940. *Franklin*, b. June 3, 1846.

896. *David III. of Essex, Vt., m. Zilpha Griffin, Dec. 29, 1829, and d. Dec. 9, 1845. Children—
1950. *Sylvia*, b. Sept. 16, 1827; d. Dec. 7, 1846.
1951. *Asa B.*, b. July 10, 1830; d. July 28, 1842.
1952. *Edgar G.*,
1953. *Ellen G.*, } Twins, b. Feb. 19, 1833.
1954. *John F.*, b. Oct. 20, 1835.
1955. *Celia*, b. Jan. 10, 1838; d. Sept. 21, 1844.
1956. *Albert B.*,
1957. *Alfred B.*, } Twins, b. Aug. 25, 1842: d. Nov. 28, 1842.
1958. *David S.*, b. Dec. 14, 1844.
1959. *Olivia*, b. July 15, 1846.

898. Irad, of Bloomington, Iowa, son of David 2d, m. Zetta Mead, July, 1839, and has two sons and one daughter.

901. *Jube C. of Centreville, Mich., son of Asa, m. Demetrias Willson, Feb. 8, 1824, and d. Dec. 15, 1847, aged   Children—
1970. *Octavius*, b.
1971. *Delia*, b.
1972. *Martha*, b.
1973. *Marinda*, b.
1974. *John*, b.
1975. *Robert*, b.

904. Robert, of Lockport, N. Y., son of Asa, m. Susan Church, Dec. 10, 1824.

913. **Samuel,** of Essex, Vt., son of Hezekiah, m. Mary Thayer, in 1833. Children—

1990. *Eliza,* b. Jan. 16, 1835.
1991. *Mary,* b. Nov. 14, 1836.
1992. *Sarah A.,* b. Oct. 6, 1839.
1993. *Harriet,* b. June 22, 1842.
1994. *Samuel* 2d, b. March 8, 1845; d. July 8, 1845.
1995. *Martia,* b. Aug. 12, 1847.

914. **Chester,** first of Essex, Vt., then of Underhill, Vt., son of Hezekiah, m. Esther D. Pattrill, Oct. 15, 1832. Children—

2000. *Martha Rosanna,* b. Oct. 30, 1833.
2001. *Henry C.,* b. Feb. 9, 1836.
2002. *Eliza Ann,* b. May 8, 1837.
2003. *Ellen R.,* b. Dec. 6, 1838.
2004. *Elizabeth,* b. Sept. 10, 1840; d. Nov. 27, 1842.
2005. *Joseph,* b. Jan. 19, 1842.
2006. *Alfred L.,* b. Feb. 6, 1844.
2007. *William P.,* b. Sept. 27, 1846.
2008. *Isabella J.,* b. Aug. 27, 1848.

917. **Jonathan,** of Essex, Vt., son of Hezekiah, m. Hannah Page, Aug. 1, 1843. Children—

2010. *Jane,* b. March 4, 1844.
2011. *Ellen,* b. Feb. 22, 1846.

926. **Brigham II.** of West Springfield, (Ireland Parish,) m. Nancy Ann Cilley of Canada:—and has one child—

930. **Eleazer,** of Somerset, Vt., son of Eleazer M., m. Amarilda Hitchcock of Springfield, Jan. 5, 1830. Children—

2030. *Alonzo,* b. Aug. 31, 1832.
2031. *John C.,* b. Dec. 7, 1835.
2032. *Ellen,* b. Sept. 25, 1840.

941. **Sylvester,** of Springfield, Mass., son of Hosea, m. Eliza Ely, Feb. 18, 1827. Children—

2050. *Joseph,* b. March 1, 1838.
2051. *Eliza Jane,* b. May 3, 1839; d. Jan. 12, 1841.
2052. *Charles Henry,* b. Sept. 27, 1842.
2053. *Homer Sylvester,* b. Jan. 24, 1846.

942. **Eldridge,** of West Springfield, son of Hosea, m. Miriam S. Ardoway of that town. Children—

2060. *Julia M.,* b. July 9, 1844.
2061. A daughter, b. Oct. 2, 1848.

955. **William H.** of New York City, son of Joseph 3d, m. Mercy C. Church of Brattleboro', Vt., Jan. 4, 1847. Children—
2070. *William Plummer*, b. Sept. 30, 1848.

962. **Norman,** of Chicopee, (Willimansett,) son of Sylvester, m. Jane E. Reed of Granville, Conn., Nov. 28, 1845. Children—
2090. A daughter, b. Aug. 1848.

980. **Roswell,** of Searsburg, Vt., son of Solomon, m. Eliza Filllmore of Bennington, Vt., Oct. 21, 1841. Children—
2100. *Albert*, b. July 31, 1842; d. Sept. 2, 1842.
2101. *Almon F.*, b. Sept. 20, 1843.
2102. *Henry L.*, b. June 3, 1847.

981. **Henry B.** of Fair Haven, Conn., son of Solomon, m. Mary F. Ives of West Springfield, April 22, 1833. Children—
2110. *Henry Bishop*, b. June 29, 1834: d. Nov. 14, 1836.
2111. *Henrietta L.*, b. Oct. 29, 1836.
2112. *Joseph Leverett*, b. March 20, 1838.
2113. *Josephine Ophelia*, b. Nov. 11, 1840.
2114. *Prosper Randall*, b. Oct. 17, 1844.

983. **Lyman,** formerly of Columbus, Ohio, now of Blendon, Franklin Co., Ohio, m. Fanny Watson of Troy, N. Y., April 19, 1837. Children—
2120. *George W.*, b. March 27, 1838.
2121. *Harriet M.*, b. July 11, 1841; d. Nov. 17, 1841.
2122. *Lovina*, b. Jan. 12, 1844.
2123. *Mary F.*, b. Sept. 20, 1845.

985. **Newton,** of North Granby, Conn., son of Roswell, m. Sybil Pease, Oct. 27, 1834. Children—
2130. *Diana S.*, b. July 28, 1835.
2131. *Diedrik M.*, b. Nov. 17, 1836.
2132. *Maria H.*, b. Nov. 30, 1841.

992. **Giles L.** of Johnston, Ohio, son of Giles 2d, m. Eunice C. Root, April 27, 1842.
2140. *Mary Rheuma*, b. Sept. 20, 1842; d. Nov. 5, 1843.
2141. *Emma Adilla*, b. Feb. 20, 1846.
2142. A daughter, b. Aug. 7, 1848.

993. **Willard,** of Mesopotamia, Ohio, son of Giles 2d, m. Marilla Stevens, Nov. 3, 1841. Children—

2150. *Helen*, b. April 26, 1843.
2151. *Maria*, b. Aug. 21, 1848.

994. Edward N. of Mesopotamia, Ohio, son of Giles 2d, m. Catharine Spangler, Dec. 1, 1844. Children—
2160. *Hannah E.*, b. Dec. 1, 1845.
2161. *Milo E.*, b. May 18, 1848.

996. Leicester, of Johnston, Ohio, son of Giles 2d, m. Christine Curly of that town, Dec. 30, 1844.

1020. William H. of Moravia, N. Y., son of Hon. Rowland, m. Mary A. Tallman, Sept. 23, 1841.

1030. Horatio, of Summer Hill, N. Y., son of Harvey, m. Abigail F. Baker, Feb. 13, 1840. Children—
2200. *Charles G.*, b. Jan. 7, 1841.
2201. *Jarvis*, b. June 15, 1845.

1031. Oscar, of ———, Wisconsin, son of Harvey, m. Abigail Royce, and has two daughters.

1034. Charles, of Springport, N. Y., son of Harvey, m. Jane Billings, Children—
2220. *Charles 2d*, b.

1075. Benjamin H. of New York City, son of Henry, m. Eveline Shepard, Sept. 13, 1831. Children—
2250. *Henry*, b. July 8, 1832.
2251. *Mary Ely*, b. Oct. 27, 1833; d. Feb. 23, 1838.
2252. *Benjamin*, b. March 7, 1838.
2253. *Clarence Shepard*, b. Aug. 9, 1844.

1100. William F. of Franklin, Portage Co., Ohio, son of David, licensed to preach Nov. 9, 1844; m. Ann D. Grover, May 19, 1847. Children—
2300. *Harriet E.*, b. March 29, 1848.

1150. *Frederic, son of William, removed to Canada, and perished in the conflagration of a hotel at Toronto, while there on business; m. Anna Wood of Rutland, Vt. Children—
2350. *Cynthia*, b. Dec. 1, 1810: m. ——— Kenyon of Michigan.
2351. *Harriet Ann*, b. Sept. 25, 1812; m. Abel Beach of Conewango, N. Y.
2352. *Henry M.*, b. Nov. 4, 1814.
2353. *Ira Frederic*, b.   d. in infancy.

1151. Henry, of Kosciusco Co., Ind., son of William, m. Sophia Spear of Ellington, (N. Y.?) Children—

2360. *William*, b. May 20, 1819.
2361. *Ursula Ann*, b. Feb. 1821; m. James Jacoby of Oswego, Ind.
2362. *Lucinda*, b. d. in infancy.
2363. *Nelson Leonard*, b. May 1823.
2364. *Louisa Jane*, b. Nov. 17, 1825; m. George Harton of Oswego, Ind.
2365. *Henry McIntire*, b. Feb. 1828.
2366. *Cyrus Shepard*, b. March 1830; d. Feb. 23, 1842.

1157. *William, of Conewango, N. Y., son of William, m. Maria Bates, Nov. 23, 1820, and d. Feb. 22, 1842, aged 41. Children—

2370. *Josephine Eliza*, b. Sept. 29, 1832.
2371. *William Leonard*, b. Nov. 3, 1834.
2372. *Arad I.*, b. Dec. 21, 1836.
2373. *Francis Ellsworth*, b. March 16, 1838.
2374. *Harlan Blake*, b. Dec. 24, 1840.

1240. Almon, of South Hadley, (Canal,) son of Ezekiel 2d, m. Betsey Ashley, Oct. 17, 1822. Children—

2400. *Mary Elizabeth*, b. Sept. 3, 1823; m. George J. Bartlett, Nov. 16, 1848.
2401. *Sophronia M.*, b. June 27, 1825.
2402. *Harriet Angeline*, b. Oct. 25, 1827; m. James Lathrop of South Hadley Falls.

1242. Elihu, of Newark, N. J., son of Ezekiel 2d, m. Harriet E. Beach of Newark, in 1828. Children—

2410. *Eliza Beach*, b.	1829.	
2411. *Harriet Climena*, b.	1832; d.	1836.
2412. *Albert Charles*, b.	1834; d.	1836.
2413. *Harriet Climena*, b.	1837.	
2414. *Jane Louisa*, b.	1839.	
2415. *Albert Elihu*, b.	1841; d.	1842.
2416. *Cleone Taylor*, b.	1843.	

1246. Ezekiel III., for some years of Newark, N. J., now in West Springfield, m. Mary Albright of Madison, N. J., Feb. 9, 1843. Children—

2420. *Ezekiel* 4th, b. Aug. 1845.

1253. Sylvester, of Lowville, N. Y., son of Justin, m. Mabel Babcock of Lowville, March 30, 1834. Children—

2430. *Warren W.*, b. Oct. 22, 1834.

2431. *Amanda*, b. June 6, 1836.
2432. *Harry*, b. Feb. 15, 1838.
2433. *Lydia*, b. Oct. 29, 1839.
2434. *Algernon*, b. June 16, 1842.
2435. *Franklin*, b. Dec. 24, 1844.
2436. *Jane*, b. Aug. 26, 1847.

1254. **Justin II.**, residing near Fairport, Ohio, m. Abby Briggs of Martinsburgh, N. Y. Children—
2440. *Arœtus*, b.

1255. **Harvey,** of Oneida Lake, N. Y., son of Justin, m. Dorothy Ann Markham, Children—
2450. *Henry*, b.   and four daughters.

1270. **Horace II.** of Villenova, N. Y., m. Sarah Chase, Children—
2480. *Theodosia Ely*, b. June 29, 1823.
2481. *Mary Chase*, b. April 24, 1825.
2482. *Horace 3d*, b. Feb. 17, 1827.
2483. *Esther Chase*, b. Dec. 9, 1828.
2484. *Emily Miller*, b. Dec. 19, 1830.
2485. *Benjamin Franklin*, b. June 28, 1833.
2486. *Alceste*, b. Nov. 14, 1835.
2487. *Lydia Matilda*, b. March 23, 1838.
2488. *Harriet*, b. Feb. 16, 1841.

1271. *****Luke**, of Springfield, son of Horace 1st, m. Harriet Chapin of that town, Sept. 1826, and d. Nov. 4, 1836, aged 32. Children—
2490. *Levi Ely*, b. July 24, 1827.
2491. *Harriet Chapin*, b. Aug. 30, 1829.
2492. *Jael Holmes*, b. Jan. 27, 1832.
2493. *Elizabeth Ann*, b. April 7, 1833.

1282. *****Asher H.** of ———, son of Kelsey, m. Delina Stiles of Westfield, Aug. 1839, and d. Feb. 5, 1847. Children—
2500. *William Henry*, b. April 7, 1841.

1290. **Thomas S.** of New York City, son of Luke 3d, m. Ann Maria Thompson of Springfield, N. J., who was b. Sept. 5, 1805. Children—
2510. *Joshua S.*, b. March 4, 1828.
2511. *****Thomas*, b. March 5, 1830; d. March 22, 1830.
2512. *Thomas Benton*, b. Oct. 18, 1834.
2513. *George Matsell*, b. June 25, 1838.

SPRINGFIELD BRANCH—SEVENTH GENERATION.   59

1293. Henry, of New York City, son of Luke 3d, m. Elizabeth Vanderwater of Hempstead, L. I., who was b. in 1816. Children—
2520. *Hester Ann*, b. March 20, 1837.
2521. *Elizabeth*, b. Aug. 12, 1839.

1320. Frederic, of Northampton, Mass., son of Noble, m. Phirilla Searl of Southampton, July 15, 1827. Children—
2540. *Joseph Sheldon*, b. Aug. 23, 1828.
2541. *Julia Elvira*, b. Dec. 10, 1830.

1340. Volney, of ———, son of Linus, m. ——— ———,
Children—
2560. *Mary S.*, b. Nov. 8, 1836.
2561. *Harrison V.*, b. April 22, 1840.
2562. *Florence E.*, b. Oct. 17, 1847.

1350. Asa II. of Zanesville, Ohio, son of Linus, m. Mary Ann Stewlock, Jan. 8, 1832. Children—
2570. *Lucy*, b. April 1, 1833.
2571. *Margaret*, b. Feb. 10, 1835.
2572. *Mary Ann*, b. Aug. 19, 1839.
2573. *William H.*, b. Dec. 25, 1840.
2574. *Stephen B.*, b. June 11, 1843.

1351. Almon, of Waterford, N. J., son of Asa I., m. ——— ———, and has four children—

1370. Judson H. of Lima, Ohio, son of Horatio, m. Susan L. Clark of Buffalo, N. Y., Aug. 25, 1838. Children—
2630. *Nancy Amelia*, b. April 15, 1839.
2631. *Francis Leora*, b. June 1, 1843.

1381. Ralph, of Deerfield, Ohio, son of Alva, m. Polly Laughlin, in 1832. Children—
2660. *Sarah B.*, b. Jan. 18, 1823; m. L. N. Wann, June 12, 1845.
2661. *John M.*, b. Oct. 29, 1826.
2662. *Elvira U.*, b. Oct. 9, 1831.
2663. **Judson R.*, b. Sept. 21, 1834; d. Aug. 30, 1847.

1390. Heman E. of Deerfield, Ohio, son of Mun, m. (1st) Maria M. Scranton, April 12, 1830, who d. July 18, 1838, aged 30; (2d) Martha Wakefield, April 10, 1840. Children—
2670. *Dudley M.*, b. Jan. 10, 1831.
2671. *Edgar M.*, b. Oct. 2, 1834.
2672. *Lucy A.*, b. April 8, 1837.

2673. *Ewing W.*, b. July 3, 1841.
2674. *Minerva Louisa*, b. July 1, 1845.

1392. **Mortimer L.** of ———, son of Mun, m. Lorinda Card, Sept. 29, 1833. Children—
2680. *Edward M.*, b. March 27, 1843.

1393. **Julius H.** of Deerfield, Ohio, son of Mun, m. Nancy Brisbane, Children—
2690. *Harrison*, b.

1395. **Roswell M.** of ———, son of Mun, m. Minerva M. Murrell, Aug. 29, 1839. Children—
2700. *Merrick E.*, b. July 23, 1840.
2701. *Sarah B.*, b. Nov. 5, 1842.
2702. *Homer L.*, b., Oct. 18, 1844.
2703. *Adelbert E.*, b. June 1, 1846.
2704. *George E.*, b. Oct. 12, 1848.

1410. **Alva O.** of Deerfield, Ohio, son of Lewis 2d, m. Minerva Higby, Children—
2730. *Edna*, b. April 16, 1835.
2731. *Lewis*, b. Aug. 1837.

EIGHTH GENERATION.

1612. **Spencer,** of Waukesha, Wis., son of Rev. Ambrose, m. Caroline Burchard of Hamilton, N. Y., May 1842. Children—
3000. *Helen Caroline*, b. March 1844.
3001. *James Henry*, b. Aug. 1846.

1621. **Albert F.** of Hartford, Conn., son of Albert, m. Annie W. Bulkley of New York, July 1, 1846. Children—
3030. *Annie Clendeling*, b. Oct. 15, 1848.

1801. **Francis,** of Lowville, N. Y., son of Chester, m. ——— Hogh, Dec. 8, 1840. Children—
3200. *Edward Chester*, b. May 8, 1841.
3201. *Aurelia*, b. May 18, 1842.
3202. *Martha Marinda*, b. April 5, 1844.

1810. **Dwight,** of Lisbon, N. Y., son of Edward, m. Johanna Towns of Lockport, N. Y., Dec. 25, 1838. Children—
3220. *Sarah Jane*, b. Dec. 25, 1840.
3221. *Aurelia*, b. July 10, 1846.

SPRINGFIELD BRANCH—EIGHTH GENERATION. 61

1811. **Joseph,** of Massena, N. Y., son of Edward, m. Eliza Proctor,
Children—
3230. *Laura,* b. Sept. 28, 1844.
3231. *Philena,* b. Nov. 12, 1847.

1833. **Ebenezer W.** of Northampton, (South Farms,) Mass., son of Eli 2d, m. Mary S. Burt of Otisco, N. Y., Jan. 31, 1845. Children—
3260. *George Newton,* b. March 4, 1847.

1860. **Edwin E.** of Gill, Mass., son of James 2d, m. Mary F. Blaisdell of Sidney, Me., Dec. 8, 1847.

1880. **Joseph E.** of Burke, N. Y., son of Nathaniel, m. Emily Mott of Malone, N. Y., Sept. 6, 1848.

1890. **Henry S.** of Chateaugay, N. Y., son of John, m. Caroline Smith of that town, Jan. 1, 1848. Children—
3370. *Cynthia L.,* b. Nov. 1, 1848.

1920. **Charles E.** of Luzerne, N. Y., son of Horatio, m. Harriet A. Spaulding, Oct. 27, 1844. Children—
3460. *Albert C.,* b. April 24, 1848.

2352. **Henry M.** of Ellington, N. Y., son of Frederic, m. Sarah C. Abbey of Ellington, Children—
3860. *Frederic,* b. died young.
3861. *Lucretia Anna,* b. March 1842.
3862. *Laura Ann.*
3863. *Martha Aurelia,* b.
3864. *Albert Evington,* b. March 1848.

SUPPLEMENT

DESCENDANTS

OF

CAPT. JOHN DAY

OF

SHEFFIELD, MASS.,

WHO MOVED TO

SHEFFIELD, OHIO

in 1816

Prepared by
SUMNER DAY and FRANK DAY

SUPPLEMENT

194 *John of Sheffield, Mass. son of Capt. William removed to Sheffield, O., in 1816, m. Lydia Austin of Sheffield, Mass., in 1794. He d. Oct. 8, 1827. She d. Oct. 9, 1854. Children—

500. *Rhoda, b. Nov. 26, 1794; d. Nov. 24, 1795.
501. *William, b. Dec. 15, 1796.
502. *Rhoda Maria, b. March 20, 1799; d. Oct. 10, 1825.
503. *John II., b. March 3, 1801.
504. *Norman, b. Jan. 24, 1803.
505. *Fanny, b. Apr. 3, 1805.
506. *James, b. Aug. 27, 1807.
507. *Lydia, b. March 5, 1810.
508. *Kellogg, b. Jan. 23, 1813.
509. *Frederick, b. Feb. 12, 1815.
510. *Edmund, b. Feb. 24, 1818.
511. *Eleanor, b. July 13, 1820.

SIXTH GENERATION.

501. *William of Sheffield, O., son of John 1st, m. Augusta Burrell of Sheffield, O. May 6, 1832 who d. Oct. 9, 1887. He d. Nov. 9, 1889. Children—

1160. *Huldah Maria, b. March 5, 1833.
1161. *William Augustus, b. June 14, 1835.
1162. Henry Kellogg, b. Aug. 22, 1837.
1163. Marietta, b. Sept. 30, 1839.
1164. Sumner Burrell, b. April 19, 1842.
1165. *Eugene I., b. April 12, 1847.
1166. Everett E., b. Nov. 3, 1850.

SEVENTH GENERATION.

1160. *Huldah Maria, of Sheffield, O., daughter of William, m. Rev. G. Frederick Wright of Whitehall, N. Y., Aug. 28, 1862. He was a member of Company C, 7th O. V. I., for 5 months in 1861, pastor in Bakersfield, Vt., 1861-72, in Andover, Mass., 1872-81, professor in Oberlin Theological Seminary and College from 1881, member of Pa. Geol. Survey, 1881-2, and of the U. S. Geol. Survey, 1884-92, president of the Ohio Archæol. and Hist. Soc. since 1907, fellow of the Geological Society of America, the American

Association for the Advancement of Science, Boston Society of Natural History, etc., author of "Logic of Christian Evidences," "Ice Age in North America," "Scientific Confirmations of Old Testament History," "Origin and Antiquity of Man," besides other books and magazine articles. She died July 21, 1899. Children—

Mary Augusta, b. Sept. 1, 1867.
Etta Maria, b. Jan. 18, 1870.
Frederick Bennett, b. Nov. 4, 1873.
Helen Marcia, b. Dec. 7, 1879.

1161. *William Augustus, of Sheffield, Ohio, son of William, m. Mary Steele of Oberlin, O., Mar. 14, 1861, and died May 4, 1910. Children—

3870. *Maude*, b. Feb. 8, 1862; m. George, son of Jas. Day of Sheffield, O., Oct. 9, 1901.
3871. *William Steele*, b. Aug. 6, 1863.

1162. Henry Kellogg, of Elyria, O., son of William, m. Elizabeth C. Pomeroy of Strongsville, O., May 5, 1862, who d. Dec. 23, 1911. Children—

3880. *Arthur Pomeroy, b. Nov. 1, 1866; d. Aug. 21, 1870.
3881. *Alice Elizabeth*, b. Jan. 30, 1884.

1163. Marietta, of Sheffield, Ohio, daughter of William, m. Hiram A. Disbrow of Atlantic, Ia., Oct. 14th, 1875, who d. Apr. 27th, 1910. He enlisted in Co. I, 23d Iowa Infantry, July 27, 1862, mustered out Aug. 25th, 1865. Was Grand Commander of the G. A. R. of Iowa for years. Children—

Greta, b. July 11, 1878.
Ruth, b. March 27, 1881.
Albert, b. Dec. 27, 1882.
**Louise*, b. Aug. 25, 1885; d. Nov. 3, 1888.

1164. Sumner Burrell, of Elyria, Ohio, son of William, m. Sue M. Knox of Russell, N. Y., May 28, 1867. Children—

3890. *Lee S.*, b. Aug. 21, 1870.
3891. *Edith M.*, b. Dec. 2, 1874.

1165. Eugene I., of Weeping Water, Neb., son of William, m. Mary Carter of Sheffield, O., Feb. 21, 1872. He d. July 5, 1894. Children—

3900. *Carl Eugene*, b. Oct. 9, 1876.
3901. **Carrie Augusta*, b. Oct. 18, 1885; d. June 30, 1886.
3902. **Mildred Louise*, b. July 9, 1889; d. Nov. 30, 1893.

LYDIA AUSTIN DAY (194),
Wife of Capt. John Day of Sheffield, Ohio.

SUPPLEMENT.

1166. Everett E., of Weeping Water, Neb., son of William, m. Jennie M. Norton of Atlantic, Ia., Dec. 15, 1881. Children—

3910. *Harold E.,* b. Feb. 22, 1883.
3911. *Mabel,* b. Feb. 25, 1887.
3912. *Margaret,* b. Jan. 30, 1890.
3913. *Elizabeth,* b. March 25, 1891.
3914. *Augusta,* b. June 12, 1893.
3915. *Helen,* b. Sept. 13, 1894.
3916. *Seward P.,* b. May 3, 1897.

EIGHTH GENERATION.

3871. William S. of Sheffield, O., son of William A., m. Maggie Pigg of London, Ky., Feb. 17, 1898. Children—

4000. *Sumner William,* b. Dec. 13, 1899.
4001. *Helen Maude,* b. July 22, 1902.
4002. **Howard Eugene,* b. June 27, 1910; d. Feb. 18, 1911.
4003. *Walter Benjamin,* b. Nov. 19, 1912.

3890. Lee S., of Elyria, Ohio, son of Sumner Burrell, m. Maude Allen of Gouverneur, N. Y., Oct. 1, 1910. Children—

4010. *William Allen,* b. June 27, 1911.
4011. **Bernice Elizabeth,* b. June 1, 1912. She d. June 7, 1913.

3891. **Edith Maria,** of Elyria, Ohio, daughter of Sumner Burrell, m. Asaph Jones of Elyria, Ohio, Nov. 9, 1898. Children—
Ernest Lee, b. Apr. 1, 1901.
Sumner Richard, b. Nov. 6, 1903.
Roderic Orlando, b. June 4, 1911.

3900. **Carl,** of Weeping Water, Neb., son of Eugene I., m. Ida Laura Cowles of Cambridge, Neb., Aug. 6, 1903. Children—
4020. *Eugene Cowles,* b. Dec. 19, 1904.
4021. *John Robert,* b. Apr. 29, 1912.

3910. **Harold,** of Cambridge, Neb., son of Everett E., m. Marie L. Brown of Cambridge, Neb., Sept. 14, 1910. Children—
4030. *Clara Brown,* b. Aug. 14, 1911.
4031. *Harold Everett,* b. June , 1913.

JUDGE WILLIAM DAY (501).
This picture was taken in his 89th year.

3911. **Mabel,** of Weeping Water, Neb., daughter of Everett E., m. Osman M. Card of Logan, Ia., Apr. 20, 1910. They reside in Weeping Water. Children—
Everett Day, b. March 7, 1911.

3916. **Seward P.,** of Weeping Water, Neb., son of Everett E.

SIXTH GENERATION.

503. *John II., of Sheffield, O., son of John I., m. Cornelia Ann Sackett of Avon, O., Mch. 24, 1831, who d. Mch. 11, 1881. He d. Mch. 22, 1871. Children—

1170. *John Ingersoll,* b. Sept. 4, 1832; d. Oct. 15, 1838.
1171. *Sophia Ann,* b. May 21, 1834; d. Oct. 1, 1838.
1172. *Harriett Cornelia,* b. May 2, 1836; d. Oct. 26, 1837.
1173. *Alfred,* b. July 28, 1837.
1174. John Ingersoll, b. Nov. 27, 1838.
1175. *Robert Ithamar,* b. Nov. 16, 1842; d. June 7, 1850.
1176. Hubert, b. Aug. 11, 1844.
1177. *Lillie Sophia,* b. Jan. 31, 1856.

SEVENTH GENERATION.

1173. *Alfred, of Mondovi, Wis., son of John II. Served three years in the 23d O. V. I. during the Civil War, m. Lida Augusta Holmes of Mondovi, Wis., Oct. 10, 1869, and d. Aug. 24, 1910. Children—
3920. *Addie C.*, b. Sept. 22, 1870.
3921. *John W.*, b. Apr. 19, 1872.
3922. *Edith May*, b. June 10, 1879; d. Dec. 16, 1884.
3923. *Hubert*, b. Feb. 28, 1881.
3924. *Alice June*, b. June 18, 1882.
3925. *Lida Augusta*, b. Mch. 31, 1884.
3926. *Lillie Pearl*, b. Aug. 27, 1885.

1174. John Ingersoll, of Denmark, Ia., son of John II., m. Mary Elizabeth Brown of Denmark, Ia., Feb. 7, 1870, who d. Feb. 14, 1911. Children—
3930. *Lillian Anna*, b. Aug. 9, 1879. Adopted by them in 1879.

1176. Hubert, of Elyria, O., son of John II., m. Annie Louise Chambers of Elyria, O., Nov. 26th, 1878. Children—
3940. *Mildred Eleanor*, b. Sept. 17, 1879.
3941. *Hubert Kellogg*, b. Sept. 12, 1881.
3942. *George Myron*, b. Oct. 14, 1885.
3943. *Harlan Harrison*, b. June 7, 1888; d. July 2, 1908.
3944. *Cora Mabel*, b. Dec. 6, 1890; d. Feb. 3, 1891.
3945. *Anne Dorothy*, b. Mch. 11, 1895.

1177. Lillie Sophia, daughter of John II., m. Sidney Freeman of Greeley, Col., Feb. 28, 1884. He d. in 1885. (Second) she m. James A. Barnes of Greeley, Feb. 21, 1886, and removed to Aberdeen, Wash., in 1907. Children—
Ralph Emerson, b. Jan. 23, 1890.

EIGHTH GENERATION.

3920. Addie C., of Mondovi, Wis., daughter of Alfred, m. Sidney G. Nogle of Mondovi, Wis., Sept. 22, 1895. Children—
Augusta Pearl, b. May 5,. 1896; d. Dec. 31, 1902.
Clair LeRoy, b. Oct. 3, 1897.
Earl LeVergne, b. Mch. 4, 1900.
Lennie Edward, b. Mch. 16, 1902.
Vivian Vesta, b. Oct. 8, 1903.
Cecil, b. Feb. 27, 1907.
Kenneth, b. Oct. 27, 1909.

JOHN DAY II. (503).

SUPPLEMENT. 71

3921. John William, of Mondovi, Wis., son of Alfred, m. Alice Edith Taylor of Sandusky, O., Nov. 23, 1897. Children—
4040. *Galen Augustus*, b. May 26, 1899.
4041. *Mara Eleanor*, b. Jan. 13, 1901.
4042. *Edna May*, b. July 8, 1902.
4043. *John Hubert*, b. July 19, 1903.
4044. *James Bernard*, b. Mar. 4, 1906.
4045. *Maude Lucile*, b. Sept. 22, 1908.

3923. Hubert, of Mondovi, Wis., son of Alfred, m. Eva Cripe of Mondovi, Wis., Mch. 8, 1905, who d. July 8, 1906. Children—
4050. *Eva, b. July 8, 1906; d. Oct. 8, 1906.

3925. Lida Augusta, of Mondovi, Wis., daughter of Alfred, m. D. J. Keyes of Mondovi, Wis., Dec. 25, 1906. Children—
Vincent Day, b. June 29, 1908.
Malcolm Wayne, b. Feb. 26, 1911.
Charlotte Edith, b. July 30, 1912.

3930. Lillian Anna, of Denmark, Ia., adopted daughter of John Ingersoll, m. Charles Wharton of Denmark, Ia., Feb. 5, 1902. Children—
Mildred Day, b. May 20, 1903.
Edith Marie, b. Oct. 29, 1904.
Irene Elizabeth, b. Nov. 13, 1906.

3941. Hubert Kellogg, of Elyria, O., son of Hubert, m. Ethel Belle Hancock of North Ridgeville, O., June 10, 1908.

3942. George Myron, of Elyria, O., son of Hubert, m. Silver H. Geldmacher of Denmark, Ia., June 14, 1911.

SIXTH GENERATION.

504. *Norman, of Sheffield, O., son of John I., m. Julia Ann Root of Sheffield, O., Aug. 10, 1830, who d. Jan. 18, 1869. He d. Oct. 12, 1880. Children—

1180. *Delia Maria,* b. July 3, 1831.
1181. *Richard William,* b. Mch. 26, 1833.
1182. *Laura Jane,* b. July 20, 1835.
1183. Eliza Florentine, b. Mch. 10, 1839.
1184. Lydia Amelia, ⎫ Twins, b. Dec. 9, 1841.
1185. Mary Cornelia, ⎬ Of Wellsville, N. Y.
1186. Charles Norman, b. Feb. 8, 1847.

SEVENTH GENERATION.

1180. *Delia M., daughter of Norman, m. Judge George Steele of San Luis Obispo, Cal., May 19, 1868, member of the Cal. State Constitutional Convention in 1877-78, member of the State Legislature one term and the State Senate two terms. He d. Oct. 1901. She d. Feb. 20, 1912.

1181. *Richard W., of Toledo, Ohio, son of Norman, m. Catharine A. Smith of Elyria, O., Jan. 25, 1859, who d. June 25, 1887. He d. Mch. 10, 1901. Children—

3950. Edith, b. Jan. 7, 1860.
3951. Clarence P., b. Jan. 28, 1862.
3952. *Dollabella,* b. Nov. 3, 1864; d. Aug. 13, 1897.
3953. *Julian R.,* b. Jan. 14, 1870; d. Mch. 31, 1911.
3954. Katherine S., b. Nov. 21, 1874.
3955. Edward B., b. Feb. 23, 1878.

1182. *Laura Jane, of Sheffield, O., daughter of Norman, m. Theron P. Otis of Wellsville, N. Y., Jan. 29, 1873. She d. Jan. 8, 1901. Children—

Norman Day, b. Jan. 11, 1877.

1183. Eliza Florentine, of Sheffield, O., daughter of Norman, m. Henry C. Bacon of Prairie Depot, O., Apr. 17, 1866. He was a member of the 103d O. V. I. for three years. First Lieut. of Co. F. Children—

Julia Davis, b. June 3, 1867; d. July 16, 1893.
Louis Henry, ⎫
Laura Alice, ⎬ Twins, b. Mch. 20, 1871.

1184. Lydia Amelia, of Sheffield, O., daughter of Norman, m.

NORMAN DAY (504).

SUPPLEMENT. 73

Henry M. Fitch of Sheffield, O., Mch. 20, 1861. Removed to Sheridan, Montana, in 1864. He d. Jan. 20, 1898. Children—
Willard, b. Aug. 9, 1862.
Laura Eleanor, b. May 21, 1871.

1186. **Charles Norman** of Wellsville, N. Y., son of Norman, m. Helen S. Lyman of Wellsville, N. Y., Feb. 1st, 1874. Children—
3960. *Charles Lyman*, b. Nov. 23, 1874.

EIGHTH GENERATION.

3950. **Edith**, daughter of Richard W., m. Dr. Asa A. Allen of Providence, R. I., Jan. 28, 1882. Children—
Harold, b. Apr. 6, 1884; d. Oct. 6, 1894.
Alfred, b. Nov. 6, 1885; d. Dec. 22, 1890.
Richard D., b. May 18, 1887.
Arthur, b. June 12, 1889.
Edgar, b. May 2, 1892.
Donald, } Twins, b. May 16, 1894. d. Aug. 5, 1894.
**Dorothy*,* }
Hugh, b. Jan. 7, 1897.
Eleanor, b. Feb. 16, 1902.

3951. **Clarence P.**, of Yonkers, N. Y., son of Richard W., m. Ida O. Chase of Baltimore, Md., Aug. 2, 1894. Children—
4060. *Chase L.*, b. May 14, 1895.
4061. *Lenox C.*, b. Aug. 14, 1896.
4062. *Claire A.*, b. Apr. 9, 1901.
4063. *Richard F.*, b. Apr. 3, 1904.
4064. *Natalie*, b. July 21, 1908.
4065. **Clarence P. Jr.*, b. Nov. 3, 1909; d. Dec. 31, 1909.

3954. **Katherine S.**, daughter of Richard W., m. Frank S. Bunnell of Norwich, Conn., Jan. 30, 1904. Children—
Richard D., b. June 14, 1906.
Catherine S., b. May 23, 1910.

3955. Edward B., of Pittsburgh, Pa., son of Richard W., m. Jessie S. Austin of Edgewood, Pa., June 18, 1903. Children—
4070. *Elizabeth S.*, b. Apr. 5, 1904.

3960. Charles Lyman, of Buffalo, N. Y., son of Charles Norman, m. Clara Louise Bowler of Boston, Mass. Children—
4080. *Colette Lyman*, b. Mch. 15, 1901.
4081. *Helen Frances*, b. Apr. 28, 1903.
4082. *Mary Louise*, b. Dec. 14, 1906.

SIXTH GENERATION.

505. *Fanny, of Sheffield, O., daughter of John I., m. Wm. H. Root of Sheffield, O., Apr. 15, 1834, who d. June 27, 1889. She d. Oct. 11, 1878. Children—
Orville, b. Oct. 23, 1837.
William,
*Walter, } Twins, b. Dec. 4, 1846. Walter d. Jan. 12, 1907.

SEVENTH GENERATION.

Orville, son of Fanny Day and Wm. H. Root of Sheffield, O., m. Sara A. Howes of Sheffield, O., Apr. 3rd, 1878. Children—
Fanny Elizabeth, b. Oct. 27th, 1880; m. Albert K. Hibbard, Sept. 28th, 1910.
Harriett Maria, b. Aug. 27, 1885.

FANNY DAY ROOT (505).

*Walter, son of Fanny Day & Wm. H. Root of Sheffield, O., m. Vira Watkins of Norvell, Mich., Sept. 6, 1871, who d. Aug. 14, 1900. He d. Jan. 12, 1907. Children—
*Alice Blanch, b. Oct. 19, 1872; d. Dec. 18, 1885.

William, of Lorain, O., son of Fanny Day and Wm. H. Root of Sheffield, O. m. Sara H. Hackett of Sheffield, O., Sept. 17th, 1873, who d. July 1881. For his second wife he m. Mrs. Mary Carey Hackett of Elyria, O., Oct. 1895. Children—
Florence, b. July 30th, 1876. She m. Ernest Brackett of Elyria, Oct. 7, 1896.

SIXTH GENERATION.

506. *James, of Sheffield, O., son of John I., m. Ann Eliza Austin of Sheffield, Ohio, Sept. 18, 1835, who d. Jan. 13, 1873. He d. Mch. 19, 1896. Children—
1190. *Charles Eugene, b. Dec. 24, 1836; d. Apr. 13, 1837.
1191. *Oscar, b. Nov. 1, 1838; d. Jan. 16, 1846.
1192. Frank, b. Mch. 20, 1841.
1193. George W., b. Aug. 25, 1843.
1194. Celia C., b. Nov. 19, 1845.
1195. *Arabella, b. Oct. 18, 1848.; d. Oct. 12, 1849.
1196. May Eliza, b. Oct. 10, 1850.
1197. Caroline Elizabeth, b. Feb. 22, 1854.

SEVENTH GENERATION.

1192. Frank, son of James, settled in Weeping Water, Neb., in 1874, m. Linda Fuller of Mt. Pisgah, Ind., Mch. 20, 1878. Children—
3970. Clyde J. Wyman, b. July 19, 1880.
3971. *James, b. Apr. 18, 1882; d.
3972. Milo F., b. May 6, 1886.

1193. George, of Sheffield, O., son of James, m. Maude Day, daughter of William A. of Sheffield, O., Oct. 9th, 1901.

1194. Celia, of Sheffield, O., daughter of James, m. Oct. 30, 1867, Cyrus Yale Durand of Romeo, Mich., who served three years in the 103d O. V. I. during the Civil War. They removed in 1883 to Huron, S. Dak., where he died Aug. 5, 1887. Children—
George Harrison, b. Dec. 31, 1868.
Edward Dana, b. Oct. 18, 1871; Director of the Thirteenth U. S. Census taken in the year 1910.
Walter Yale, b. July 26, 1874.

Albert Cyrus, b. Aug. 1, 1879.
Alice May, b. Nov. 14, 1884.

EIGHTH GENERATION.

3970. Clyde J. Wymen, of Sheffield, S. Dak., son of Frank, m. Eleanor C. Conkling of Osceola, Neb., Jan. 21st, 1904, who d. May 1st, 1904. Second marriage to Ida M. Thurston of Sheffield, S. Dak., Jan 1st, 1909. Children—

4090. *Alta May*, b. Feb. 12, 1910.

3972. Milo F., of Delta, Colo., son of Frank.

SIXTH GENERATION.

507. *Lydia, of Sheffield, O., daughter of John I., m. Kendrick K. Kinney of Sheffield, Ohio, Sept. 17, 1840, who d. Oct. 2, 1889. She d. Apr. 22, 1891. Children—

Kellogg, b. July 4, 1842; d. July 19, 1845.
Myron, b. July 10, 1845.

SIXTH GENERATION.

508. *Kellogg, of Denmark, Ia., son of John I., m. Mary L. Ingalls of Napoli, N. Y., Aug. 11, 1841, who d. Oct. 28, 1897. He d. Jan. 20, 1887. Children—

1200. *Mary Ermina*, b. Oct. 10, 1843.
1201. *Laura Ellen*, b. Sept. 5, 1845.
1202. *Harriett Caroline*, b. Dec. 20, 1847.

JAMES DAY (506).

SUPPLEMENT. 77

SEVENTH GENERATION.

1200. Mary Ermina, of Denmark, Ia., daughter of Kellogg, m. Latham Hull Ayer of Keokuk, Ia., June 21, 1876. Children—
*Ernest, b. Jan. 18, 1878; d. Jan. 19, 1878.
Latham Hull II., b. Aug. 21, 1879.
*Faith, b. July 6, 1881; d.

1201. Laura Ellen, of Denmark, Ia., daughter of Kellogg, m. Rev. Henry L. Bullen of Moline, Ill., Oct. 9, 1867. Children—
Laura Day, b. Jan. 17, 1869.
Henry Webster, b. Jan. 18, 1882.

1202. Harriett Caroline, of Denmark, Ia., daughter of Kellogg, m. Aug. 19, 1880, Rev. Thomas McClelland of Mendon, Ill., President of Pacific University, Forest Grove, Ore., 1891-1900, and Knox College, Galesburg, Ill., since 1900. Children—
*Harry, b. Nov. 12, 1881; d.
Kellogg Day, b. Mch. 26, 1884.
Cochran Bruce, b. Aug. 22, 1887.
Ruth Marjorie, b. Oct. 16, 1890.

SIXTH GENERATION.

509. *Frederick, of Sheffield, O., son of John I., m. Mary A. Sackett of Avon, O., Aug. 18, 1835, and d. Aug. 11, 1840. Children—
1210. Helen Amelia, b. May 5, 1836.
1211. Frederic Oliver, b. Mch. 2, 1840.

SEVENTH GENERATION.

1210. Helen Amelia, daughter of Frederick, m. Arora James Burrell of Spring Brook, Mich., Oct. 21st, 1858. He d. Nov. 4, 1909. Children—
Rose Day, b. Jan. 13, 1864.
Royal Orange, b. Aug. 15, 1870.

1211. Frederic O., Washington, D. C., son of Frederick, served during the Civil War in the 56th Illinois Inafntry and the First Illinois Light Artillery from Oct. 2, 1861, to July 26, 1865; m. Emma M. Tower of the State of Mich. Feb. 22, 1873, who d. Apr. 15, 1885. Children—
3980. Halsy Tower, b. Jan. 17, 1875.
3981. Frederic Allen, b. July 18, 1876.
3982. Carl Edmond, b. Mch. 19, 1880.

EIGHTH GENERATION.

3980. Halsey Tower, of Detroit, Mich., son of Frederic O., m. Sarah E. Johnston, Aug. 27th, 1902; m. second wife Gertie A. Oldfield of Detroit, Mich., July 21, 1910. Children—
4100. *Emma Euphemia,* b. July 2, 1903.
4101. *Gertie Jane,* b. Feb. 2, 1906.

3981. Frederic Allen, of Portland, Ore., son of Frederic O., m. Mable Adelle Fuller in 1896 of Greenville, Mich. Children—
4110. *Clare Allison,* b. Feb. 1, 1897.
4111. *Frederic Orville,* b. Apr. 4, 1900.
4112. *Evelyn Mable,* b. Sept. 16, 1906.

3982. Carl Edmond, of Portland, Ore., son of Frederic O., m. Clare D. Christianson June 12, 1906. She d. Dec. 10, 1909; m. second wife, Ada Elizabeth Hastings, Nov. 30, 1911. During the war with Spain in 1898 he served in the 32d Mich. Infantry and the 7th U. S. Cavalry.

LYDIA DAY KINNEY (507).

SUPPLEMENT. 79

SIXTH GENERATION.

510. *Edmund, of Sheffield, Ohio, son of John I., m. Camilla Austin of Sheffield, O., Sept. 2, 1846, who d. Dec. 15, 1892. He d. Oct. 17, 1898. Children—
1212. *Dell Mary, b. Feb. 28, 1849; m. D. T. Johnson Oct. 26, 1873, and d. Feb. 21, 1874.
1213. Quincy Dorr, b. Jan. 26, 1852.
1214. Dwight R., b. May 7, 1860.
1215. Dewey, b. Oct. 9th, 1863.

SEVENTH GENERATION.

1213. Quincy Dorr, of Toronto, Canada, son of Dr. Edmund, m. Fannie Maria Barrett of Cleveland, O., Jan. 27, 1874. She died Nov. 2nd, 1900. Children—
3990. Louise D., b. Jan. 28, 1876.
3991. Harriett Barrett, b. July 1, 1877.
3992. Clarence Austin, b. Apr. 2, 1879.
3993. Harold Otis, b. Oct. 12, 1881.
3994. Edmund Alphens, b. Jan. 21, 1892.
3995. Helen Gertrude, b. Dec. 3, 1896.

1214. Dwight R., of Cleveland, O., son of Dr. Edmund, m. Nettie Townsend of Cleveland, O., Oct. 18th, 1883. Children—
3997. Beulah May, b. Aug. 11th, 1890. Adopted 1892.

EIGHTH GENERATION.

3992. Clarence Austin, of Detroit, Mich., son of Quincy Dorr, m. Bertha Holden of the same place May 6, 1903. She d. Dec. 20, 1912. Children—
4130. Dorothy A., b. Apr. 13th, 1904.

3993. Harold Otis, of Calgary, Alberta, son of Quincy Dorr, m. Clara Dennison July 1st, 1906. Children—
4140. *Helen Alberta, b. July 19, 1907; d. aged one month.
4141. *Marjory May, b. Sept. 7, 1908; d. Dec. 29, 1908.
4142. *Norman Clarence, b. Dec. 25, 1909; d. May 3, 1912.
4143. Edward Barrett, b. Mch. 2, 1912.

SIXTH GENERATION.

511. *Eleanor, of Sheffield, O., daughter of John I., m. James Austin of Sheffield, O., Apr. 3, 1840, who d. Feb. 6, 1908. She d. July 30, 1902. Children—

Arthur Quinn, b. Aug. 22, 1844.

SEVENTH GENERATION.

Arthur Quinn, son of Eleanor Day and Jas. Austin of Sheffield, O., m. Fanny Smith of Stevensville, Mich., Jan. 19, 1870. Children—
Edith Eleanor, b. Jan. 31, 1874; m. Capt. Geo. L. Cudeback of Lorain, Ohio, Jan. 6th, 1897.
*George Quinn, b. Jan. 15, 1876; d. Aug. 3, 1877.
Harry William, b. Dec. 7, 1882.

KELLOGG DAY (508).

Notable Things in the Genealogical Register of the Springfield Branch of the Day Family

BY G. FREDERICK WRIGHT

In his summary of the second edition of this genealogical register Rev. George Day, one of the most distinguished members of the family, then of Northampton, Massachusetts, remarked that "very few of the family have been in any way distinguished." But it is fair to add that those few have been so distinguished as to add luster to the whole family name, and that the general average of those who bear the name is so high that while not individually distinguished they are as a class worthy of the highest esteem. Especially has the family been prominent in the pioneer work which has opened America to civilization and given to it its high character.

Mr. Thomas Day, born in Springfield in 1659, was the son of a woman of distinguished name, Sarah Cooper, whose father was killed by the Indians when the town was burnt. The will which is given under his name in this volume bears witness to his high character and broad accomplishments. As we come down in the list there is a constant succession of large families gradually subduing the wilderness lying west of the Connecticut River.

Fourth Generation.

Of the fourth generation Samuel II. of West Springfield, Massachusetts, was deacon of the church. Aaron of West Springfield graduated at Yale College in 1738. Benjamin of West Springfield was a colonel during the French and Indian wars. Most distinguished of all, perhaps, was William born in West Springfield, October 23, 1715. "Most of his life was spent in the sea-faring business and was filled up with stirring events, and thrilling adventures, 'as those who go down to the sea in ships and do business in great waters usually are.' He was in the service during the French War, holding his commission under the King of England. His vessel was captured at one time and he was carried a prisoner to France and was in prison there for two years. When released he begged the privilege of taking his old boots with him, which was granted; the boot heels were filled with guineas. For meritorious service during the war in capturing four French frigates, and bringing them into Plymouth harbor, he was in honor of his bravery and achievement, presented by the admiralty of England, with a large painting by Copley, commemorative of the event of his bringing them all into port. He is represented standing on the deck of his ship, spy glass in hand, calmly viewing the scene with the conscious pride of the victorious hero swelling in his breast, and lighting up his features." ("History of the Day Family read at the 80th Birthday Celebration of James Day, August 27, 1887." By Mrs. E. D. Austin.)

When on shore William made his home in Sheffield, Berkshire County, Massachusetts, and was active in town affairs up to his death in 1797 at the age of 82. Afterwards another branch of the family removed his remains to the Peabody Cemetery in Springfield, Massachusetts, and erected there a monument to his memory. On the first face of this there is the following inscription,—the poetical portion having been copied from the original monument in Sheffield, consisting of lines which had been composed by the aged patriot himself.

"In memory of Capt. William Day Born in Springfield Oct. 25, 1715. died in Sheffield March 22, 1797 aged 82 years. The action represented here was fought during the French War about the year 1760 by Capt. William Day."

[Picture—Five French boats one American.]

"Through various climes and tempests tossed,
From sea to sea and coast to coast,
Through dangers of the deep profound,
Each scene kind Heaven with safety crowned,
The storms and trials of life now o'er,
In death I reach a peaceful shore;
And when that sleeping dust shall rise
To meet my Saviour in the Skies,
May I appear in bright array,
And with him spend an endless day."

On the third face is the following:—

"In memory of Mrs. Rhoda Day wife of Capt. William Day, daughter of Major John Hubbell of Litchfield, Conn. died July 25, 1795 at Sheffield aged 47 years.

"Capt. William Day sailed in command of a frigate with a picked crew, encountering a fleet of five French ships in the Bay of Biscay. The Admirals Ship larger than his own was considerably in advance of the others. He engaged and captured her before the others came up, and neither vessel being much injured he divided his force with the captured ship and the others coming he attacked them with such spirit that they all surrendered and he brought them all safe into Plymouth. (The scene on the

DR. EDMOND A. DAY (510).

SUPPLEMENT. 83

other side of this monument is taken from a portrait painted at the time, now in possession of his family.) Capt. William Day soon after the war retired from the sea and settled in Sheffield, Mass. where he died. He was an active patriot in the revolution. He lived and enjoyed the esteem and respect of his friends and neighbors. His remains with those of his wife were removed from Sheffield and placed under this monument. This Monument is placed here by his Grandson Thomas D. Day of St. Louis."

Fifth Generation.

Thomas D. who erected the monument just described was the son of James of the fifth generation. James, like his father, won renown in naval warfare. In the war of 1812 he was in command of a vessel which was so hard pressed by an overpowering British squadron that he only escaped by running his vessel upon the rocks at Point Judith in Long Island Sound. For a short time he came to Sheffield, Ohio, to reside near his brother.

Jeremiah of New Preston, Connecticut, was graduated at Yale College in 1756, and settled in Sharon, Connecticut, which town he represented in the General Assembly for two successive terms. He was ordained pastor of the Congregational church in New Preston in 1770. His son Jeremiah, born in New Preston, became President of Yale College. To his career we will return under the sixth generation. Benjamin II. of West Springfield was graduated from Yale College in 1768. John, the son of Captain William, removed to Sheffield, Ohio, in 1816 and was the progenitor of the branch of the family whose genealogy is given in the supplement to this volume. Ithamar H. removed to Hull, Canada, where he became the father of the distinguished Charles Dewey to be noticed hereafter.

Sixth Generation.

Of the sixth generation the Rev. Jeremiah Day, D.D., LL.D., was graduated from Yale College in 1795, was elected tutor in Williams College in 1796, became professor of mathematics and natural history in Yale College in 1801, and was president of the College from 1817-1846. Besides a series of mathematical textbooks he wrote "An Inquiry concerning the Self Determining Power of the Will," and "An examination of President Edwards on the Will." The first of these books passed into a second edition, and both continue to be standard works upon the subjects treated. Hon. Thomas Day, LL.D., brother of the preceding, also was graduated at Yale College and was for a while tutor at Williams College. He was admitted to the bar in 1799, and from 1810-1835 was secretary of the state of Connecticut, and was for a long time president of the Connecticut Historical Society. Hon. Roland Day of Moravia, N. Y., was elected a member of the state legislature of that state in 1821, and in the following year was a member of the Constitutional Convention of the state. In 1832 he was a member of Congress. Benjamin, son of Heman, was graduated at Yale College in 1812. Hon. Charles D. Day of Montreal, Canada, was one of her majesty's executive counsel for the province of Canada; solicitor general; member of the provincial parliament; and one of the judges of the Queen's Bench at Montreal. Of the children of John who came to Sheffield in 1816, William, John II., Norman, and James became farmers in that township, William having been for some time one of the county judges. Kellogg was for some time a missionary to the Cherokee Indians, and Edmund for a considerable portion of his life practised medicine. Eleanor, the youngest of the two children born in Sheffield, Ohio, became practically the historian of the family as is indicated by the quotation which we have taken from the historical sketch written by her and read at the eightieth birthday celebration of James Day on the 27th day of August, 1887. Altogether this sketch is a model piece of literature, and indicates the qualities of the writer which won for her so high a place in the esteem of the whole circle of relatives. To the day of her death "Aunt Eleanor" as she was called continued to be the center of attraction in the August picnics which were annually held, for the most part at her house.

Seventh Generation.

Of the seventh generation, Rev. Henry N. Day of Hudson was graduated at Yale College in 1828, and for three years was tutor in the college. In 1837 he was ordained to the Congregational ministry and in 1840 elected professor of sacred rhetoric in the theological department of Western Reserve College. Rev. Ambrose Day of Westfield, Mass., was ordained an evangelist in 1830. Rev. George E. Day, D.D., was graduated at Yale College in 1833, and at Yale Divinity School in 1838, in which he was assistant instructor for two years in sacred literature. After pastorates in Marlborough and Northampton, Mass., he was professor of Biblical literature in Lane Theological Seminary, Cincinnati, Ohio, from 1851-1866, when he was elected professor of the Hebrew language and Biblical theology in Yale Divinity School, a position which he held until his death. He was secretary, from its organization, of the American Bible Revision Committee, in which he served as a member of the Old-Testament Company. Having taught in the New York Institution for the Deaf and Dumb for two years after graduating from college, he became deeply interested in deaf mute instruction and published two extended reports of his personal examination of the condition of deaf mute instruction in Europe, especially in regard to mechanical articulation. These reports appeared in 1845 and 1861. From 1863 to 1870 he edited the *Theological Eclectic*, a repertory of foreign theological liter-

ELEANOR DAY AUSTIN (511).

ature, for which he translated from the Dutch and also published separately, Van Oosterzee's "Biblical Theology of the New Testament." He also translated with additions Van Oosterzee on "Titus" for Dr. Schaff's edition of Lange's Commentary, and edited the American issue of Oehler's "Biblical Theology of the Old Testament" with an introduction and additional notes. In his last years he was associated with Professor Charles M. Mead in preparing the American edition of the revised version of the Old Testament, published in 1901.

Horace Day of New Haven, brother of George E., was graduated from Yale College in 1836.

Pioneer Services of the Descendants of Thomas Day.

Students of sociology cannot fail to be impressed with the debt we owe to the descendants of Thomas Day of Springfield, for the work which they have done as pioneers, both in opening up a new country for settlement and in laying foundations wherever they went for the advancement of all the higher forms of civilization. In glancing over the genealogy we see first a remarkable succession of large families who at length filled the Connecticut Valley to overflowing, and then spread in successive waves westward into Connecticut, Massachusetts, and Vermont. A little later the families appear in New York, and at the opening of the 19th century they appear in full force on the Western Reserve of Ohio.

Here it will be in place to notice more particularly the careers of the descendants of John Day, who removed from Sheffield, Massachusetts, to Sheffield, Ohio, in 1816. In 1794 John Day and Lydia Austin were married in Sheffield, Massachusetts, where they resided for twenty-one years until their removal to their new home in Ohio. Meanwhile ten children had come into the household. How in the world the mother who at the time of her marriage is described as "a frail delicate girl of nineteen summers" could care for so large a family and look after the affairs of the household as they had to be looked after in those days it is difficult for us of this generation to comprehend. The youngest one of her children, Eleanor, thus describes these duties. "In the spring the flax was to be spun, woven into cloth and whitened for the family supply of linen. That is a very short statement of the matter of supply, and conveys to those of the present day no idea of the amount and severity of the labor to be performed, of the many, many weary steps to be taken, the aches to be endured to accomplish all this. Later in the season the same process of spinning and weaving the wool, was to be gone through with for their winter clothing; all this cloth had to be made up of course. The modern woman even with the aid of a good sewing machine considers it a great task, a burden she can scarce endure to do the family sewing and her housework too. What would they think if they had to make their cloth as well, as our mothers did? Besides there was the butter, and cheese to make, a large family to be fed and cared for, washing, ironing, mending, baking, brewing, cleaning and the many other things all housekeepers find to do, went on continually in the old home, the theater of our mother's unceasing industry. Into this home with its stirring activities came every two years or more, a consignment of responsibility, with its attendant supply of love, and a demand for care and they called it John or Norman or Fanny, and so on as it pleased them, and proceeded forthwith to make a place in the Day family for this fresh arrival of pink humanity.

"There is always room, warm welcome and willing service in mother love, so the Day babies were all cordially received and the added burden of their care cheerfully taken up, although by what we have heard, we should judge the twelve of them all told did not receive as much attention, as one modern baby often gets. Still they got enough to make strong selfreliant men and women of them, and that was all that was needful."

The journey from Massachusetts to Ohio, which now can be made with comfort in sixteen hours, required then twenty-two days of arduous exertion and strenuous self-denial. In January 1815 Captain John Day joined with Jabez Burrell in the purchase of the tract of land now known as Sheffield, Lorain County, Ohio. After persuading several other persons to share the purchase with them they came to Sheffield in June to explore the township and to select lots for themselves and friends. On the 27th of the following July, Captain Day and his wife and his nine children arrived at their destination in Ohio, after a journey in covered wagons of more than three weeks. The heavy household goods and farming utensils had at Schenectady, New York, been loaded on a small half decked schooner of about fifteen tons burden which was sailed up the Mohawk, locked around the obstruction of Little Falls and thence drawn through the rude canal which led into Oneida Lake and thence through the Oswego River to Lake Ontario. At Queenston the schooner was unloaded, put upon cart wheels and drawn past Niagara Falls to Chippewa and there launched. Her cargo followed in like manner and was there reloaded. The schooner then proceeded through the lake and up Black River to the mouth of French Creek, where her cargo of salt and goods was landed on the Big Bottom.

A log house was soon built and the slow work of clearing a heavy forest begun. Here in the course of four years two other children were added to the household, making twelve in all. But they were surrounded with other households of proportionate size. Captain Burrell with his eight children arrived a few days after. Henry Root and his wife and six children had preceded them by two or three months, while Captain Smith with his eight children was already on the ground. Deer, and bears abounded in the forest and fish were abundant in the river, thus affording ready made a considerable portion of the food which was required. But bears were not altogether pleasant neighbors. Norman Day relates that in 1821 Peter Miller, a lad of 17, who was working for someone at the center of Sheffield, started to go home through the wilderness to his father's on the lake shore at Avon, five miles away. When he had gone one third of the way he met a bear and two cubs. To escape from the elder bruin that was coming towards him he hastily climbed a small smooth elm tree; but the bear followed him and seized one of his feet, when letting go her hold on the tree she fell to the ground, but quickly climbed the tree again with the same result as before. A third time the bear ascended when the boy frightened and exhausted lost his hold and both tumbled to the ground together. While the bear was collecting her thoughts amid the confusion, Peter ran back to the center of Sheffield, when the neighbors including Norman Day set out on a vain effort to find and secure the animal which had caused the trouble.

True to their traditions the Day family in Sheffield immediately set up religious and educational institutions. In the winter of 1816 religious meetings were commenced at the house of Captain Burrell, and in the absence of clergymen a sermon was read. In the spring of 1817 Alvan Coe preached the first sermon. In the fall of the same year Rev. Alvin Hyde began regular services in Sheffield and adjoining towns, and in 1818 the Congregational Church was formed, William Day being one of the original members. A log school house was soon built, near where the church now stands, and the first school in it was taught by Preston Pond from Keene, N. H. In June 1824 the town of Sheffield was organized by the County Commissioners, and John Day chosen as one of the trustees. The interest in religion and education thus shown has continued in all the descendants of this pioneer family. At one time or another nearly all those who were born in Sheffield have pursued their higher education in Oberlin College, and it still remains true that nearly all the members of the family are professors of religion, and with Aunt Eleanor we can point with pride to the fact that the descendants of John Day "have never from their number furnished a criminal, or a drunkard, or a disreputable person of any kind." Not satisfied with knowledge attained in school, May, daughter of James Day, became a recognized authority in the botany of Lorain County so that she was constantly consulted by professors of Oberlin. The herbarium which she presented to the College contains some specimens that had not before been discovered in the County. Lydia, daughter of Norman, became an equal authority in the botany of the Rocky Mountain region.

In due time the new hive swarmed; and as pioneers went out from Sheffield in Massachusetts, so again they went out from Sheffield, Ohio, to carry with them their habits of industry, economy, and upright life, and spread broadcast the leaven so successfully brought from the ancestral home.

As already remarked Kellogg Day was for many years a missionary among the Cherokee Indians. Alfred, a son of John II., after having served three years in the Civil War took up his residence and has reared a large family in Mondovi, Wisconsin. His brother John I. early removed to Denmark, Iowa. Their sister Lillie Sophia after marriage settled in Aberdeen, Washington. Della M., daughter of Norman, after her mariage to Judge George Steele, was for more than forty years a resident of San Luis)Obispo, California. Lydia Amelia, daughter of Norman, removed to Montana in 1864, and narrowly escaped the Indian massacres which followed the Civil War. Frank, son of James; and Eugene and Everett, sons of William, were early settlers in Weeping Water, Nebraska. Their sister Marietta, after teaching for some time in Tabor College, Iowa, married and with her husband settled for life in Atlantic, Iowa. Celia, daughter of James, was one of the early settlers of Dakota, where she reared a family who have all become distinguished. Mary, Laura, and Harriet, daughters of Kellogg, have all been active in promoting the good things in the Mississippi Valley, Harriet having spent most of her life as the wife of a college president who was first at Pacific University, Forest Grove, Oregon, and is now at Knox College, Galesburg, Illinois. Harold Otis, son of Quincy Dorr, is rearing a family in Calgary, Alberta.

Those who have served their country in the Civil War are Hiram A. Disbrow, husband of Marietta; G. F. Wright, husband of Maria; Alfred, son of John; Henry C. Bacon, husband of Eliza F.; Cyrus Yale Durand, husband of Celia; and Frederic O., son of Frederick; while Carl Edmund, son of Frederic O., served in the Cuban War. (It is interesting also to note that Mr. Disbrow's father was in the Mexican War, while two grandfathers were in the War of 1812, and two great grandfathers in the War of the Revolution.)

Though the size of the families like those of nearly all of the native born population of the United States has greatly diminished since 1850, so that the rate of increase has been less than when the first edition of this volume was published, there have been during the century since John Day and Lydia Austin were married 208 descendants (without counting those of the female line after the first generation) of whom more than 150 are now living.

HARTFORD BRANCH

DESCENDANTS OF JOHN, SON OF ROBERT.

SECOND GENERATION.

2. *John Day, of Hartford, son of Robert and brother of Thomas, (1) m. Sarah Maynard of Hartford, and died probably in 1730. His will was proved May 5, 1730.† His children were—

‡5000. *Joseph, b. (probably about 1675;) d. in 1696.
5001. *John 2d, b. 1677.
5002. *Thomas, b.
5003. *Mary, b.   ; m. William Clark, Nov. 14, 1699.
5004. *Maynard, b.   ;m. Elizabeth Marsh in 1714: made his will in 1759, in which year he probably died: had no issue.

---

† The will is as follows:—
November 16, 1725. In the name of God, Amen. I John Day of Hartford, being advanced in years and weak in body, not knowing the day of my death, and being willing to set my house in order, I do ordain and make this to be my last will and testament, hereby making void all former wills by me made or declared. *Impri*, I give my soule to God who I hope hath redeemed it by the precious blood of his Son, Jesus Christ. *Item.* After my debts and funeral charges are discharged out of my moveable estate, I give to my loving wife two cows, with a third part of the remainder of my moveable estate, as also all my right in the mill, and after her decease, I give it to my son William and his heirs: *Item.* I give to my son John Day forty shillings to be paid out of my [wearing or weaving]. I do confirm to my several sons the deeds of gift I have formerly made to them, of my lands to them and their heirs. *Item.* I give to my son William and to his heirs my three acre lot in the Long meadow. I give to my son Joseph my teame, with all the appurtenances thereunto belonging. *Item.* All the rest of my moveable estate not before given, I give to my daughters equally to be divided among them, only my daughter

‡ As these numbers are merely *designatory*, and not at all enumerative, (except in the individual families,) the Hartford branch is made to begin with the number 5000 in order to leave room for future additions to be made to the Springfield branch, according to the same system of notation.

5005. *Sarah, bapt. Sept. 19, 1686; m. Garrett (or Jared) Spencer, June 10, 1708.
5006. *William, bapt. April 24, 1692.
5007. *Joseph, bapt. June 14, 1699.

THIRD GENERATION.

5001. John II. of Colchester, Conn., m. Grace Spencer of Hartford, Jan. 21, 1696. She was probably "the wife of John Day, (who) died May 12, 1714," in Colchester. For his second wife, he m. Mary ———, who d. Nov. 2, 1749, aged 74. He d. Nov. 4, 1752, aged 75. He must have removed to Colchester after 1701, as his three elder children were born in Hartford. Children—
5010. *Lydia, b. April 11, 1698; m. Joseph Fuller of Kent, Conn.
5011. *Mary, b. Aug. 14, 1699; m. Jonathan Northam of Colchester, Dec. 20, 1722.
5012. *John 3d, b. June 6, 1701.
5013. *Joseph, b. Sept. 27, 1702.
5014. *Benjamin, b. Feb. 7, 1704.
5015. *Editha, b. Sept. 10, 1705; m. David Bigelow of Colchester, Dec. 11, 1729.
5016. *Daniel, b. March 9, 1709; d.   1712.
5017. *David, b. July 18, 1710.
5018. *Abraham, b. March 17, 1712.
5019. *Isaac, b. May 17, 1713.
5020. *Daniel, b.   d. probably unmarried on or before June 3, 1746. His moveable estate was divided among his brothers and sisters, April 9, 1747.

5002. *Thomas, of Hartford, son of John I., m. Hannah Wilson, Sept. 21, 1696, and d. probably in Dec. 1724 or Jan. 1725. Children—
5030. *Thomas 2d, b. June 8, 1699; m. and had a family; d. before 1729.
5031. *Hannah, bapt. Feb. 2, 1701.
5032. *John, bapt. Aug. 20, 1704.
5033. *Nathaniel, bapt. July 3, 1715.
5034. *Mehitable, b.   ; m. Amos Field of Hatfield, in 1739.

Sarah shall have the value of four pounds more than either of her sisters. And I do hereby nominate and appoint my loving wife Sarah to be sole Executrix of this my last Will. It being before omitted, I add, I give to my wife the use of half my house during her widowhood, and half the cellar, the housing to be on the south part.   JOHN DAY.

5006. *William, of Hartford, son of John I., m. Elizabeth Andrus, d. probably in 1768. Children—

5040. *Samuel, bapt.	1720.
5041. *Elizabeth, bapt.	1723.
5042. *William 2d, b.	

FOURTH GENERATION.

5012. *John III. of Colchester, deacon of the Congregational church in that town, m. Sarah Loomis of Colchester, Aug. 20, 1725, who d. April 8, 1780, aged 76. He d. Aug. 25, 1780, aged 79. On his grave stone in the Westchester Society is the following inscription:—

Death Reigns.

This stone stands to memorialize the death and burial of the aged, humane and pious Deacon John Day, who in the 80th year of his age and on August 25, 1780 quitted this mortal and entered on the immortal state.

> An honest man (rare to be found,)
> Lies buried deep within this ground,
> Whose soul to God has winged her flight,
> And dwells in everlasting light.

Children—
5060. *John 4th, b. Nov. 20, 1738.
5061. *Noah, b. June 10, 1740.
5062. *Sarah, b. March 12, 1742.
5063. *Lois, b. March 13, 1744; m. Joshua Bulkley of Colchester, Nov. 19, 1761.
5064. *Stephen, b. Feb. 20, 1746.

5013. Joseph, of Colchester, son of John 2d, m. Esther Hungerford, April 1, 1729, who d. May 7, 1790, aged 81. He d. Oct. 26, 1793, aged 92. Children—
5070. *Ezra, b. June 18, 1730; d. July 23, 1730.
5071. *Joseph 2d, b. May 6, 1731.
5072. *Esther, b. March 12, 1783.
5073. *Grace, b. March 12, 1736.
5074. *Mary, b. July 2, 1738.
5075. *Ezra, b. July 20, 1740; d. March 17, 1742.
5076. *Asa, b. March 13, 1743; d. Sept. 10, 1760.
5077. *Rachel, b. Nov. 22, 1745; m. Stephen Brainard.
5078. *Jesse, b. Jan. 16, 1748.

5014. *Benjamin, of Colchester, son of John 2d, m. Margaret Foote of Colchester, March 6, 1729, and d. Dec. 22, 1777, aged 73. His widow d. April 1801, aged nearly 90. Children—

5080. *Anna, b. Feb. 27, 1730; m. —— Pepoon of Stockbridge, Ms.
5081. *Benjamin 2d, b. Sept. 13, 1731.
5082. *Adonijah, b. July 16, 1733.
5083. *Asa, b. May 16, 1735; d. May 26, 1735.
5084. *Asa, b. June 1, 1736; d. June 13, 1736.
5085. *Margaret, b. Oct. 27, 1737; m. Joel Jones of Hebron, Conn., Oct. 24, 1754.
5086. *Aaron, b. Sept. 14, 1740.
5087. *Amasa, b. April 21, 1742.
5088. *Lydia, b. April 21, 1744; m. Asa Beebe, Aug. 4, 1763.
5089. *Daniel, b. July 21, 1747.
5090. *David, b. Aug. 4, 1749.
5091. *Editha, b. Jan. 5, 1752; m. Elijah Williams.
5092. *Russel, b.   d. Sept. 16, 1756.
5093. *Russel, bapt. Oct. 24, 1756.

5017. *David, of Colchester, son of John 2d, m. Hannah Kellogg, and d. without issue, Sept. 5, 1775, aged 66, leaving a large estate, which he "gave for the support of the gospel ministry in the Presbyterian way and order," in the different parishes where his land lay, viz. in the Westchester Parish in Colchester, Hartland, and Rumney, N. H., and for the maintenance of a high school "for the instruction of youth in the Latin and Greek languages, reading, writing and arithmetic," in the town of Colchester, (Westchester.) His widow m. John Eliot of Middletown, Conn., May 5, 1766, and d. in 1812, aged 95.

5018. *Abraham, of Colchester, son of John 2d, m. Irene Foot, Nov. 20, 1740, and d, March 18, 1792, aged 80. His widow d. Aug. 7, 1809. Children—
5100. *Ephraim, b. July 10, 1741.
5101. *Ezra, b. April 22, 1743. (Family Record, May 3, New Style)
5102. *Nehemiah, b. March 5, 1745.
5103. *Abraham 2d, b. Sept. 20, 1747.
5104. *Elisha, b. Jan, 30, 1749.
5105. *Lucy, b. May 14, 1752; m. William Brainard of Westchester Society, Dec. 31, 1792, and d. in 1831, aged 79.
5106. *Elijah, b. Dec. 1, 1754.
5107. *Irene, b. March 7, 1757; m. David Yeomans of Westchester Society, Jan. 7, 1774.
5108. *Sarah, b. March 26, 1759; m. Samuel Northam of Westchester Society, April 8, 1779.
5109. *Oliver, b. Sept. 12, 1761.

5019. *Isaac, of Colchester, son of John 2d, m. Anna Foot, July 23,

1740, who d. June 22, 1760, aged 45. He d. March 7, 1765, aged 52. Children—

5110. *Anna, b. Nov. 7, 1742; m. Joseph Skinner of Hebron, Sept. 30, 1762; d. June 3, 1815, aged 73.
5111. *Mary, b. Dec. 27, 1744; m. David Otis, Nov. 30, 1766.
5112. *Daniel, b. Nov. 14, 1746.
5113. *John, b. Dec. 14, 1748.
5114. *Isaac, b. Nov. 15, 1750; d. Aug. 26, 1753.
5115. *Jacob, b. Aug. 31, 1753; d. March 28, 1777, of small pox, aged 24.
5116. *Hannah, b. Aug. 26, 1756; m. Daniel Horsford of Charlotte, Vt.

For his second wife, Isaac m. Widow Dorothy Bigelow, Oct. 12, 1762, by whom he had one son—

5117. Charles, b. July 14, 1763.

5032. *John, of Hartford, son of Thomas; m. ——— ———, Children—

5130. *Thomas, bapt.		1728.
5131. *Sarah, bapt.		1731.
5132. *Eunice, bapt.		1733.
5133. *Mary, bapt.		1736.

5033. *Nathaniel, of Northampton, Mass., son of Thomas, m. Thankful Clesson, Jan. 20, 1737, who d. in 1754. Children—

5140. *Nathaniel 2d, b. Oct. 1737.
5141. *Simeon, b. Dec. 12, 1738; d. Feb. 3, 1739.
5142. *Thankful, b. March 31, 1740; m. Joseph Fairfield of Pittsfield.
5143. *Hannah, b. 1743; m. Oliver Strong of Northampton; then John Bullard of Westhampton,

For his second wife, he married Experience Birge, in 1757, who d. Aug. 3, 1783, aged 50. He d. Sept. 26, 1787, aged 72. Children—

5144. *Simeon, bapt. Feb. 19, 1758.
5145. *Joel, b. Aug. 16, 1759.
5146. *Luke, b. May 24, 1761.
5147. *Experience, b.   m. —— Crandall of Norwich.
5148. *Thomas, b. Feb. 19, 1769.

5040. *Samuel, of Hartford, son of William, m. Hannah Ashley, and was living in 1757. Children—

5150. *Samuel 2d, b.
5151. *Joseph, b.
5152. *Hannah, b.
5153. *Jerusha, b.

FIFTH GENERATION.

5060. *Noah, of East Menden, N. Y., son of John 3d, m. Ann Loomis of Colchester, Conn., Dec. 6, 1759, and d. April 22, 1813, aged 73. His widow d. in 1831. Children—

5180. *Sarah, b. Dec. 26, 1760; m. Charles Foot, Jr., Dec. 17, 1778.
5181. *John, b. May 6, 1762.
5182. *Ann, b. March 4, 1764; m. James Bigelow, and d. Oct. 25, 1825, aged 51.
5183. *Noah 2d, b. May 27, 1766.
5184. *Lois, b. March 4, 1768; m. Joseph Carrier, 1789.
5185. *Lydia, b. May 1770; d. June 5, 1773, aged 3.
5186. *Lucy, bapt. July 12, 1772; m. Abel Baldwin of Clarendon, N. Y.
5187. *Hannah, bapt. April 17, 1774; m. Benjamin Botsford, and d. March 15, 1814.
5188. *David, b. May 7, 1775.
5189. Lydia, b. m. Joseph Peters of Pittstown, and lives in Portland, N. Y.
5190. *Sophia, b. m. Ralph Strong of East Mendon, and d. Oct. 12, 1810, aged 23.
5191. *Eli, b. March 13, 1781; d. March 24, 1781.
5192. *Eli, b.
5193. Erastus, b. March 4, 1787.
5194. Charles, b. March 15, 1789.

5064. *Stephen, son of John 3d, resided successively in Tolland, Colchester, and Wallingford, in the State of Connecticut, and in 1791 removed to Catskill, N. Y., where he died, April 11, 1820, aged 74. He married Dimmis Ransom of Kent, Conn., March 27, 1766, who died March 8, 1824, aged 74, and had ten children, viz.—

5200. *Ira, b. May 5, 1767.
5201. *Sodema, b. July 6, 1769; m. Ashly Gilbert; d. May 10, 1813.
5202. *Pamela, b. April 18, 1772; d. July 4, 1774.
5203. *Orrin, b. May 11, 1776.
5204. *Philo, b. June 18, 1779.
5205. Electa, b. March 27, 1783; m. Lyman Hall; after his decease, m. John C. Johnson.
5206. Julia, b. June 16, 1785; m. Robert Gardiner, who was lost at sea a few months afterwards; then m. Henry McKinstry.
5207. *Nancy, b. Oct. 5, 1787; m. James Powers, and d. Jan. 14, 1826.
5208. *Russell, b. Oct. 10, 1789.
5209. Betsey, b. Sept. 22, 1791; m. Rev. Thomas Punderson of Huntington, Conn.

HARTFORD BRANCH—FIFTH GENERATION.

5071. *Joseph II. of Colchester, m. Susanna Brainard, Nov. 13, 1754, who d. Oct. 22, 1817, aged 87. He d. April 8, 1819, aged 88. Children—

5210. *Susanna*, b. Jan. 27, 1755; m. Elisha Kellogg of Colchester, June 9, 1776.
5211. *Joseph*, } b. Aug. 2, 1756; d. Aug. 2, 1772, aged 20.
5212. *Rhoda*, } b. twin; m. John Staples.
5213. *Asenath*, b. April 2, 1759; m. Daniel Williams, Dec. 14, 1780, and d. April 27, 1841.
5214. *Asa*, b. Aug. 12, 1761.
5215. *Esther*, b. Oct. 1, 1763; d. April 6, 1829, aged 65.
5216. *Mary*, b. Oct. 14, 1765; m. John Kellogg, Dec. 26, 1791, and d. Dec. 10, 1848, aged 83.
5217. *Eli*, b. Nov. 12, 1768; d. Sept. 10, 1776, aged 8.
5218. *Jonathan*, b. Jan. 6, 1772; d. Sept. 17, 1776.
5219. *Talitha*, b. April 12, 1774; d. Oct. 17, 1775.
5220. *A son, b. Sept. 17, 1776.

5078. *Jesse, of Sing Sing, (?) N. Y., son of Joseph I., m. Mary Kellogg of Colchester, March 7, 1771, who d. Sept. 10, 1776, aged 23.

5081.*Benjamin II., first of Colchester, Conn., then of Hebron, Conn., removed to Royalton, Vt., about 1774; m. Abigail Day, daughter of Samuel Day of Colchester, by whom he had five children: for his second wife, m. Widow Eunice Young, by whom he had six children, and d. Jan. 26, 1811, aged 79. Children—

5230. *Samuel*, bapt. June 10, 1753.
5231. *Benjamin* 3d, bapt. April 6, 1755.
5232. *Mary*, bapt. Feb. 29, 1759; m. —— Clapp.
5233. *Asa*, bapt. March 8, 1761.
5234. *Solomon*, b.
5235. *Standish*, b.   1765.
5236. *Ralph*, b.
5237. *Alfred*, b.   d. young.
5238. *Sylvester*, b. May 17, 1770.
5239. *Ebenezer*, b.
5240. Ira, b. Dec. 4, 1777.

5082. *Adonijah, first of Colchester, Conn., then of Ellington, Conn., son of Benjamin I., m. Sarah Loomis in 1753, and d. Oct. 1, 1799, aged 66. His widow d. Jan. 28, 1802. Children—

5250. *Charles*, b. Sept. 18, 1753.
5251. *Sarah*, b. Feb. 9, 1755; m. Ozias Benton; d. March 23, 1816.
5252. *Lucy*, b. June 12, 1756; m. Benjamin Chamberlin of Dalton.
5253. *Margaret*, b. Feb. 12, 1758; m. Caleb Kelton of Stafford, Conn.

5254. *Adonijah, b. Dec. 28, 1759; d. in the Army at New York, Sept. 8, 1776, aged 17.
5255. *Rachel, b. Aug. 6, 1761; d. March 14, 1772.
5256. *Alvin, b. May 20, 1763.
5257. Levi, b. March 14, 1765.
5258. Lydia, b. Jan. 12, 1767; m. Zadoc Benton of Stafford, Conn.
5259. Erial, b. July 20, 1768.
5260. Elihu, b. May 7, 1770.
5261. *Epaphroditus, b. May 9, 1772.
5262. Rowena, b. April 23, 1774; m. Darius Sabin of Greenwich, Ms.
5263. *Clarissa, b. Nov. 1, 1775; m. Charles Newell of Ellington; d. Aug. 1840.
5264. Adonijah 2d, b. March 14, 1778.
5265. *Ira, b. March 29, 1780; d. March 3, 1783.
5266. *Oliver, b. Aug. 16, 1783; probably died in infancy.

5086. *Aaron, of Spencertown, N. Y., son of Benjamin I., m. Mary ———, Children—
5270. *Lucia, bapt. March 28, 1742.
5271. Aaron 2d, b.
5272. Lewis, b.
5273. A daughter, b.   m. ——— Schuyler.
5274. A daughter, b.   m. Gideon Curtis.
5275. Lydia, b.
5276. Edissa, b.

5087. *Amasa, of Stockbridge, Mass., son of Benjamin I., m. ——— Beebe,   Children—
5280. *Clarissa, b.   1771; d. Feb. 19, 1775.
5281. *Minoris, b.   1773; d. Jan. 14, 1775.
5282. *Erastus, b.   1774; d. Sept. 9, 1776.
5283. Clarissa, b.   m. Ebenezer Carrier, April 14, 1795.
5284. Eleanor, b.   m. Flavius Pease of Stockbridge.
5285. *David, b.   1778; d. May 18, 1789
5286. Roderic, b.
5287. Minoris, b.   of Charlton, N. Y.
5288. Matilda, b. 1782; m. Justin Day, (5391), Nov. 5, 1800.

5089. *Daniel, of Lima, N. Y., son of Benjamin I., m. Elizabeth Chamberlin, Dec. 10, 1772, and d. in 1835, aged 88. His widow d. July 10, 1826, aged 80. Children—
5290. *Daniel 2d, b.   1773.
5291. *Erastus, b. Aug. 4, 1780.
5292. David, b.   of Wastenaw, Mich.
5293. Harry, b. May 1, 1786.

5294. *Russell*, b.
5295. *Elisha*, b.
5296. *Eunice*, b.
5297. *Elizabeth*, b.
5298. *Anna*, b.
5299. *Margaret*, b.   d. in 1838.

5090. *David, of Spencertown, N. Y., son of Benjamin I., m. ——
——, Children—
5300. *Daniel*, b.   m. —— Spencer: removed to the West: d. aged 68.
5301. *Jerusha*, b.   m. Elias Jones of Hebron, Conn.
5302. *Charlotte*, b.
5303. *Betsey*, b.   m. —— Abel.
5304. *Polly*, b.

5093. *Russell, of Winhall, Vt., son of Benjamin I., m. Anna Chapman of Colchester, Conn., and d. in 1829, aged 73. Children—
5310. *Warren*, b. Nov. 24, 1787.
5311. *Russell* 2d, b.   1791.
5312. *Azel*, b.   1794.
5313. *Jabez*, b.   1798; d. unm. at Schuyler, N. Y., July 6, 1829.
5314. *Christiana*, b.   m. J. G. Fergeson.
5315. *Electa*, b.   m. Daniel Newcomb.
5316. *Rosina*, b.   m. Josiah Clarke of Whitesboro, N. Y.
5317. *Nancy*, b.   m. Dr. Silas Clark.
5318. *Sophia*, b.   m. Joel Wright.
5319. *Clarissa*, b.   m. Dr. Dudley Beebe.

5100. *Ephraim, son of Abraham I., m. Sarah Ackley: removed to Winhall, Vt., and then to Parma, N. Y., where he d. Deacon of the Congregational Church. Children—
5320. *A son b.   d. April 15, 1764.
5321. *Dudley*, b. Dec. 1, 1764; d. in Canada.
5322. *Sarah*, b.   m. Asa Beebe of Parma.
5323. *Ephraim* 2d, b.
5324. *Eli*, b.
5325. *Abraham*, b.
5326. *Salmon*, b.

5101. *Ezra, of South Hadley, Mass., son of Abraham I., m. Hannah Kendall, Oct. 3, 1767, and d. Nov. 21, 1823, aged 80. His widow d. Oct. 23, 1827. Children—
5330. *Asa*, b. May 16, 1768.

5331. *Hannah*, b. May 7, 1769; m. Eldad White of South Hadley.
5332. *Sarah*, b. June 7, 1771; m. Abiathar Vinton.
5333. *Ezra* 2d, b. June 7, 1773.
5334. *Rhoda*, b. Dec. 18, 1774; m. Sylvester Moody.
5335. *Clarissa*, b. Sept. 14, 1777; m. Charles Chapin; d. June 18, 1813.
5336. *Justin*, b. March 30, 1778.
5337. *Alvin*, b. Nov. 18, 1780.
5338. *Plin*, b. May 27, 1782.
5339. *Roswell*, b. June 2, 1784.
5340. *Ashbell*, b. Aug. 6, 1786.
5341. *Polly*, b. Nov. 15, 1789; m. Dr. Amos Taylor of Warwick, Ms.
5342. *Sophia*, b. April 9, 1791; m. Samuel Alvord of South Hadley; d. Dec. 7, 1816.

5102. *Nehemiah, of Dalton, Mass., son of Abraham I., m. Dimmis Kilborn of Colchester, Conn., Aug. 21, 1766, and d. Children—
5350. *Amasa*, b.
5351. *Hezekiah*, b.
5352. *Abraham*, b.
5353. *Nehemiah* 2d, b. March 5, 1772.
5354. *Diadema*, b.
5355. *Elijah*, b. May 10, 1780.

5103. *Abraham II. of Chester, Mass., m. Irene Jackson, Oct. 16, 1769, and d. in 1797, aged 50. Children—
5360. *Irene*, b. Oct. 20, 1770; m. Salithan Judd of South Hadley.
5361. *Abraham* 3d, b. May 9, 1772.
5362. *Lucy*, b. Nov. 28, 1773; m. John Leonard of West Springfield, April 4, 1814.
5363. *Joshua*, b. Sept. 11, 1775.
5364. *Erastus*, b. Feb. 14, 1777; of or near Great Bend, Pa.: m.
5365. *Anna*, b. Feb. 2, 1779.
5366. *Ira*, b. April 28, 1781.
5367. *Chauncey*, b. April 24, 1783.
5368. *Rachel*, b. April 16, 1785.
5369. *Selah*, b. March 23, 1788.
5370. *Calvin*, b. June 12, 1790.

5104.*Elisha, of South Hadley, Mass., son of Abraham I., m. Sybil Williams, July 15, 1771, who d. June 8, 1778. He d. in South Hadley, Children—
5380. *Elisha* 2d, b.

HARTFORD BRANCH—FIFTH. GENERATION. 99

5381. *Zachariah, b.
5382. Hannah, b.

5106. *Elijah, of Winhall, Vt., son of Abraham I., m. Dorothy Olmsted, March 10, 1776, and d. April 22, 1798, aged 44. Children—
5390. *Dr. Stephen O., b. Aug. 21, 1777; d. Oct. 26, 1802, aged 26.
5391. Justin, b. April 2, 1781.
5392. *Fanny, b. Aug. 20, 1783; m. Augustus Williams; d. Oct. 7, 1839.

5109. *Oliver, of Holly, (?) N. Y., son of Abraham I., m. ———
———, Children—
5400. Austin, b.
5401. Justin, b.
5402. Oliver 2d, b.
5403. Silas, b.
5404. Lucy, b.   m. Paphyrus Beebe.
5405. Diadema, b.   m. ——— Sprague.
5406. Sarah, b.
5407. Sylvia, b.
5408. Minerva, b.
5409. Ruby, b.
5410. Amarilla, b.

5112. *Daniel, son of Isaac, m. Martha Isham of Colchester, Sept. 10, 1774: removed first to Williamstown, Mass., then to Cazenovia, N. Y., and finally to Rome, N. Y., where he d. in 1830, aged 84. Children—
5420. Mary, b. 1774; m. Daniel A. Noble in 1793, then, Gershom Bulkley in 1798, both of Williamstown.
5421. Alfred, b.   1776.
5422. *Jacob, b. July 11, 1779.
5423. Sophia, b.   m. James Sherman of Rome, N. Y.
5424. Ralph, b.   1783; unmarried.
5425. Daniel, b.   1786; of Williamstown: unmarried.
5426. Martha, b.   1788; m. Dea.—Miller of Pompey, N. Y.
5427. Anna, b.   1791; m. Orrin Chandler of Cazenovia.
5428. Maria, b.   1797; m. Daniel Faxton of Stonington, Ct.

5113. *John, of Williamstown, Mass., son of Isaac, m. Abiah Noble, and d. in 1814, aged 66. Children—
5430. *Erastus, b. Feb. 26, 1775
5431. John Bennet, b. Sept. 26, 1775; grad. at Williams Col. in 1804.

100   DESCENDANTS OF ROBERT DAY.

5117. Charles, of Colchester, Conn., son of Isaac, m. Anna Worthington, Jan. 17, 1796. Children—
5440. *Nancy, b. Jan. 25, 1797; d. Feb. 6, 1797.
5441. Charles Frederic, b. Jan. 12, 1798; of Colchester: unm.
5442. Elijah Worthington, b. Sept. 17, 1799.
5443. Anna Lovett, b. July 31, 1801.
5444. *Albert, b. March 16, 1803; d. March 28, 1803.
5445. Eliza Maria, b. Sept. 21, 1804.
5446. Justin Edwin, b. Oct. 7, 1806.
5447. Isaac Henry, b. Nov. 10, 1808.
5448. Erastus, b. Nov. 13, 1810.
5449. Artemas, b. Dec. 11, 1812.
5450. *John, b. May 16, 1815; d. Dec. 12, 1835.
5451. Guy Bigelow, b. July 21, 1818; graduated at Yale College in 1845, and in the Theological Department in 1848.

5140. *Nathaniel II. of Northampton, Mass., m. Adah Marshall of that town, Nov. 25, 1761, and d. July 5, 1806, aged 68. Children—
5460. *Clarissa, bapt. Nov. 23, 1766; d. April 6, 1788.
5461. Nathaniel 3d, b. July 26, 1769.
5462. *Samuel, b. Feb.   1774; of Hartford, where he married and died.
5463. *Dudley, bapt. June 25, 1775.
5464. *Grace, bapt. Nov. 5, 1780; m. Samuel May of Northampton, May 9, 1811.
5465. *Deborah, bapt. Sept. 29, 1782; m. Jesse Randall of Northampton, June 20, 1799.
5466. Clarissa, b. July 9, 1791; m. Elihu Strong of Northampton.

5144. *Simeon, of Northampton, Mass., son of Nathaniel I., m. Eleanor Hurlbert, April, 1784, who d. March 30, 1785. For his second wife, he m. Phebe Goff, April 13, 1786, and d. Children—
5470. *Simeon, bapt. March 25, 1785; d. March 26, 1785.
5471. *Phebe, bapt. April 5, 1789; m. —— Greene.
5472. *Spencer, bapt. May 6, 1792.
5473. Pamela, bapt. April 26, 1795; m. —— Humiston.

5145. *Joel, of Hatfield, Mass., son of Nathaniel I., m. Martha Murray of that town, March 10, 1783, who was b. July 14, 1761, and d. Nov. 21, 1838. He d. April 8, 1835, aged 76. Children—
5480. *William, b. Feb. 11, 1784; d. Dec. 16, 1805.
5481. Martha, b. Sept. 6, 1786; m. Joseph Morton, Feb. 10, 1810.
5482. Pliny, b. March 4, 1789; of Hatfield; m. Chloe Cowles of Williamsburg, Jan. 3, 1815.
5483. Zelotes, b. June 24, 1791.

5484. *Elijah,* b. Sept. 6, 1793.
5485. *Obed,* b. May 6, 1796; drowned June 24, 1804.
5486. *Alonzo,* b. July 31, 1799.
5487. *Mercy M.,* b. Nov. 23, 1801; m. Amos Narramore of Goshen, Sept. 6, 1824.

5146. *Luke, of Northampton, Mass., son of Nathaniel I., m. Prudence Phelps of that town, June 10, 1794, and d. June 2, 1848, aged 87. Children—
5490. *Electa,* b. April 20, 1795; m. Horace Lyman of Northampton, Dec. 1, 1820.
5491. *Lucy,* b. Nov. 1, 1796.
5492. *George,* b. June 19, 1798; m. Susan King of Westhampton, Nov. 17, 1831, and d. without issue, Oct. 27, 1834, aged 36.
5493. *Experience,* b. June 1, 1800; m. Jonathan D. Kellogg of Northampton, Dec. 25, 1823.
5494. *Jonathan,* b. April 1, 1802.
5495. *David Seward,* b. May 14, 1804; m. Amaranda Hotchkiss of Utica, N. Y., Nov. 11, 1831, and d. without issue, Nov. 10, 1834, aged 30.
5496. *Laura,* b. Oct. 8, 1806; d. Sept. 19, 1829.

5148. *Thomas, of Lanesboro', Mass., son of Nathaniel I., m. Betsey Strong of Pittsfield, Nov. 22, 1798, and d. June 2, 1827, aged 58. Children—
5500. *Thomas Lyman,* b. Aug. 20, 1799.
5501. *Betsey,* b. Oct. 21, 1800.
5502. *Daniel,* b. Feb. 27, 1802; d. June 8, 1802.
5503. *Polly,* b. June 7, 1803; d. Sept. 20, 1803.
5504. *Mary Strong,* b. March 12, 1805.
5505. *William,* b. March 28, 1809.
5506. *Daniel,* b. Sept. 18, 1815.

5150. *Samuel II., m. Charity Pease of Glastenbury, Conn.: resided some years in Hartford, Conn., but removed about the year 1809 to Great Barrington, Mass., where he d. in 1813, aged Children—
5510. *Samuel H.,* b. July 30, 1783; m. Rachel Sickles of New Brunswick, N. J., in 1819, and d. in Great Barrington, in 1845, aged 62.
5511. *Sarah,* b. Aug. 14, 1784; m. Samuel Cook of Hartford.
5512. *William,* b. Aug. 20, 1786.
5513. *George,* b. Aug. 28, 1790; killed in the battle of Queenstown.
5514. *Daniel,* b. Jan. 4, 1794; d. on board the U. S. ship Columbia in the Mediterranean, in 1827.

5151. *Joseph, of Hartford, Conn., son of Samuel I., m. Rhoda Steele, in 1786, and d. July, 1799. Children—
5520. *Edward*, b. April 7, 1788.
5521. *Joseph 2d*, b. June 9, 1790.
5522. *Amelia*, b. Dec. 1792; m. Peter Peck of Albany, N. Y.
5523. **Horace*, b.   d. young.
5524. **Horace*, b. June 16, 1796.

SIXTH GENERATION.

5181. *John, of Williamstown, Mass., son of Noah, m. Catharine Jones of Hebron, Conn., Dec. 20, 1792, and d. June 26, 1828, aged 66. Children—
5530. *Maria L.*, b. Jan. 30, 1794.
5531. *Catharine J.*, b. Feb. 5, 1796; m. Samuel Kellogg.

5183. *Noah II. of Winfield, N. Y., m. Milly Graves of Hoosick, and d. 1847, aged 79. Children—
5540. *Eli*, b.
5541. *Daniel*, b.
5542. *Orrin*, b.
5543. *Dudley*, b.
5544. *Mills*, b.
5545. *Lois*, b.

5188. *David, of New Albion, N. Y., son of Noah I., m. Polly Lee of Pittstown, N. Y., Jan. 6, 1800, and d. Aug. 30, 1844, aged 69. Children—
5547. *Anna*, b. Nov. 4, 1800; m. John Harton.
5548. **Charles*, b. Feb. 28, 1803.
5549. **Eli*, b. Jan. 28, 1813; d. Feb. 12, 1815.

5192 *Eli, of Royalton, Vt., (?) son of Noah I, m. Mary Phelps of Winfield, March, 1801, and d.   Children—
5550. *Prudence*, b.
5551. **Jeremiah*, b.
5552. *Eli 2d*, b.
5553. **Mary*, b.
5554. *Hannah*, b.
5555. *Willet*, b.

5193. Erastus, of New Albion, N. Y., son of Noah I., m. Marion Lee, in 1812. Children—
5560. *Asahel*, b. June 4, 1813.
5561. **Eli*, b. May 10, 1815.

HARTFORD BRANCH—SIXTH GENERATION.   103

5562. *Hudson*, b. Aug. 28, 1816.
5563. *Wealthy*, b. July 11, 1818; m. John Davis of New Albion, 1836.
5564. *Orrin*, b. Jan. 10, 1821.
5565. *Elias*, b. July 18, 1827.

5194. Charles, of East Mendon, N. Y., son of Noah I., m. Sally Phelps of Pittsford, May 13, 1810. Children—
5570. *Mary S.*, b. June 18, 1811; m. William Silstry of Hartland.
5571. *John*, b. May 1, 1814.
5572. *Charles 2d*, b. Feb. 14, 1820.
5573. *George*, b. May 4, 1822.
5574. *Sarah J.*, b. Oct. 14, 1829.
5575. *Judson*, b. Oct. 20, 1833.

5200. *Ira, of Catskill, N. Y., son of Stephen, m. (1st) Eunice Mc-Cleave: (2d) Lucy Atwater of Wallingford, Conn., and d. Nov. 17, 1818, aged 51. Children—
5580. *John*, b. Oct. 26, 1796.
5581. *Caleb*, b. April 7, 1798.
5582. *Delia*, b. March 28, 1800; m. Rev. Samuel C. Aikin of Utica, N. Y., then of Cleveland, Ohio.
5583. *Henrietta*, b. Feb. 25, 1802; m. Rev. Samuel C. Aikin.
5584. *William*, b. March 13, 1804.
5585. *Ira Ransom*, b. March 1, 1807.
5586. *Emeline*, b. Nov. 14, 1811; m. Flavel W. Bingham of Cleveland.

5203. *Orrin, of Catskill, N. Y., son of Stephen, m. Mary Burr Hall of Greenfield, Conn., April 25, 1802, and d. Dec. 26, 1846, aged 70. Children—
5590. *Edgar Burr*, b. Sept. 1, 1803.
5591. *Henry Ransom*, b. May 9, 1805; d. May 4, 1808.
5592. *Samuel Sherwood*, b. April 3, 1807.
5593. *Julia R.*, b. April 6, 1809.
5594. *Mary H.*, b. May 16, 1811; m. Joshua Atwater, now of Catskill, N. Y.
5595. *Caroline E.*, b. April 24, 1813.
5596. *George B.*, July 21, 1816.
5597. *Charlotte M.*, b. Aug. 30, 1818; m. Curtis Noble of New York, Jan. 6, 1848.
5598. *Emily C.*, b. Sept. 25, 1821; m. Jeremiah Day, (662) Nov. 10, 1846.
5599. *Charles H.*, b. Sept. 22, 1828.

5204. *Philo, of Catskill, N. Y., son of Stephen, m. Emma Eason

Gardiner of that place, May 20, 1800, and d. Aug. 24, 1809, aged 30. Children—

5600. *Rodman Gardiner, b. April 4, 1801.
5601. *Augusta Ann, b. June 7, 1803.
5602. Robert, b. Feb. 17, 1805.
5603. *Harriet, b. Sept. 24, 1806; d. Nov. 1835.
5604. *Nelson, b. Sept. 24, 1808.

5208. *Russell, of Catskill, N. Y., son of Stephen, m. Harriet Gardiner of Newport, R. I., Nov. 6, 1810, and d. Sept. 12, 1832, aged 43. Children—

5610. *Philo, b. Feb. 16, 1812; d. April 16, 1825.
5611. John Gardiner, b. Nov. 8, 1813.
5612. Stephen, b. Sept. 6, 1815.
5613. Sarah G., b. Oct. 8, 1817; m. Dennis Casey, now of New Orleans.
5614. *Harriet A., b. Oct. 9, 1820; m. Oliver P. Haswell of Burlington, Vt., and d. Feb. 18, 1848.
5615. Jane C., b. Dec. 1, 1826.
5616. Mary R., b. March 25, 1829.
5617. Emma E., b. Oct. 15, 1831.

5214. *Asa, of Colchester, Conn., son of Joseph 2d, m. Anna Marvin, April 25, 1790, who d. Nov. 20, 1817, aged 53. He d. Oct. 1841, aged 80. Children—

5620. Anna, b. Jan. 28, 1791; m. Dea. Warren A. Skinner of Chatham, (Easthampton Parish,) Conn., Nov. 28, 1810.
5621. *Joseph, b. Nov. 28, 1792.
5622. Almira, b. Aug. 18, 1794; m. Erastus Sheldon of New Marlboro', Mass., Nov. 27, 1835.
5623. Talitha, b. June 21, 1796; m. Warren West of Colchester, April 30, 1821.
5624. *Susanna, b. Sept. 14, 1798; d. March 21, 1834.
5625. Elizabeth, b. July 30, 1800; m. William E. Tracy of Colchester, Nov. 3, 1826.
5626. Asa 2d, b. Oct. 20, 1802.
5627. Mary Octavia, b. Aug. 18, 1804; m. David C. Buel, Feb. 4, 1829.
5628. Elihu Marvin, b. Jan. 25, 1807.
5629. Stephen Brainard, b. Nov. 2, 1808.

5230. *Samuel, of Cambridge, N. Y., son of Benjamin 2d, m. ———— ————, Children—

5650. Samuel 2d, b. ———————— of White Creek, N. Y.; m. ———— Herroun: no children.

5651. *Eliphalet*, b.   of Oak Hill, N. Y.
5652. *Asa*, b.
5653. *Solomon*, b.
5654. *Joseph Spencer*, b.
5655. *Hezekiah*, b.   of Cambridge, N. Y.

5231. **Benjamin III.**, removed in 1780 from Hebron, Conn. to Royalton, Vt., of which town he was one of the first settlers, and though obliged to retire on account of the hostility of the Indians, returned in 1783; m. Hannah Northam of Hebron, March 28, 1784, and d. March 28, 1829, aged 74. His widow d. Sept. 16, 1834. Children—

5660. *Alfred, b. April 21, 1786.
5661. *Spaulding*, b. Jan. 15, 1788.
5662. *Mary*, b. Dec. 22, 1789; m. Wm. S. Shepherd of Randolph, Vt.
5663. *Dan, b. Jan. 22, 1791.
5664. *Gad*, b. Dec. 6, 1793.
5665. *Benjamin* 4th, b. Sept. 5, 1795.
5666. *Asa*, b. Aug. 7, 1797.
5667. *Ira*, b. Aug. 17, 1799.
5668. *Joel*, b. Sept. 12, 1801; of Royalton, Vt.; m. Rebecca Wheeler of Bethel, Vt., Feb. 28, 1828.

In Sept. 1827, this family after a separation of twenty five years, assembled once more under the paternal roof, and enjoyed a festival of ten days with their old neighbors and friends.

5233. *Asa, of Stockbridge, Mass., son of Benjamin 2d, was graduated at Dartmouth College in 17—: was a teacher for some time in Pittsfield, Mass. One child—
5670. *Margaret, b.

5234. *Solomon, of Sandy Hill, N. Y., son of Benjamin 2d, m. ———
———,   Children—
5680. *Ralph, b.
5681. *John, b.   and three daughters.

5235. *Dr. Standish, of Woodstock, Vt., son of Benjamin 2d, studied Medicine with Dr. Nathan Smith; m. (1st) Priscilla Pierce, Dec. 29, 1785, who d. without issue: (2d) Deborah Sturtevant of Halifax, Mass., March, 1791, and d. Aug. 19, 1799, aged 34. Children—
5690. *Lucia, b. April 1, 1794; m. Samuel Marcy, Jan. 8, 1823, and d. Jan. 8, 1831.
5691. *Fanny, b. Oct. 1795; d. Oct. 1796.
5692. *Fanny, b. Jan. 1797; d. Jan. 1798.

5693. *Polly May*, b. Dec. 10, 1799; m. Luther Cross of Montpelier, Vt., May 31, 1827.

5236. *Ralph, first of Royalton, Vt., then of Troy, N. Y., son of Benjamin 2d, m. (1st) Eunice Pierce of Royalton, Aug. 17, 1788: (2d) Eunice King of Windsor, Vt., and d. Children—
5700. *Ralph*, b.   d. young.
5701. *Danforth*, b. lived in Royalton and had several children.
5702. *Harvey*, b.   d. young.
5703. *Ira*, b.
5704. *Emeline A.*, b.   m. William F. Mead, and d. at New Orleans, Sept. 6, 1847.

5238. *Sylvester, of Royalton, Vt., son of Benjamin 2d, m. Rachel Parkhurst, Dec. 4, 1794, and d. July 26, 1813, aged 43, Children—
5710. *Eunice*, b. April 13, 1796.
5711. *Standish*, b. March 31, 1799.
5712. *George*, b. Jan. 16, 1801.
5713. *Edmund*, b. Dec. 24, 1803.
5714. *Charles*, b. Jan. 12, 1805.
5715. *Oel*, b. Jan. 7, 1807.
5716. *Sharly G.*, b. Feb. 11, 1809.
5717. *Benjamin*, b. Aug. 23, 1811.
5718. *Sylvester* 2d, b. Nov. 6, 1813.

5239. *Ebenezer, of Royalton, Vt., m. Polly Robinson, Oct. 29, 1801, and d. Children—
5720. *Laura*, b. April 11, 1804.
5721. *Betsey*, b. April 5, 1806.
5722. *Alfred*, b. Dec. 14, 1807.
5723. *Albert*, b. Nov. 29, 1814.
5724. *Charles Rood*, b. May 4, 1821.
5725. *Martha*, b. Jan. 10, 1824.

5240. Ira, of South Barre, Vt., son of Benjamin 2d, m. (1st) Martha Clark of Boston, Oct. 17, 1808, who d. July 1, 1813: (2d) Olive Smith of Plainfield, N. H., Nov. 1, 1814. Children—
5730. *Ira*, b. Nov. 3, 1809; d. May 14, 1822.
5731. *Clark*, b. Feb. 5, 1811.
5732. *Martha*, b. May 11, 1813; m. Hon. Lucius B. Peck, M.C., May 10, 1832.
5733. *Joseph S.*, b. Dec. 31, 1818; an officer in the U. S. Navy.
5734. *Benjamin, b. Oct. 30, 1820; a merchant in Montpelier, Vt.; d. Feb. 1, 1845.

HARTFORD BRANCH—SIXTH GENERATION.

5735. *Ira, b. Sept. 5, 1826; d. Sept. 27, 1826.
5736. *Ira, b. April, 7, 1830; d. June 12, 1832.

5250. *Charles, of Burlington, Otsego Co., N. Y., son of Adonijah, m. Susanna ——— in 1779, who was b. Sept. 22, 1753, and d. Feb. 4, 1844. He d. Feb. 26, 1814, aged 61, Children—

5740. *Charles* 2d, b. April 15, 1780.
5741. *Rachel*, b. July 15, 1782; m. Daniel Willard of Paris, N. Y., Jan. 5, 1809.
5742. *Sylvia*, b. Sept. 12, 1784; m. John Willard of Chili, N. Y., 1804.
5743. *Ira*, b. Oct. 25, 1786.
5744. *Sarah*, ⎫ Twins, b. May 29, 1789: m. Wm. Campbell of Pembroke, N. Y., 1814.
5745. **Mary*, ⎭ m. Dea. Levi Campbell, 1816; d. in Riga, N. Y., Oct. 13, 1845.
5746. *Susanna*, b. Aug. 25, 1791; m. Joel Baldwin, 1821; d. in Riga, Dec. 31, 1837.
5747. *Flavel*, b. March 10, 1794.

5256. *Alvin, of Wilbraham, Mass., son of Adonijah, m. Temperance Snow in 1789, and d. Aug. 26, 1836, aged 73. His widow d. Sept. 29, 1839. Children—

5750. *Marcia*, b. Aug. 3, 1790; m. Obed Wright.
5751. *Lucia*, b. March 4, 1792; m. John Calkins of Wilbraham, April 20, 1812.
5752. *Alfred*, b. May 20, 1794.
5753. *Lovisa*, b. Aug. 25, 1796; m. Moses Hancock of Wilbraham.
5754. *Temperance*, b. Feb. 7, 1798; m. Nathaniel Knowlton of Wilbraham.
5755. *Cyrena*, b. July 23, 1801; m. Ezra H. Beebe of Wilbraham, Sept. 9, 1828.
5756. *Alvin* 2d, b. March 7, 1806.
5757. *Lyman*, b. March 20, 1812.

5257. Levi, of Lima, N. Y., son of Adonijah, m. Abiah Chamberlin of Dalton, Mass., Feb. 10, 1792. Children—

5760. *Lyman*, b. May 11, 1794.
5761. *Lois*, b. April 1, 1796; m. Stephen Barrett of Mendon, N. Y., Dec. 1817.
5762. *Abiah*, b. May 22, 1798; m. Chauncey Baldwin of Sangerfield, N. Y., Feb. 1819.
5763. *Levi*, b. Sept. 10, 1800; d. Feb. 9, 1802.
5764. *Harriet*, b. Dec. 20, 1802; m. Asa Carter of Sangerfield, Oct. 19, 1825.
5765. *Dan*, b. Dec. 1, 1805.

5766. *Levi C.*, b. May 11, 1808.
5767. *Mary Ann*, b. Jan. 20, 1811; m. Heman Rugg of Springfield, N. Y., March 25, 1832.

5259. Erial, of Monson, Mass., son of Adonijah and deacon of the Baptist Church in that town, m. (1st) Eunice Russel in 1790: (2d) Lydia Snow, May, 1796. Children—

5770. *Roxanna*, b. Oct. 9, 1791; m. Joshua Stanton of Wilbraham, March 12, 1812.
5771. *Lucy*, b. March 2, 1793; m. Solomon Hawes of Tolland, Conn., Jan. 20, 1814.
5772. *Eunice*, b. Dec. 6, 1794; m. Amos Crandall of Tolland, Dec. 5, 1822.
5773. *Royal*, b. Sept. 22, 1797.
5774. *Russel*, b. June 16, 1799.
5775. *Lydia*, b. Nov. 20, 1801; m. Hiram Allard of Georgetown, N. Y., Oct. 11, 1825.
5776. *Cyrus*, b. Nov. 20, 1804; of Munson, Mass.
5777. *Armenia*, b. April 28, 1807; m. Isaac F. Allard of Roxbury, Mass., May, 1833.
5778. *Gideon*, b. May 18, 1812.

5260. Elihu, of Burlington, N. Y., son of Adonijah, m. (1st) Hannah King, May 7, 1794, who d. Feb. 15, 1809: (2d) Widow Lydia Smith, April 1, 1810. Children—

5780. *Selden*, b. Jan. 7, 1795.
5781. *Warren*, b. April 25, 1796; d. May 15, 1800.
5782. *Jerusha Warren*, b. Sept. 5, 1798; m. Dyer C. Johnson, Dec. 9, 1820.
5783. *Sophronia*, b. Nov. 4, 1802; m. Luther Chase, May, 1822.
5784. *Austin*,) Twins, b. Jan. 20, 1805.
5785. *Laura*,) m. Daniel Blackman, 1825, and d. March 31, 1840.
5786. *Harlem*, b. April 15, 1808.
5787. *Elihu* 2d, b. June 6, 1811.
5788. *Ezra*, b. June 28, 1813.
5789. *Lydia*, b. Aug. 21, 1817; d. Oct. 12, 1822.

5261. *Epaphroditus, of Ellington, Conn., son of Adonijah, m. Nancy Bestar, Oct. 26, 1801, and d. in Buffalo on his way to Ohio, Sept. 15, 1815, aged 43. Children—

5790. *Mirandis*, b. Aug. 29, 1804; m. Russel Day, (5774) May 21, 1829.
5791. *Nancy B.*, b. Aug. 9, 1806; d. Nov. 15, 1826.
5792. *Sally S.*, b. March 11, 1809; d. July 10, 1810.
5793. *Horace L.*, b. Aug. 21, 1811; d. Feb. 14, 1813.
5794. *Sally L.*, b. Sept. 9, 1813; m. Orrin Wilson.

HARTFORD BRANCH—SIXTH GENERATION. 109

5264. Adonijah II. of Burlington, N. Y., m. Elizabeth Marvin, Feb. 10, 1802. Children—
5800. *Marvin,* b. Dec. 26, 1802.
5801. *Adonijah* 3d, b. June 20, 1805.
5802. *Orril,* b. March 7, 1807; d. May 11, 1808.
5803. *Betsey,* b. Feb. 15, 1809; d. April 1835.
5804. *Hiram,* b. April 25, 1811; d. Nov. 26, 1812.
5805. *Hiram,* b. April 6, 1813.
5806. *Epaphroditus,* b. Oct. 9, 1815.
5807. *Ira,* b. Oct. 6, 1818.

5286. Roderic, of Stockbridge, Mass., son of Amasa, m. Elizabeth Wilson.

5290. *Daniel II. of Colchester, (Westchester Parish,) Conn., m. Anna Morgan, and d. April 24, 1842, aged 69. Children—
5820. *Sarah,* b. March 30, 1799; m. Ansel Brainard, Jr., Dec. 14, 1826.
5821. *David,* b. Aug. 30, 1801.
5822. *Eliza,* b. Dec. 14, 1803; m. John Brainard.
5823. *Jerusha,* b. Feb. 1806; m. Ezekiel Root, Jan. 2, 1831.
5824. *Lucretia,* b. 1808; m. Wm. E. Arnold, Oct. 20, 1829.
5825. *Benjamin,* b. 1810.
5826. *Abby,* b. 1813; m. Justin Smith.
5827. *Daniel* 3d, b. April 12, 1816.
5828. *Adaline,* b. March 24, 1821
5829. *Colatinus,* b.

5291. *Erastus, of Washtenaw, Mich., son of Daniel I., m. Lucy Willard, who was b. Aug. 22, 1780. He d. July 14, 1836, aged 56. Children—
5830. *Erastus* 2d, b. Oct. 15, 1808.
5831. *John W.,* b. Sept. 13, 1810.
5832. *Russel,* b. May 24, 1813.
5833. *Daniel W.,* b. Dec. 5, 1814.
5834. *Levi,* b.
5835. *Lucinda,* b. Jan. 13, 1820.
5836. *Lucy,* b.   d. young.

5293. Harry, of ———, Pennsylvania, son of Daniel I., m. Nancy Chamberlin, who was b. Feb. 13, 1786. Children—
5850. *William,* b. Dec. 11, 1809; d. Dec. 12, 1809.
5851. *Urial,* b. Dec. 1810.
5852. *William C.,* b. Sept. 16, 1812.
5853. *Betsey,* b. Oct. 17, 1813.

5854. *Esther*, b. Sept. 4, 1816; m. Daniel W. Day, (5833) March 13, 1839.
5855. *Emily*, b. March 17, 1819; d. June, 1821.
5856. *Elvira*, b. Oct. 2, 1821; m. Dr. L. D. Whitney of Lakeville, Mich., March, 1847.
5857. *Erastus*, b. March 20, 1824.
5858. *Lucetta*, b. July 12, 1826.
5859. *Lavinia Ann*, b. Aug. 31, 1828.
5860. *Augustus B.*, b. Aug. 22, 1830.

5294. Russel, of Kalamazoo, Mich., son of Daniel I., m. Lavinia Hubbard of Burlington, N. Y. Children—
5870. *Fanny*, b. Jan. 31, 1813; m. Norton Frost in 1845.
5871. *Phebe*, b. Nov. 21, 1816; m. John Mershon of Springfield, Pa., 1834.
5872. *Eri H.*, b. June 5, 1817.
5873. *Philetus*, b. Feb. 3, 1819.
5874. *Volney*, b. May 25, 1821.
5875. *Chauncey*, b. April 1824.
5876. *Arthurton*, b. July 1827.
5877. *Paullona*, b. Dec. 15, 1832.

5295. Elisha, of Lima, N. Y., son of Daniel I., m. Eunice Hopkins of that town. Children—
5880. *Cordelia*, b. 1827; m. —— Dyer of Springfield, N. Y.
5881. *Horace*, b. 1829.
5882. *Angelina*, b.

5310. Dr. Warren, son of Russel I., removed in 1808 to Granville, N. Y., where he studied Medicine with Dr. Eli Day, (5324); m. Eleanor Gould of that town, Feb. 13, 1813, and removed to Schuyler, N. Y. Children—
5890. *Clarissa Gould*, b. June 4, 1814; d. Sept. 5, 1815.
5891. *Erastus Warren*, b. Oct. 19, 1815.
5892. *Fayette Gould*, b. Feb. 23, 1817; was graduated at Union College in 1838: admitted to the Bar in 1842, and now an Attorney at Law in Auburn, N. Y.
5893. *Horace Burch*, b. Aug. 27, 1820.
5894. *Russel Jabez*, b. May 9, 1829.

5311. Russel II., Attorney at Law, in Dansville, N. Y., m. —— Bostwick, Children—
5900. *Ann*, b.
5901. *Flora*, b.

HARTFORD BRANCH—SIXTH GENERATION. 111

5312. *Dr. Azel, of Sparta, N. Y., son of Russel I., m. Flora Pierpont, and d. at Dansville, July 4, 1828. Children—
5910. *Dr. Pierpont*, b. resides in Kentucky.
5911. *Frances*, b.
5912. *Franklin*, b. of Rochester, N. Y.
5913. *Caroline*, b.

5323. *Ephraim II. of Murray, N. Y., m. Lucinda Beebe, Children—
5920. *Asa*, b.
5921. *Ephraim*, b.
5922. *Hiram*, b.
5923. *Daniel*, b.
5924. *Irene*, b.
5925. *Margaret*, b.

5324. Dr. Eli, of Rochester, N. Y., son of Ephraim I., m. Mary Sprague of Winhall, Vt.
5930. *Jesse*, b.
5931. *Eli 2d*, b.
5932. *Warren*, b.
5933. *Dorothea*, b. m. —— Morse.

5325. Abraham, of Winhall, Vt., son of Ephraim I., m. —— Sawyer, Children—
5940. *Flavilla*, b.
5941. *Marinda*, b.
5942. *Eli*, b.
5943. *Albert*, b.
5944. *Abraham 2d*, b.

5326. Salmon, of Ashford, N. Y., son of Ephraim I., m. ——
——, Children—
5950. *Sophia*, b.
5951. *Elvira*, b.
5952. *Sylvia*, b.
5953. *Amaritta*, b.
5954. *Abigail*, b.
5955. *Dudley*, b.
5956. *Marshall*, b.
5957. *Salmon 2d*, b.

5330. Asa, of Granby, Mass., son of Ezra, m. Lydia Tuttle of West Springfield, March 8, 1792. Children—
5960. *Lysander*, b.

5961. *Asenath,* b.
5962. *Pamela,* b.
5963. *Lydia,* b.
5964. *Lorraine,* b.

5333. Ezra II. of Greenfield, N. Y., m. ——— ———,
Children—

5970. *Sally,* b. Nov. 12, 1797; m. Ira Ormsby; d. 1830.
5971. *Ezra* 3d, b. Nov. 13, 1800; m. Betsey Hodges of Greenfield, in 1821.
5972. *William Whipple,* b. May 25, 1803; of Waterford, N. Y., m. Mary H. Horton of Norton, Mass., Dec. 18, 1827.
5973. *Hannah,* b. Sept. 9, 1805; d. April 5, 1839.
5974. *Alvin,* } Twins, b. July 5, 1807; m. Sally Jane Ensign, 1837.
5975. *Almeida,* } m. James Cooper, 1826.
5976. *Saburna,* b. May 25, 1809; m. Edward Parkman of Corinth, N. Y., 1837.
5977. *David D.,* b. July 7, 1811; m. Adaline Webb of Lansingburgh, 1834.
5978. *Horace W.,* b. June 10, 1813; of Lansingburgh, N. Y., m. Julia B. Hanford, 1839.

5336. Justin, of South Hadley, Mass., son of Ezra I., m. Patty Bracket, Feb. 12, 1800, who d. Aug. 21, 1842. Children—

5980. *Justin 2d,* b. Oct. 26, 1803; m. Julia Moody of South Hadley, Jan. 22, 1825; and d. without issue, Feb. 19, 1837, aged 33.
5981. *Plin,* b. June 1, 1806
5982. *Pamela,* b. Oct. 22, 1808; m. John M. Chapin, April, 1831.
5983. *Alfred, (Dr.)* b. Feb. 22, 1811.
5984. *Fidelia,* b. July 2, 1813; m. Phinehas White of Napier, Mich.
5985. *Sophia D.,* b. Jan. 1, 1816; m. Charles H. Smith of Northampton.
5986. *Clarissa E.,* b. April 25, 1818; d. Dec. 15, 1819.
5987. *Horace R.,* b. Dec. 17, 1820.
5988. *Austin S.,* b. Oct. 4, 1822.

5337. *Alvin, of South Hadley, Mass., son of Ezra I., m. Hannah Butts of that town, Oct. 31, 1802, and d. Nov. 8, 1806, aged 26. Children—

5990. *Asaph Butts,* b.
5991. *Alvin* 2d, b.

5338. *Plin, of West Springfield, Mass., son of Ezra I., m. Deborah Butts of South Hadley, May 15, 1805, and d. Aug. 31, 1846. Children—

HARTFORD BRANCH—SIXTH GENERATION. 113

6000. *Plin B.*, b. April 21, 1806.
6001. *Sherubiah*, b. Jan. 30, 1808.
6002. *Samuel*, b. Oct. 12, 1809.
6003. *Deborah Ann*, b. Sept. 9, 1813.
6004. *Alvin*, b. Sept. 3, 1815.
6005. *Eliza Maria*, b. Feb. 18, 1819; m. Abel F. Hildreth of Derry, N. H., July 24, 1844.
6006. *Henry*, b. Dec. 25, 1820.
6007. *Addison*, b. April 4, 1823.
6008. *Catharine*, b. June 4, 1825; m. Richard W. Swan of Exeter, N. H., Dec. 1845.

5339. *Roswell, of Malta, N. Y., son of Ezra I., m. Eldula Fellowes, in 1814, and d. July 3, 1848, aged 64. Children—
6010. *Lorenzo*, b.   1816; d. young.
6011. *Samuel, b.   1818; d.   1834.
6012. *Andrew*, b.   1821.
6013. *Elizabeth*, b.   1826; m. —— ——, Sept. 1848.

5340. Ashbel, of Greenfield, N. Y., son of Ezra I., m. Lucretia Stewart of Chester, Mass., about 1807. Children—
6020. *Ashbel*, b. about 1809; d.   1835.
6021. *Amanda*, b.   1811.
6022. *Olive*, b.   1814.
6023. *Almira*, b.   1819.
6024. *Samuel Findlay*, b. about 1826.

5350. Amasa, of Dalton, Mass., son of Nehemiah, m.
Children—
6030. *Elisha*, b.   of Dalton.
6031. *John*, b.   and two others.

5353. Nehemiah II, of South Hadley, Mass., m. Thirza Alvord of that town, Aug. 16, 1792, who d. Aug. 5, 1837. Children—
6060. *Walter*, b. Feb. 16, 1793.
6061. *Porter, b. June 18, 1795; d. in Catskill, N. Y., in 1847.
6062. *Abigail*, b. Dec. 7, 1796.
6063. *Major*, b. Feb. 16, 1799.
6064. *Minerva*, b. Oct. 29, 1802; m. Ebenezer S. Goldthwait, Nov. 4, 1819; d. July 20, 1822.
6065. *Melancthon*, b. March 18, 1808.
6066. *Franklin*, b. March 5, 1810.
6067. *Alonzo*, b. Dec. 17, 1813.

5361. *Abraham III., first of Chester, Mass., then of Triangle, N.

Y., m. Anna Brooks in 1794, who d. April 25, 1843. He d. Nov. 7, 1844, aged 72. Children—

6080. *Irene*, b. Dec. 2, 1795; m. Asa Taft of Triangle, N. Y., Dec. 22, 1816.
6081. *Abraham* 4th, b. Jan. 17, 1799.
6082. *Clarendon*, b. Aug. 1801; d. Feb. 12, 1826.
6083. *Electa*, b. April 1, 1803; m. John W. Taft of Union, Ind., Nov. 29, 1822.
6084. *Ira*, b. March 22, 1804.
6085. *Eliza*, b. March 9, 1806; m. Dexter Whitney of Triangle, Nov. 23, 1822.
6086. *Charlotte*, b. Oct. 9, 1807; m. Abraham Taft of Elkland, Pa., Oct. 18, 1822.
6087. *Joshua*, b. Jan. 9, 1809.
6088. *John G.*, b. March 10, 1812.
6089. *Mary*, b. May 1814; m. Isaac Taft of Triangle, April, 1834; d. Dec. 1839.
6090. *William W.*, b. Aug. 27, 1816.
6091. *Seymour S.*, b. July 1, 1819.

5366. *Ira, of Chester, Mass., son of Abraham II., m. Clara Cady, (b. Aug. 18, 1786,) Oct. 11, 1807, and d. May 14, 1837, aged 56. Children—

6110. *Clarissa*, b. Dec. 17, 1808; m. Joseph Kelso of Chester, Sept. 1827.
6111. *Esther*, b. July 26, 1810; m. Alonzo Clapp of Chester, and d. April 12, 1823.
6112. *Ira* 2d, b. Aug. 8, 1812.
6113. *Asa C.*, b. March 24, 1815.
6114. *Joshua*, b. Feb. 20, 1817; of Pulaski, Ill.
6115. *Calvin*, b. Oct. 24, 1818; of Chester.
6116. *Alvin*, b. Feb. 1, 1820.
6117. *Erastus*, b. Feb. 2, 1822; d. young.
6118. *Louisa*, b. Dec. 19, 1822.
6119. *Martha A.*, b. April 13, 1824; m. Edw. Sampson, June 14, 1842.
6120. *John*, b. Aug. 2, 1825; of Hinsdale, Mass.
6121. *Edwin Munroe*, b. June 5, 1828; of Westfield, Mass.

5380. *Elisha II. of Easthampton, Mass., m. ———— ————,
Children—

6150. *William*, b.   of Northampton.
6151. *Norris*, b.
6152. *Deborah*, b.   m. Josiah Snow of South Hadley.
6153. *Betsey*, b.   m. ———— Miller of Westfield.

5391. Justin, of Colchester, (Westchester Society,) son of Elijah,

HARTFORD BRANCH—SIXTH GENERATION. 115

resides on the farm formerly owned by his grandfather Abraham; m. Matilda Day, (5288) of Stockbridge, Nov. 5, 1800. Children—

6160. *Elijah*, b. June 13, 1802.
6161. *Eleanor Louisa*, b. Feb. 18, 1804; m. Ansel Hungerford of Hadlyme, Feb. 19, 1833.
6162. *Stephen Olmsted*, b. Jan. 7, 1806.
6163. *Amasa*, b. May 12, 1808.
6164. *Sarah Maria, b. Aug. 10, 1810; m. John J. Worthington, May 6, 1830; d. Sept. 24, 1832.
6165. *Dorothy Olmsted*, b. Sept. 16, 1813; m. Brainard D. Kellogg, March 13, 1834.
6166. *Justin* 2d, b. Dec. 26, 1815.
6167. *Roderic, b. Nov. 16, 1817; d. Dec. 16, 1821.
6168. *Frances Matilda*, b. April 16, 1820; m. Jared C. Kellogg, Oct. 1, 1839.
6169. *Laura*, b. Oct. 16, 1822.
6170. *Roderic*, b. May 16, 1825.

5400. **Austin**, of Holly, N. Y., son of Oliver, m. ―――― Chapman, Children—

6180. *Mary Ann*, b.   m. Hiram Buel.
6181. *Catharine*, b.
6182. *Ferdinand A.*, b.
6183. *Corydon Chapman*, b.

5401. **Justin**, of Granville, N. Y., son of Oliver, m. ―――― ――――, Children—

6190. *Charles*, b.
6191. *Minerva*, b.
6192. *Edward*, b.

5402. **Oliver II.** of Murray, N. Y., m. ―――― ――――, Children—

6200. *Philura*, b.
6201. *Elijah*, b.
6202. *Justus*, b.
6203. *Diodate Brockway*, b.
6204. *Cerintha*, b.
6205. *Cornelia*, b.
6206. *Oliver* 3d, b.

5421. **Alfred**, of Rome, N. Y., son of Daniel, m. Anna Smith, Children—

6220. *William*, b.
6221. *Thomas*, b.
6222. *Dwight*, b.
6223. A daughter, b.

5422. *Jacob, successively of Cazenovia and Granville, N. Y., and Sherman, Mich., son of Daniel, m. Abigail Bulkley, Nov. 28, 1801, and d. Oct. 15, 1839. aged 60. His widow d. Feb. 20, 1840. Children—

6230. *Gershom Bulkley*, b. Oct. 28, 1802.
6231. *Henry Jacob*, b. June 4, 1804.
6232. *William Addison*, b. April 23, 1806.
6233. *Daniel Isham*, b. Nov. 15, 1808.
6234. *Elizabeth Abigail*, b. June 20, 1810; m.―――― Rice.
6235. *Martha Ann, b. June 4, 1815.
6236. *Charles Tayntor, b. June 9, 1811; d. young.
6237. *John Edward, b. Nov. 28, 1812; d. aged 19.
6238. *Edwin Tayntor, b. Twin; d. young.
6239. *Charlotte Maria, b. May 4, 1817; d. Dec. 18, 1846.
6240. *Sarah Tayntor, b. May 12, 1820.
6241. *Charles Chester, b. Jan. 1, 1823; d. Jan. 9, 1823.

5430 *Erastus, of Williamstown, Mass., son of John, m. Louisa Skinner of Hebron, Conn., who d. July 14, 1824. He d. Aug. 1, 1830, aged 55. Children—

6250. *Henrietta A. C.*, b.   m. Joseph Skinner 3d.
6251. *Mary Ann*, b. March 20, 1807.
6252. *John W.*, b. Feb. 2, 1808.
6253. *Louisa S.*, b. Jan. 15, 1811.
6254. *Harriet B.*, b. Feb. 21, 1814.
6255. *George W., b. Dec. 21, 1816; d. Aug. 15, 1825.
6256. *William F.*, b. June 30, 1819.
6257. *Thompson H., b. April 10, 1822; d. March 10, 1823.

5442. Elijah W. of Port Tobacco, Md., son of Charles, m. Annie Baillie, (b. in Edinburg, Scotland, in 1793,) July 20, 1834, who d. May 17, 1845, aged 52. Children—

6260. *John Baillie, b. June 27, 1835; d. Oct. 11, 1836.

5446. Justin E. of Colchester, Conn., son of Charles, m. Eliza Maria Ransom of Colchester, Nov. 10, 1835. Children—

6270. *Frances Ann*, b. Jan. 28, 1837.
6271. *Elijah Worthington*, b. Nov. 25, 1840.

5447. Isaac H. of Colchester, son of Charles, m. Sarah Ellis Williams of Chatham, (b. June 10, 1817,) Oct. 10, 1842. Children—

6280. *Ann Eliza*, b. April 29, 1844.
6281. *Sparrow Williams*, b. Feb. 22, 1846.

5448. Erastus, son of Charles, studied Theology in the Theological Department of Yale College, where he completed his studies

HARTFORD BRANCH—SIXTH GENERATION. 117

in Aug. 1844; m. Maranda Matilda West, (b. Oct. 13, 1812,) daughter of Rev. Joel West of Chatham, (Easthampton Parish,) Conn., Sept. 15, 1846. Children—
6290. *Mary*, b. Aug. 24, 1847.

5461. **Nathaniel III.** of Northampton, Mass., m. Achsah Strong, Nov. 29, 1792, who d. July 31, 1847. Children—
6300. *Eunice*, b. Jan. 11, 1795; m. Phinehas Owens of Westfield, Sept. 1, 1820.
6301. *Huram*, b. April 11, 1796.
6302. *Hiram*, b. Oct. 1797; d. May 11, 1819, aged 22.
6303. *Eliza*, b. May 11, 1804; m. William Smith of Northampton.
6304. *Wealthy*, b. Jan. 1806; m. Levi Pond of Hatfield.
6305. *Almira*, b. m. Wm. Leonard of Ashfield.
6306. *Samuel*, b. March 1810.
6307. *Deborah*, b. Nov. 1813; m. Wm. Wolcott of Williamsburg.

5462. ***Samuel**, of Hartford, Conn., son of Nathaniel II., m ——
Brewster, Children—
6310. *Samuel*, b. and two daughters, who removed to Illinois.

5463. *Dudley, of Northampton, Mass., son of Nathaniel II., m. Ruth Nichols of that town, and d. May 9, 1818. Children—
6320. *Rosanna*, b. 1812?
6321. *Dudley*, b. Jan. 25, 1814.
6322. *George*, b. June 13, 1818; d. in 1845.

5472. *Spencer, of Northampton, Mass., son of Simeon, m. Martha Hall of Easthampton, and d. in Sept. about 1826. Children—
6330. *Frances Eleanor*, b. d. young.
6331. *Julia*, b. d. about 1844.
6332. *Simeon*, b.
6333. *Frances Eleanor*, b.
6334. *William Hall*, b.
6335. *Martha*, b.

5483. **Zelotes**, of New Haven, Conn., son of Joel, m. Eliza Atwater of that city, July 23, 1817. Children—
6340. *Sarah Ann*, b. June 12, 1818; m. Ezekiel H. Trowbridge of New Haven, June 20, 1840.
6341. *Alonzo Murray*, b. March 22, 1822; d. Dec. 11, 1823.
6342. *Eliza Jane*, b. Jan. 27, 1823; m. Sylvester Tuttle, May 2, 1849.
6343. *Zelotes* 2d, b. June 25, 1825.

118   DESCENDANTS OF ROBERT DAY.

6344. *Frances Rebecca*, b. March 28, 1832.
6345. *Augustus Pliny*, b. May 9, 1834.
6346. *Wilbur Fisk*, b. Jan. 9, 1838.

5484. **Elijah**, formerly of Waterloo, N. Y., now of Hennepin, Ill., son of Joel, m. (1st) Eliza Strong of Northampton, May 16, 1816: (2d) Eliza Parsons of Waterloo, March 2, 1824: (3d) Ann Swift in 1828. Children—

6350. *William Henry*, b. March 1817.
6351. *Edward Lewis*, b. July 4, 1819.
6352. *Frederic Augustus*, b. Sept. 12, 1821.
6353. *Elijah* 2d, b. March 1846.

5486. **Alonzo**, of Savannah, Ga., son of Joel, m. Jane Elizabeth Corey, Aug. 14, 1825. Children—

6360. *Elizabeth*, b. June 12, 1826; m. Clarence Lawrence, Jan. 1846.
6361. *Alonzo Murray*, b. June 1828.

5494. **Jonathan**, of Northampton, Mass., son of Luke, m. Laura O. Hubbard of Cummington, Feb. 18, 1830. Children—

6370. *Laura*, b. Nov. 26, 1830.
6371. *Myron*, b. Nov. 6, 1832.
6372. *Mary*, b. April 17, 1836.
6373. *Susan*, b. Aug. 4, 1839.
6374. *William Hubbard*, b. May 5, 1842.
6375. *Ellen Czrina*, b. July 12, 1847.

5500. **Thomas L.** of Guilford, Chenango Co., N. Y., son of Thomas, m. Sally White of Torringford, Conn., Feb. 1830. Children—

6380. *William White*, b. Feb. 1834.
6381. *Helen*, b. May 1843.

5505. **William**, of Bristol, Conn., son of Thomas, m. Emeline C. Hitchcock, (b. Jan. 18, 1815,) of Southington, Conn., May 2, 1836. Children—

6390. *Mary Elizabeth*, b. April 29, 1837.
6391. *Harriet Eliza*, b. May 8, 1843.

5506. **Daniel**, of Lanesboro', Mass., son of Thomas, Principal of the Academy in that town, m. Jane Eliza Smedley of Williamstown, Mass., Oct. 14, 1840. Child—

6400. *Ellen Maria*, b. Oct. 5, 1842.

5512. **William**, of Great Barrington, Mass., son of Samuel II., m. Mary Pixley in 1808. Children—

HARTFORD BRANCH—SEVENTH GENERATION. 119

6410. *Samuel, b. Jan. 2, 1809; d. young.
6411. *William, b. April 15, 1810; d. young.
6412. Guy, b. Aug. 12, 1811.
6413. Horace H., b. July 10, 1813.
6414. *Sarah, b. April 13, 1815; d. 1821.
6415. *Mary, b. Nov. 20, 1816; d. young.
6416. *Mary, b. Jan. 24, 1818; m. Miles Avery; d. May 28, 1839.
6417. Elizabeth, b. Oct. 24, 1819; m. Geo. L'Hommedieu, April 23, 1839.
6418. *Charity, b. Aug. 8, 1825; m. Jonathan F. Franklin of East Hartford, Conn., Oct. 10, 1844, and d. March 1846.

5520. Edward, of Hartford, Conn., son of Joseph, m. Alice Rogers of Montville, Conn., May 16, 1813, and d. Sept. 30, 1842, aged 54. Children—
6420. *Thomas Steele, b. July 12, 1814; d. Sept. 3, 1814.
6421. *Edward Steele, b. March 13, 1815; d. June 18, 1816.
6422. Edward Thomas, b. May 13, 1817.
6423. Amelia Jenette, b. April 30, 1818; m. Joseph S. Williams of Hartford, in 1840.
6424. Aurelia Rhoda, b. Aug. 11, 1819.
6425. Harriet, b. Jan. 31, 1821; m. Moseley S. Roberts of Hartford, in 1840.
6426. Catharine Alice, b. June 1, 1822; m. Horace H. Day, (6413) Sept. 14, 1844.
6427. Wheaton, b. Sept. 21, 1826.

5521. Joseph II. of Monticello, Ind., m. Mary Ann Griffith of Barbersville, Va., June 15, 1820, who d. March 8, 1846. Children—
6430. John, b. Jan. 16, 1823.
6431. *Amelia, b. Nov. 14, 1825; d. March 4, 1827.
6432. Edward Horace, b. Oct. 26, 1829.
6433. *Joseph, b. Aug. 14, 1834; d. Nov. 22, 1840.

5524. *Horace, of Hudson, N. Y., son of Joseph, m. Melliscent Hildreth of that place, Nov. 12, 1818, and d. Oct. 1, 1822, aged 25. One child—
6440. Rev. Horace G., b. Sept. 13, 1819; Pastor of the Baptist Church in Skenectady, N. Y., Jan. 1, 1847.

SEVENTH GENERATION.

5548. *Charles, of Alabama, Niagara Co., N. Y., son of* David, m. Jane Lewis of Murray, N. Y., and d. Dec. 26, 1847. Children—
6500. Eli, b. and two others.

5560. Asahel, of New Albion, N. Y., son of Erastus, m. Charlotte Waite of Cataraugus, N. Y., in 1838. Children—
6540. *Persis*, b. June 5, 1839.
6541. *Wealthy*, b. June 26, 1841.
6542. *Alonzo E.*, b. March 20, 1843.
6543. *Esther R.*, b. Feb. 2, 1846.

5561. *Eli, of New Albion, N. Y., son of Erastus, m. Cyrene Chase of Cataraugus, N. Y. in 1838, and d. in 1846, aged 31. Children—
6550. *Harriet A.*, b. Dec. 6, 1844.

5562. Hudson, of New Albion, N. Y., son of Erastus, m. Eliza Gray of Cataraugus, N. Y., in 1837. Children—
6560. *Ozro E.*, b. May 26, 1839; d. 1841.
6561. *Cordelia*, b. April 6, 1842.
6562. *Mary E.*, b. Oct. 18, 1844.

5564. Orrin, of New Albion, N. Y., son of Erastus, m. Brooksanna Jones of Cataraugus, N. Y., in 1845. Children—
6570. *Alvin C.*, b. April 13, 1848.

5571. John, of Royalton, son of Charles, m. Catharine Watson, Children—
6590. *Dudley Watson*, b.
6591. *John 2d*, b.
6592. *Mary*, b.
6593. *Charles*, b.

5573. George, of East Mendon, N. Y., son of Charles, m. Harriet Fisher, Children—
6609. *Harriet*, b.

5580. John, of Cleveland, Ohio, son of Ira, m. Mary Powers, Oct. 2, 1817. Children—
6610. *Cornelia H.*, b. Aug. 13, 1818; m. Henry C. Kingsley, Esq. of Cleveland, Sept. 6, 1841, and d. Aug. 31, 1843.
6611. *Maria E.*, b. Nov. 23, 1821; m. M. C. Younglove of Cleveland, Sept. 15, 1840.
6612. *James P.*, b. May 10, 1827; d. July 18, 1848.

5581. Caleb, of Catskill, N. Y., son of Ira, was graduated at Yale College in 1818; m. Lucretia Lyman of Goshen, Conn., Children—
6620. *Moses Lyman*, b. Nov. 3, 1826; d. April 29, 1833.
6621. *Caleb Atwater*, b. Oct. 23, 1829.

6622. *Edward Lyman*, b. Feb. 2, 1835.
6623. *Elizabeth Henrietta*, b. March 27, 1837.
6524. *Ellen Augusta*, b. July 15, 1840.

5584. Rev. William, Bethel-Chaplain in Cleveland, Ohio, son of Ira, was ordained Sept. 29, 1840; m. Elizabeth Waldo Allen of Lancaster, N. H., Nov. 8, 1842. Children—
6630. *Mary Elizabeth*, b. Oct. 11, 1846.
6631. *Lucy Waldo*, b. July 26, 1848.

5585. Ira R. of Atwater, Ohio, son of Ira, m. Harriet Field of Atwater, March 1, 1829. Children—
6640. *William Sherwood*, b. June 17, 1831.
6641. *Edgar Field*, b. June 27, 1835.
6642. *Helen Maria*, b. May 5, 1840.
6643. *Mary Lavinia*, b. July 16, 1842; d. July 17, 1845.
6644. *Sarah Lavinia*, b. March 6, 1847.

5590. Edgar B. of Catskill, N. Y., son of Orrin, was graduated at Yale College in 1824; m. Sophia A. Camp of Sacketts Harbor, Sept. 24, 1835. Children—
6650. *Sophia Hale*, b. Feb. 24, 1838.
6651. *Ella M.*, b. April 20, 1844.
6652. *Isabel H. M.*, b. Sept. 6, 1846.

5592. Samuel S. of Catskill, N. Y., son of Orrin, m. (1st) Catharine A. De Forest of Huntington, Conn., Sept. 26, 1833, who d. Aug. 20, 1837: (2d) Cornelia E. Spencer of Utica, N. Y., June 16, 1842. Children—
6660. *Walter De Forest*, b. Oct. 27, 1835.
6661. *Benjamin W.*, b. June 11, 1837; d. March 9, 1838.
6662. *Orrin*, b. Sept. 24, 1845.
6663. *Joshua Spencer*, b. Dec. 11, 1846.
6664. *Ellen Spencer*, b. Sept. 22, 1848.

5600. *Rodman G. of New York City, son of Philo, m. (1st) Cornelia W. Hoag of Chatham, N. Y., Sept. 3, 1823: (2d) Mary Hoag of Nassau, N. Y., Dec. 3, 1832, and d. Oct. 12, 1835, aged 34. Children—
6670. *Thomas Hoag*, b. March 3, 1825.
6671. *Robert Henry*, b. Aug. 21, 1826.
6672. *Caroline*, b. Oct. 17, 1828.
6673. *Emma Cornelia*, b. April 22, 1831.
6674. *Gardiner*, b. Dec. 20, 1833.

5602. Rev. Robert, of Nassau, N. Y., son of Philo, m. Eliza Hoag of that town, June 1833. Children—
6680. *Edward,* b. March 1834.
6681. *Caroline H.*, b. Sept. 1844.

5621. *Dea. Joseph,* of Colchester, (Westchester Parish), Conn., son of Asa I., m. Eliza Adams of Colchester, May 24, 1825, and d. in 1846, aged 54. Children—
6700. *Mary Ann,* b. Feb. 14, 1827.
6701. *Heman,* b. Nov. 6, 1831.
6702. *Laura Adams,* b. March 11, 1833.
6703. *Henry Norman,* b. Jan. 29, 1836.
6704. *Caroline Elizabeth,* b. May 7, 1839.

5626. Asa II. of Marlborough, Conn., m. Charlotte P. Jones of Marlboro', Dec. 31, 1834. Children—
6710. *John W.*, b. March 9, 1836.
6711. *Samuel Jones,* b. Nov. 5, 1840.
6712. *Florena Wilson,* b. May 6, 1844.

5628. Elihu M. of Colchester, (Westchester Parish,) Conn., son of Asa I., m. Elizabeth Jane Buel of Marlborough, Conn., May 29, 1833. Children—
6720. *Susan,* b. June 3, 1834.
6721. *Erastus Sheldon,* b. July 7, 1836.
6722. *Jane Maria,* b. March 19, 1842.
6723. *David Buel,* b. Oct. 15, 1844.

5629. Stephen B., of Colchester, (Westchester Parish,) Ct., son of Asa I., m. Clarissa L. Brainard, Nov. 27, 1834. Children—
6730. **Hobart,* b. and d. Jan. 4, 1837.
6731. **Abby,* b. Aug. 4, 1838; d. Dec. 6, 1838.
6732. *Everett William,* b. May 25, 1840.
6733. *Margaret Foot,* b. May 23, 1843.
6734. *Almira Sheldon,* b. Nov. 1846.

5652. Asa, of Ogden, N. Y., son of Samuel, m. ——— ———,
Children—
6750. *Ira,* b.
6751. *M'Lauren,* b.
6752. *Jane,* b.
6753. *Alma,* b.
6754. *Elizabeth,* b.
6755. *Mary,* b.

5160. *Alfred,* first of Milton, Vt., then of Burlington, Vt., son of

Benjamin 3d, m. Mary Richmond of Woodstock, Vt., Feb. 20, 1812, and died suddenly from being thrown from a wagon, Dec. 8, 1834, aged 48. His widow d. July 23, 1839, aged 47. Children—

6790. *Angelina A.*, b. Nov. 9, 1812; m. William B. Munson of Colchester, Vt., May 16, 1831.
6791. *Mary E.*, b. Jan. 15, 1814; m. George W. Cobb of Chicago, Ill., Jan. 26, 1836.
6792. *Franklin O.*, b. Oct. 31, 1815.
6793. *Alfred* 2d, b. Oct. 24, 1817; of Exeter, Ill.
6794. *Louisa M. R.*, b. Aug. 3, 1820; m. John S. Munson of Colchester, Vt., May 13, 1841.
6795. *Ira*, b. April 15, 1822; not known to be living.
6796. *Richmond L.*, b. Feb. 14, 1824; of Colchester, Vt.
6797. *Margaret M.*, b. Nov. 8, 1826.

5661. **Spaulding**, first of Enosburg, Vt., now of Orangeport, N. Y., son of Benjamin 3d, m. Sarah Fasset, (b. Jan. 8, 1792) of Enosburg, Feb. 15, 1810. Children—

6800. *Silas Benjamin*, b. Nov. 2, 1812.
6801. *Julia*, b. Sept. 24, 1814.
6802. *Clarissa*, b. Feb. 8, 1817.
6803. *Seymour Tuller*, b. May 4, 1820.
6804. *Dan Dewey*, b. Dec. 11, 1821.
6805. *Persis*, b. Jan. 20, 1824.
6806. *Alfred*, b. Sept. 24, 1827; of Lockport.
6807. *Ira Sylvester*, b. March 11, 1830.
6808. *Sarah Parmelee*, b. Dec. 15, 1835.

5663. ***Dan**, of Burlington, Vt., son of Benjamin 3d, and Deacon of the Congregational Church in that town, m. Persis Dewey of Milton, Vt., Nov. 8, 1814, and d. instantly from ossification of the heart, Jan. 7, 1842, aged 51. Children—

6810. **Persis*, b. Oct. 28, 1816; m. James E. Brinsmade of Burlington, Vt., Sept. 9, 1834, and d. Jan. 11, 1845.
6811. **Dan Dewey*, b. Jan. 24, 1819; d. July 1, 1819.
6812. *Zebediah Dewey*, b. Aug. 22, 1820.
6813. *Harriet*, b. Oct. 21, 1822; m. William B. Rhoades of Westport, N. Y., March 11, 1840.
6814. **Abigail*, b. Nov. 30, 1825; d. Oct. 26, 1827.
6815. *Henry*, b. June 15, 1828.
6816. **Cleora*, b. Aug. 1, 1830; d. Aug. 15, 1830.
6817. *Dan Douglas*, b. Sept. 1, 1831.
6818. *Lucius*, b. March 2, 1838.

5664. **Gad**, son of Benjamin 3d, has resided successively in Carlisle, Lancaster and Harrisburg, Pa., in which places he has

been engaged in teaching nearly 30 years; m. Ann De Pui of Philadelphia, Jan. 5, 1830. Children—
6825. *Ann De Pui*, b.
6826. *Mary*, b.

5665. **Benjamin IV.** of Lockport, N. Y., m. Cynthia Freeman of Potsdam, N. Y., April 15, 1819: and has four daughters.

5666. **Asa**, of Lockport, N. Y., son of Benjamin 3d, m. (1st) Abigail Hall of Potsdam, N. Y., Dec. 23, 1824, who d. Feb. 11, 1841: (2d) Cleora Edwards of Lockport, May 26, 1842. Children—
6840. *Warren Hall*, b. Nov. 1, 1826.
6841. *Emerson*, b. July 18, 1830.
6842. *Cornelia Hortensia*, b. Oct. 10, 1834.
6843. *Fayette*, b. July 24, 1839.

5667. **Dr. Ira**, of Mechanicsburg, Pa., son of Benjamin 3d, m. Elizabeth Torrey of that place, Dec. 25, 1828. Children—
6850. *Alfred*, b. Feb. 20, 1830.
6851. *Annette*, b. July 5, 1832.
6852. *Caroline Elizabeth*, b. July 8, 1834; d. March 17, 1835.
6853. *John Emory*, b. April 1, 1836.
6854. *Mary*, b. July 8, 1838.
6855. *Susan Alice*, b. Oct. 6, 1840.
6856. *Jacob Torrey*, b. Dec. 9, 1842.
6857. *Ira*, b. Dec. 2, 1845; d. Dec. 11, 1845.
6858. *Francis Boggs*, b. May 2, 1847.

5712. **George**, of ———, ———, son of Sylvester, m. Mary Bellows of Ipswich, Vt. Children—
6910. *Charles Edward*, b.
6911. *George Washington*, b.
6912. *Mary*, b.
6913. *James Giles*, b.
6914. *Benjamin*, b.

5713. **Edmund**, of ———, ———, son of Sylvester, m. Augusta Gale of Barre, Vt., Children—
6920. *Sylvester*, b.
6921. *Dennison*, b.
6922. *Lucy*, b.
6923. *Clarissa*, b.
6924. *Julia*, b.

5712. **Benjamin**, of Royalton, Vt., son of Sylvester, m. Emily H. Goff, Jan. 19, 1847.

5731. **Clark,** of Barre, Vt., son of Ira, m. Emily Carter, June 2, 1841. Children—
7010. *Gertrude,* b. April 3, 1843.
7011. *Alvin,* b. Feb. 2, 1845.
7012. *Emily,* b. March 23, 1848.

5740. **Charles II.,** first of Burlington, N. Y., now of Sauquoit, N. Y., m. Eunice King, (b. Oct. 27, 1788,) Nov. 24, 1808. Children—
7030. *Hannah,* b. Nov. 27, 1809.
7031. *Alvord,* b. Sept. 18, 1811.
7032. *Samuel,* b. Aug. 1, 1813; d. Aug. 10, 1813.
7033. *Alvin,* b. Dec. 20, 1814.
7034. *Sophia,* b. Dec. 22, 1816; m. ——— ———, Jan. 25, 1837.
7035. *Almon,* b. Jan. 27, 1819.
7036. *Harriet,* b. Dec. 15, 1820; d. young.
7037. *Almeron,* b. April 11, 1822; of Litchfield, N. Y.
7038. *Albert,* b. July 20, 1824.
7039. *Alfayette,* b. July 30, 1826.
7040. *Rexy Alice,* b. Sept. 2, 1829.
7041. *Alfred,* b. July 16, 1831; d. March 18, 1833.

5743. **Ira,** of Ellington, N. Y., son of Charles I., m. Susanna Mather, in 1810. Children—
7050. *Daniel Willard,* b. April 29, 1811.
7051. *Stephen M.,* b. Nov. 11, 1812; d. July 21, 1815.
7052. *Mary M.,* b. July 19, 1814; m. John F. Farnam of Ellington, Jan. 6, 1836.
7053. *Lorenzo M.,* b. May 16, 1816.
7054. *Almira,* b. May 30, 1818; m. Warren Hoag, Jan. 6, 1840.
7055. *Sarah A.,* b. Sept. 12, 1821; m. Eli Perkins, Jan. 16, 1844.
7056. *Maria H.,* b. Aug. 4, 1825.
7057. *Edwin P.,* b. March 27, 1829.

5747. **Flavel,** of Burlington, N. Y., (on the homestead,) son of Charles I., m. Lucy Marvin in 1817. Children—
7060. *Lucy,* b. 1830.
7061. *Ira,* b. 1832.
7062. *Julia,* b. 1834.
7063. *La Mott,* b. 1838.

5752. **Alfred,** of Mantua, Ohio, son of Alvin, m. Lydia Calkins, Aug. 20, 1815. Children—
7070. *Epaphroditus,* b. Jan. 5, 1816; d. Oct. 29, 1816.
7071. *Ditus,* b. Oct. 10, 1817.
7072. *Sabrina,* b. April 19, 1819; m. Charles M. Taylor, Sept. 9, 1840.

7073. *Denison, b. Jan. 30, 1821; d. March 14, 1823.
7074. Temperance, b. Dec. 14, 1822; m. Jonathan Parker, Dec. 5, 1844.
7075. Lucia, b. Jan. 19, 1826.
7076. Arodine, b. June 19, 1828.
7077. Esther, b. March 24, 1830.
7078. Alfred A., b. May 29, 1834.
7079. Levi E., b. Dec. 8, 1837.

5756. Alvin II. of Wilbraham, Mass., m. Anna Maria Stebbins, June 25, 1828. Children—
7080. Harrison C., b. March 26, 1829.
7081. Nelson, b. Feb. 21, 1831.
7082. Gilford, b. May 31, 1832.
7083. Lovina, b. Feb. 22, 1834.
7084. Sanford, b. Nov. 23, 1835.
7085. George, b. Jan. 11, 1838.
7086. Alfred, b. Jan. 25, 1840.
7087. Olive Maria, b. Sept. 15, 1841.
7088. Mary Azubah, b. Dec. 9, 1843.
7089. Alvira, b. Sept. 6, 1845.
7090. Jane Eliza, b. March 28, 1847.

5757. Lyman, of Wilbraham, Mass., son of Alvin I., m. Chloe Staunton, April 28, 1835. Children—
7100. Henry Robert, b. March 1, 1836.
7101. Maranda Jane, b. Aug. 3, 1838.
7102. Ann Eliza, b. Oct. 3, 1840.
7103. Cyrus Clinton, b. Sept. 15, 1841.
7104. Lyman Morton, b. Sept. 16, 1844.
7105. Chloe Elvira, b. Sept. 24, 1847.

5760. Lyman, of Sangerfield, N. Y., son of Levi, m. Maria Preston, Dec. 6, 1820. Children—
7110. Cornelia H., b. May 23, 1822; m. N. H. Terry, Oct. 3, 1843.
7111. Charlotte R., b. July 20, 1824.
7112. Nelson C., b. June 30, 1826.
7113. Joseph A., b. Sept. 16, 1828.
7114. Lyman P., b. June 4, 1831.
7115. Henry L., b. Aug. 4, 1834.
7116. Clarissa M., b. Aug. 19, 1838.
7117. Julia Ann, b. Oct. 17, 1841.
7118. *Alice A., } b. June 9, 1844; d. Feb. 11, 1845.
7119. Amelia S., } b. Twin.

5765. Dan, of Lima, N. Y., son of Levi, m. Julia Hooker, Dec. 4, 1828. Children—

HARTFORD BRANCH—SEVENTH GENERATION. 127

7120. *Helen G.*, b. Nov. 29, 1833.
7121. *William H.*, b. Jan. 17, 1845.

5766. **Levi C.** of Lima, N. Y., son of Levi, m. Mary Hooker, Jan. 13, 1835. Children—
7130. *Charles H.*, b. Nov. 13, 1842; d. May 17, 1848.

5773. **Royal,** of Munson, Me., of which he was one of the first settlers, son of Erial, m. Love Clark of Monson, Mass., Jan. 28, 1823. Children—
7140. *Alvira*, b. April 12, 1825; m. Nelson Cushman of Munson, Me., April 12, 1842.
7141. *Lydia Annis*, b. Sept. 27, 1827; m. James Anderson, Aug. 30, 1846.
7142. *Royal Newton*, b. July 26, 1829.
7143. *Candace*, b. Jan. 27, 1833.

5774. **Russel,** of Monson, Mass., son of Erial, m. Mirandis Day, (5790) May 21, 1829. Children—
7150. *Levi Russel*, b. March 28, 1830; d. Dec. 6, 1834.
7151. *Epaphro Almanzy*, b. Oct. 2, 1833.
7152. *Erial Bestar*, b. Oct. 9, 1835; d. June 5, 1838.
7153. *Russel Morton*, b. Nov. 28, 1839.
7154. *Mary Jenette*, b. Nov. 11, 1841.

5778. **Gideon,** of Monson, Mass., son of Erial, m. Marcia Henrietta Cushman of Stafford, Conn., Nov. 24, 1842. Children—
7170. *Nancy Henrietta*, b. Sept. 14, 1843.

5780. **Selden,** of Lenox, N. Y., son of Elihu, m. Clarissa Baker 1816, and has had five sons and four daughters.

5786. **Harlem,** of Burlington, N. Y., son of Elihu, m. Salome Beardsley, June, 1824, and has five sons and two daughters.

5787. **Elihu II.** of West Winfield, N. Y., m. Cinderilla Huntington in 1837, and has three sons.

5788. **Ezra,** of Exeter, Otsego Co., N. Y., son of Elihu I., m. Polly A. Sprague, Sept. 1, 1839, and has one daughter.

5800. **Marvin,** of Lebanon, Madison Co., N. Y., son of Adonijah II., m. Eliza Dunham, Jan. 31, 1827. Children—
7220. *Jerusha*, b. Dec. 16, 1827.
7221. *Orril*, b. Oct. 22, 1829.
7222. *Cornelia*, b. May 3, 1832.

7223. *Wallis*, b. March 30, 1834.
7224. *Betsey*, b. Oct. 15, 1835.
7225. *Charles*, b. April 13, 1837.

5801. Adonijah III. of Marshall, Oneida Co., N. Y., m. Sophia Titus, Dec. 18, 1833. Children—
7230. *Ellen J.*, b. Sept. 16, 1837.
7231. *Julius A.*, b. May 3, 1840.
7232. *Jane S.*, b. Sept. 25, 1845.

5805. Rev. Hiram, of South Cornwall, Conn., son of Adonijah II., completed his studies at Oneida Institute in 1839, and at the East Windsor Theological Institute in 1842; ordained Pastor of the Congregational Church in South Cornwall, Feb. 29, 1844; dismissed Oct. 9, 1847; m. Emily L. Foster, May 7, 1844. Children—
7240. *Harriet F.*, b. March 5, 1845.
7241. *Arthur H.*, b. June 7, 1847.

5806. Epaphroditus, of Westmoreland, N. Y., son of Adonijah II., m. Achsah Scott, Feb. 15, 1837. Children—
7250. *Achsah J.*, b. Jan. 22, 1839.
7251. *Herbert L.*, b. Dec. 25, 1845.

5807. Ira, of Georgetown, N. Y., son of Adonijah II., m. Susanna Whitmore, Children—
7260. *Adaline W.*, b. April 12, 1846.

5821. David, of ———, ———, son of Daniel II.,† m. Catharine Clark, Children—
7270. *James H.*, b.
7271. *Nelson*, b.
7272. **Daniel*, b.

5825. Benjamin, of Haddam, (Neck,) Conn., son of Daniel II., m. Sylvia Brainard,

5827. Daniel III. of Great Barrington, (Housatonicville,) Mass., m. Jenette Lang, Oct. 4, 1846. Children—
7290. *Charles Lester*, b. March 28, 1848.

5830. Erastus II. of Armada, Mich., m. (1st) Catharine Smith,

---

† It is stated in a letter from Michigan, received since the last sheet was struck off, that Daniel II. resided in Bruce, Mich.; m. Anna Clark of Burlington, and had but one child, *Colatinus*, b. Sept. 13, 1809, who d. unmarried, May 9, 1836. If so, the parentage of Daniel, (5290) is not correctly given in this Register.

HARTFORD BRANCH—SEVENTH GENERATION. 129

(b. May 30, 1807,) of Mendon, N. Y. in 1833: (2d) Betsey Day, (5853) Sept. 13, 1836. Children—
7300. *Lucy C.*, b. Feb. 9, 1834.
7301. *Mary*, b. July 27, 1835.
7302. *John E.*, b. Jan. 11, 1838.
7303. *Harriet Malvina*, b. May 22, 1839.
7304. *Harry*, b. Sept. 7, 1841; d. 1844.
7305. *Sarah*, b. Aug. 22, 1843; d. 1843.
7306. *Martha*, b. June 1, 1847.

5831. **John W.** of Dryden, Mich., son of Erastus I., m. Mary Parkhurst of Mendon, N. Y. in 1836. Children—
7310. *Frances*, b. March 5, 1838.
7311. *John W.*, b. March 1846.

5832. **Russel**, of Bruce, Mich., son of Erastus I., m. Charlotte Smith of Lima, N. Y., March 1, 1841. Children—
7320. *Elizabeth*, b. Feb. 1842.
7321. *Olive*, b. Oct. 1844.
7322. *Charles*, b. July 1845.
7323. *Phebe*, b. May 22, 1847.

5833. **Daniel W.** of Otisco, Mich., son of Erastus I., m. Esther Day, (5854) March 13, 1840. Children—
7330. *Julia Elizabeth*, b. Jan. 26, 1841.
7331. *Oscar*, b. July 9, 1843.
7332. *Loren*, b. Feb. 1845.

5834. **Levi**, of Otisco, Mich., son of Erastus I., m. Clarissa Rider of Austinburg, Ohio. Children—
7340. *Helen S.*, b., Sept. 1844.

5851. **Urial**, of Armada, Mich., son of Harry, m. Olive Sporry of Springfield, Pa., Sept. 1833. Children—
7350. *Emily*, b. June 1834.
7351. *Cordelia*, b. June 1837.
7352. *Caroline M.*, b. 1840.
7353. *Lucinda E.*, b. Oct. 1842.

5852. **William C.** of Dryden, Mich., son of Harry, m. Emma Phelps of Dryden, May 1841. Children—
7360. *Gad C.*, b. Aug. 1843.
7361. *Virginia A.*, b. Feb. 1845.
7362. *William*, b. Nov. 1848.

5857. **Erastus,** of Lakeville, Mich., son of Harry, m. Caroline V. Beardsley of Albion, Pa., April 1848.

5872. **Eri H.** of the Mission to the Indians at Fond Du Lac, son of Russel, m. Harriet Brockway of Ashtabula, Ohio, in 1843, and has two sons.

5874. **Volney,** of Kalamazoo, Mich., son of Russel, m. Lucinda Day, (5835) and has one son—
7410. ———, b. 1849.

5891. **Erasmus W.** of Schuyler, N. Y., son of Dr. Warren, m. Mary Ann Root of that town in 1839. Children—
7440. *Warren,* b. July 6, 1840.
7441. *Mary Louisa,* b. Nov. 22, 1847.

5893. **Dr. Horace B.** of Schuyler, N. Y., son of Dr. Warren, completed his studies at the Albany Medical College, Jan. 23, 1844; m. Mary Richardson of Schuyler, Oct. 16, 1844, who d. June 4, 1848. Children—
7450. *Horace Eaton,* b. Aug. 21, 1845.

5981. **Plin,** of South Hadley, Mass., son of Justin, m. Jerusha Alvord of that town, Oct. 1830. Children—
7680. *Ann Jerusha,* b. Nov. 14, 1831.
7681. *Jane Eliza,* b. Jan. 1, 1833.
7682. *Clarissa,* b. Nov. 10, 1835.
7683. *Fidelia,* b. June 10, 1837.
7684. *Justin,* b. July 14, 1838; d. May 1839.

5983. *Dr. Alfred,* of Perryville, Mo., son of Justin, m. Mary Jane Fenick of that town, and d. Aug. 10, 1844, aged 33. Children—
7690. *Eliza Ann,* b.

5991. **Alvin H.** of Webster, Mass., m. Mary G. Camp of South Hadley, Nov. 8, 1838, and d. June 11, 1844. Children—
7720. *Henry Alvin,* b. March 24, 1841; d. Sept. 23, 1841.
7721. *George Alvin,* b. Jan. 1845.

6000. **Rev. Plin B.** of Derry, N. H., son of Plin, was graduated at Amherst College in 1834; ordained Pastor of the Congregational Church in Derry, Oct. 4, 1837; m. Emily Haskell of Rockport, Mass., Oct. 22, 1839. Children—
7730. *Ellen Haskell,* b. July 28, 1840.

7731. *Henry Martyn Hildreth*, b. Nov. 12, 1841.
7732. *Elizabeth Banister*, b. May 2, 1845.

6001. **Sherubiah**, of West Springfield, Mass., son of Plin, m. Harriet Sampson of Springfield, Dec. 30, 1834. Children—
7740. *Sherubiah* 2d, b. Feb. 17, 1838.
7741. *Harriet*, b. June 19, 1840.

6002. **Samuel**, of Springfield, son of Plin, m. Clarissa Hillyer of Granby, Conn., March 3, 1834. Children—
7750. *Sarah H.*, b. March 3, 1835; d. Feb. 8, 1844.
7751. *Mary Melissa,* ⎫ Twins, b. June 30, 1841; d. Sept. 25, 1842.
7752. *Martha Clarissa,* ⎭ d. June 2, 1842.
7753. *Albert Morgan*, b. June 24, 1845.

6006. **Henry**, a lawyer in New York City, son of Plin, was graduated at Yale College in 1845; m. Phebe Lucretia Lord of New York, Jan. 31, 1849.

6007. **Addison**, of Springfield, Mass., son of Plin, m. Margaret Smith of West Springfield, Dec.   1847.

6060. *Walter, of South Hadley, (Canal,) Mass., son of Nehemiah 2d, m. Lydia Kneeland of that town, April 5, 1821; d. March 17, 1844. Children—
7840. *Harvey*, b.   of South Hadley.
7841. *George*, b. May 1, 1825.
7842. *Electa Ann*, b.   m. Wm. R. Davison, Ap. 19, 1849.
7843. *Edwin*, b.
7844. *Albert*, b.

6063. *Major, of South Hadley, Mass., son of Nehemiah II., m. Maletha Mandeville of that town, June 26, 1824, and d. Oct. 1, 1830, aged 30. One child—
7850. *William Waite*, b. July 7, 1825; at Warehouse Point.

6065. *Melancthon, of Hadley, Mass., son of Nehemiah II., m. Matilda Wallis of Monchcong, Pa., and d. Oct. 2, 1845, aged 37. Children—
7860. *Elizabeth M.*, b. Dec. 30, 1832.
7861. *Albert*, b. Aug. 19, 1834.
7862. *Minerva*, b. Aug. 28, 1836; d. Jan. 30, 1838.
7863. *Henry*, b. Sept. 16, 1838; d. Aug. 20, 1839.
7864. *Henry*, b. April 16, 1841.

6066. Franklin, of South Hadley, Mass., son of Nehemiah II., m. Lavira Pendleton of Easthampton, Nov. 27, 1834. Children—

7870. *Sarah Maria,* b. Nov. 22, 1835.
7871. *Eunice Alice,* b. March 10, 1844.
7872. *Edward Franklin,* b. June 3, 1846.
7873. *Osmond Alonzo,* b. Aug. 21, 1848.

6067. Alonzo, of Warehouse Point, Conn., son of Nehemiah II., m. Elizabeth Bartlett of Hadley, Mass., Aug. 18, 1841.

6081. Abraham IV. of New Albion, N. Y., m. Johanna Guy, Children—

7880. *Laura A.,* b. April 26, 1826.
7881. *Abraham Robert,* b. June 5, 1829.
7882. *Clarendon,* b. Nov. 6, 1832.
7883. *Thomas Foster,* b. Nov. 19, 1837.
7884. *Jefferson Deroy,* b. March 15, 1839.
7885. *Mary Juliette,* b. April 4, 1842; d. March 10, 1844.
7886. *Emeline,* b. June 15, 1845.
7887. *Charlotte,* b. April 16, 1847.

6084. *Ira, of Turmona Creek, Ind., son of Abraham 3d, m. Celestia Barnes, in 1827, and d. Sept. 1846, aged 42. His widow d. in 1847. Children—

7890. *Lucy Ann,* b. Sept. 1828.
7891. *Cornelia,* b. 1829.
7892. *Joshua,* b. 1831; d. 1847.
7893. *Irene,* b. 1834.
7894. *Louisa,* b. 1837.
7895. *Charlotte,* b. 1840.
7896. *Ira* 2d, b. 1844.

6087. *Joshua, of Jamestown, N. Y., son of Abraham 3d, m. Eliza Taft, Jan. 1837, who d. July, 1847. He d. in 1847, aged 38. Children—

7900. *Lewis,* b. Feb. 1838.
7901. *William W.,* b. 1840.
7902. *Balinda,* b. 1841.
7903. *George W.,* b. 1843.

6088. John G. of La Grange, Mich., son of Abraham 3d, m. Annis Parker, Sept. 1836. Children—

7910. *Lucius,* b. Nov. 1837.
7911. *Almira,* b. Aug. 8, 1839.
7912. *Eugene,* b. May 1842.
7913. *Polly M.,* b. April 1845.

6090. William W., M.D., of Triangle, N. Y., son of Abraham 3d, m. Lucy C. Pringle, Sept. 6, 1848.

6091. Seymour S. of Triangle, N. Y., son of Abraham 3d, m. Polly McGilfrey, Nov. 14, 1841. Children—
7930. *Isaac C.*, b. May 16, 1844; d. May 7, 1846.
7931. *Lucretia*, b. July 14, 1846; d. Aug. 4, 1846.
7932. *Helen U.*, b. Dec. 2, 1846.

6112. Ira H. of Hinsdale, Mass., m. Fidelia Ramsdale, Children—
7940. *William Ira*, b.
7941. *Esther Fidelia*, b.

6113. Asa C. of Chester, Mass., son of Ira, m. Amelia S. Tucker, (b. Jan. 8, 1820,) May 8, 1842. Children—
7950. *Charles Franklin*, b. April 6, 1844.
7951. *Henry Lee*, b. March 15, 1845.

6116. Alvin, of Hinsdale, Mass., son of Ira, m. Esther Cross, in 1844. Children—
7980. *Mary*, b. June 29, 1847.

6160. Elijah, of Hadlyme, Conn., son of Justin, m. Rebecca Ely Hungerford of that town, Oct. 25, 1827. Children—
8030. *Robert Elijah*, b. July 11, 1828; in the freshman class in Yale College.
8031. *Norman*, b. June 25, 1830.
8032. *Sarah Maria*, b. Sept. 8, 1832.
8033. *Albert*, b. Oct. 14, 1835.
8034. *Almon*, b. March 16, 1838.
3035. *William Henry*, b. Nov. 26, 1840.
8036. *Matilda*, b. July 22, 1844.

6162. Stephen O. of Akron, Ohio, son of Justin, m. Mary P. Willey of Hadlyme, Oct. 6, 1834. Children—
8040. *Matilda*, b. 1836.
8041. *Mary Willey*, b. 1839.
8042. *Stephen O. 2d*, b. 1843.

6163. Amasa, of East Haddam, Conn., son of Justin, m. (1st) Ursula Maria Gates of Lyme, Conn., Sept. 30, 1838, who d. Oct. 30, 1844: (2d) Sarah Selden Spencer, Nov. 27, 1845. Children—
8050. *Charles Amasa*, b. Jan. 16, 1847.

6166. Justin II. of Rochester, N. Y., m. Jane Layton of Auburn, N. Y., Sept. 14, 1841. Children—
8060. *Henry Clay,* b. Oct. 5, 1842.
8061. *Caroline J.,* b. Aug. 24, 1847; d. June 26, 1848.

6230. Rev. Gershom B. of Sherman, Mich., son of Jacob, m. Elizabeth Benjamin of Whitehall, N. Y., Oct. 25, 1832. Children—
8180. *Sarah Charlotte,* b. 1835.
8181. *Joseph Drake,* b. d. young.
8182. *Mary Elizabeth,* b. 1840.

6231. Henry J. of Whitehall, N. Y., son of Jacob, m. Sally Thurston of Whitehall, Sept. 9, 1829. Children—
8190. *Sarah Jane,* b. April 11, 1831; d. Sept. 19, 1832.
8191. *Henry Jacob,* b. March 15, 1833.
8192. *Helen Maria,* b. Dec. 28, 1834.
8193. *Elisha Charles,* b. Aug. 9, 1836; d. Aug. 18, 1836.
8194. *Edward Bulkley,* } Twins, b. Dec. 6, 1839.
8195. *Edwin Daniel,*

6232. William A. of ———, Mich., son of Jacob, m. Emeline Pratt, Children—
8200. *William Addison* 2d, b.
8201. *Henry,* b.
8202. *Elijah,* b.

6233. Daniel I. of Granville, N. Y., son of Jacob, m. (1st) Therena Briggs of Fort Ann: (2d) Calista Carter of Fort Ann, and had one child, who died.

6301. Huram, of Northampton, Mass., son of Nathaniel 3d, m. Lucinda Owen of Westfield, Children—
8280. *Charles,* b. Sept. 16, 1822.
8281. *William,* b. Sept. 17, 1824.
8282. *Nathaniel,* b. Nov. 18, 1825.
8283. *Leonard,* b. Dec. 12, 1827.
8284. *Sarah,* b. Aug. 14, 1829.
8285. *Julia,* b. July 2, 1832; d. Sept. 13, 1833.

6306. Samuel, of Northampton, Mass., son of Nathaniel 3d, m. Lucinda Mann of that town, Feb. 12, 1833. Children—
8290. *George,* b. Feb. 9, 1834; d. July 21, 1840.
8291. *Lewis,* b. Feb. 12, 1836.
8292. *Samuel Clesson,* b. April 1, 1838.
8293. *Luke,* b. March 22, 1840.

8294. *Julia*, b. March 14, 1842.
8295. *George*, b. Dec. 17, 1845.

6321. **Dudley II.** of Northampton, Mass., m. Rebecca P. May, April 23, 1838. Children—
8310. *Amelia*, b. March 29, 1839.
8311. *Dudley*, b. March 16, 1840; d. Nov. 30, 1842.
8312. *Edward*, b. April 26, 1841; d.   1842.
8313. *Edward*, b. Oct. 18, 1842; d.   1844.
8314. *David Edward*, b. Oct. 1, 1844.
8315. *Harriet*, b. March 5, 1846; d. July   1847.
8316. *John Dudley*, b. Dec. 9, 1847.

6351. **Edward L.** of Savoy, Mass., son of Elijah, m. Ruth A. De Maranville of Windsor, Mass., Sept. 13, 1846. Children—
8370. *Warren Edward*, b. Feb. 27, 1848.

6352. **Frederic A.** of New Haven, Conn., son of Elijah, m. Melinda L. Stevens of Hamden, Conn., Feb. 12, 1843. Chidren—
8380. *Frederic Augustus* 2d, b. Jan. 4, 1846.

6412. **Guy,** of Great Barrington, Mass., son of William, m. Maria S. Stephens of that town, Feb. 11, 1839. Children—
8430. *William H.*, b. Dec. 23, 1840.
8431. *Martha A.*, b. Nov. 22, 1842.
8432. *George S.*, b. Feb. 25, 1844.
8433. *Edward G.*, b. Feb. 9, 1847.

6413. **Horace H.** of New York City, (residence in Jersey City,) m. (1st) Sarah Wyckoff, April 25, 1838: (2d) Kate Alice Day, (6426) of Hartford, Conn., Sept. 14, 1844. Children—
8440. *Nicholas Wyckoff*, b. Jan. 18, 1839.
8441. *Horace Waldron*, b. Sept. 21, 1845.
8442. *Edward Maynard*, b. Oct. 4, 1848.

EIGHTH GENERATION.

6670. **Thomas H.** of Little Falls, Herkimer Co., N. Y., son of Rodman G., m. Julia T. Marvin of Nassau, N. Y., Oct. 14, 1846. Children—
8650. *Caroline Emma*, b. Jan. 15, 1848.

6800. **Silas B.** of Lockport, N. Y., son of Spaulding, m. Lucy E. Kimball, Sept. 17, 1833. Children—
8800. *Benjamin Silas*, b. Aug. 8, 1834.

6803. Seymour T. of Royalton, Vt., son of Spaulding, m. Cornelia Marble, Jan. 27, 1842. Children—
8810. *Mary Elizabeth*, b. Jan. 27, 1844.
8811. *Byron Rosswell*, b. Jan. 24, 1846.
8812. *Frances Adell*, b. Sept. 5, 1847.

6804. Dan D. of Royalton, Vt., son of Spaulding, m. Betsey Kimball, Jan. 1, 1846. Child—
8820. *Emma Jane*, b. Nov. 16, 1848.

6806. Alfred, of Lockport, N. Y., son of Spaulding, m. Julia Tucker, Jan. 1, 1849.

7031. Alvord, of Rochester, N. Y., son of Charles II., m. Hannah Streeter, Nov. 25, 1841. Child—
9020. *Helen L.*, b. Feb. 22, 1842.

7033. Alvin, of Paris, N. Y., m. Lovina Johnson, March 25, 1841. Children—
9030. *Frelinghuysen*, b. July 21, 1844.
9031. *Nancy L.*, b. July 1, 1846.

7035. Almon, of Camden, Mich., m. Paulina Streeter, in 1845. Child—
9040. *Adrian*, b. March 1, 1848.

7050. Daniel W. of ———, ———, son of Ira, m. Cordelia A. Kinney. Children—
9080. **Sally S.*, b. Feb. 12, 1839; d. Aug. 24, 1843.
9081. *Julia A.*, b. Sept. 10, 1845.

7053. Lorenzo M. of———, Chatauque Co., N. Y., son of Ira, m. Caroline Hoag, Jan. 1, 1842. Child—
9090. *Ellen*, b. Feb. 12, 1847.

7071. Ditus, of Mantua, Ohio, son of Alfred, m. Cornelia Bissell, Aug. 26, 1840, who d. Dec. 19, 1844. Children—
9130. *Ellen M.*, b. Oct. 4, 1842.
9131. *Leander*, b. Dec. 14, 1844.

SUMMARY.

From the data furnished in the preceding lists, it is calculated that the whole number of the descendants of Robert Day, in the male line alone, during the last two hundred years, has not been less than *three thousand*. Of these, 2432 names are recorded in this register. The following table will give the number in the two branches in each generation, with the years within which each generation is included.

		Springfield Branch	*Years*	*Hartford Branch*	*Years*
Second	Generation,	1	—	1	—
Third	"	10	1662—1682.	8	1675—1699.
Fourth	"	39	1687—1725.	19	1698—1725.
Fifth	"	111	1718—1757.	63	1730—1769.
Sixth	"	233	1751—1820.	229	1753—1815.
Seventh	"	448	1782—1848.	448	1780—1847.
Eighth	"	331	1810—1848.	356	1809—1848.
Ninth	"	18	1840—1848.	15	1839—1848.
		1291		1139	

In respect to the *rate of increase*, the family has doubled its numbers, the last two centuries, on an average, once in somewhat less than every twenty five years. If the increase should continue at the same rate, the next hundred years, the descendants of Robert Day, in the male line, would amount in the year 1948, to from thirty to fifty thousand souls.

Of the nearly twenty-five hundred whose names are recorded in this register, four hundred and eighty one have become heads of families. Very few of the family have been in any way distinguished. To a great extent they have been farmers. So far as is known, they have generally been useful and respectable members of society. In some of the branches, nearly every member has been a professor of religion. From the best information the compiler has been able to obtain, he has been led to the conclusion that the continuance of families in the same place from generation to generation is not usually favorable to enterprize and the highest success in life. Nineteen have been graduated at Yale College, one at Dartmouth, one at Williams, one at Amherst and one at Brown University. Eleven have been ministers of the Gospel, all of whom, with only one exception, are still living. Seven of these are connected with the Congregational, and the remaining three with the Baptist denomination.

The average age of those who have become heads of families appears to have been about 68 years. The oldest person of the name was Col. Benjamin Day, who died in the year 1808, in his 98th year. His daughter Lydia, (b. Nov. 1, 1759,) the widow of Henry Dwight, Esq., is supposed to be the oldest member of the family now living.

CORRECTIONS.

754. REV. ISAAC G. BLISS, Missionary to the *Armenians in Turkey*, and resides in Erzeroom.

5592. S. SHERWOOD DAY, ESQ., was graduated at Yale College in 1827.

INDEX I

CHRISTIAN NAMES.

Born.	A.	No.						
1715.	Aaron,	37	1778.	"	5204	1884.	Alice E.	3881
1738.	"	123	1805.	"	5801	1882.	Alice J.	3924
1740.	"	5086	1829.	Adoniram J.	1616	——	Allethe,	855
——	"	5271	1797.	Albert,	712	——	Alma,	6753
1777.	"	291	1803.	"	5444	1807.	Almeida,	5975
1780.	"	292	1814.	"	3723	1822.	Almeron,	7037
——	"	303	1824.	"	7038	1794.	Almira,	5622
1813.	Abby,	5826	1834.	"	7861	——	"	6305
1838.	"	6731	1835.	"	8033	1818.	"	776
1836.	Abby H.	1230	——	"	7844	——	"	7054
1734.	Abel,	72	——	"	5943	1819.	"	6023
1792.	Abi,	405	1842.	"	2100	1839.	"	7911
1798.	Abiah,	5762	1842.	Albert B.	1956	1812.	Almira S.	1373
——	Abigail,	19	1834.	Albert C.	2412	1846.	"	6734
1713.	"	36	1848.	"	2460	1798.	Almon,	1240
1724.	"	140	1841.	Albert E.	2415	1803.	"	1351
1756.	"	134	1848.	"	2864	1819.	"	7085
1763.	"	342	1824.	Albert F.	1021	1838.	"	8084
1793.	"	445	1845.	Albert M.	7753	1843.	Almon F.	2101
1794.	"	884	1835.	Alceste,	2486	1799.	Alonzo,	5486
1796.	"	6062	1796.	Alden,	920	1809.	"	932
——	"	5954	1769.	Alexander,	359	1813.	"	6067
1825.	"	6814	1817.	"	875	1832.	"	2030
1813.	Abigail H.	521	1820.	Alfayette,	7039	1843.	Alonzo E.	6542
1749.	Abner,	236	1776.	Alfred,	5237	1822.	Alonzo M.	6341
1778.	"	630	——	"	5421	1828.	"	6361
1712.	Abraham,	5018	1783.	"	463	1910.	Alta May	4090
1747.	"	5103	1786.	"	5630	1781.	Alva,	591
——	"	5325	1794.	"	5752	1811.	Alva O.	1410
——	"	5352	1802.	"	468	1763.	Alvin,	5256
1772.	"	5361	——	"	1085	1780.	"	5337
——	"	5944	1807.	"	5722	1806.	"	5756
1799.	"	6081	1811.	"	5983	1807.	"	5974
1829.	Abraham R.	7881	1814.	"	1325	——	"	5991
1839.	Achsah J.	7250	1817.	"	6793	1814.	"	7033
1794.	Adah,	600	1827.	"	6806	1815.	"	6004
1821.	Adaline,	5828	1830.	"	6850	1820.	"	6116
1846.	Adaline W.	7260	1831.	"	7041	1845.	"	7011
1837.	Adaline B.	1750	1837.	"	1173	1848.	Alvin C.	6570
1846.	Adelbert E.	2703	1840.	"	7036	1825.	Alvira,	7140
1842.	Adelpha A.	1606	1834.	Alfred A.	7078	1845.	"	7089
1870.	Addie C.	3920	1842.	Alfred B.	1957	1811.	Alvord,	7031
1823.	Addison,	6007	1800.	Alfred E.	1072	1783.	Amanda,	556
——	Addison W.	1554	1838.	Alfred H.	1107	1811.	"	6021
1848.	Adrian,	9040	1844.	Alfred L.	2006	1812.	"	751
1733.	Adonijah,	5092	1842.	Algernon	2434	1881.	"	2431
1759.	"	5254	1847.	Alice,	1520	1833.	"	1821
			1844.	Alice A.	7118	——	Amarilla,	5410

INDEX I.

—	Amaritta,	5953	1812.	Artemas,	5449	—	Bede,	601
1742.	Amasa,	5087	1811.	Artentia,	915	1704.	Benjamin,	5014
—	"	5350	1847.	Arthur H.	7241	1710.	"	45
1808.	"	6163	1866.	Arthur P.	3880	1731.	"	5081
1767.	Ambrose,	282	1827.	Arthurton,	5876	1746.	"	181
1792.	"	710	1735.	Asa,	5083	1747.	"	182
1792.	Amelia,	826	1736.	"	5084	1790.	"	475
1702.	"	5522	1743.	"	5076	1795.	"	5665
1825.	"	6431	1755.	"	169	1810.	"	5825
1839.	"	8310	1759.	"	225	1811.	"	5717
1818.	Amelia J.	6423	1760.	"	372	1820.	"	5734
1844.	Amelia S.	7119	1761.	"	5233	1822.	"	918
1775.	Aminta,	620	1761.	"	5214	1823.	"	1121
1815.	Andrew,	1294	1768.	"	5330	1838.	"	2252
1821.	"	8012	1781.	"	581	1839.	"	1131
1817.	Andrew J.	785	—	"	5662	—	"	6914
—	"	1083	1797.	"	5666	1806.	Benjamin F.	676
1828.	"	1904	1800.	"	1350	1833.	"	2485
1835.	Andrew V.P.	1670	1802.	"	5626	1810.	Benjamin H.	1075
—	Angelina,	5882	—	"	5920	1834.	Benjamin S.	8800
1812.	Angelina A.	6790	1820.	"	1802	1837.	Benjamin W.	6661
1818.	Angeline,	960	1830.	Asa B.	1951	1912.	Bernice E.	4011
1825.	"	1931	1815.	Asa C.	6113	1791.	Betsey,	5209
1821.	Angeline A.	1901	1813.	Asahel,	5560	1794.	"	700
1764.	Ann,	5182	1736.	Asaph,	205	—	"	5303
1803.	"	1250	1739.	"	206	1800.	"	5501
—	"	5900	1760.	"	540	1806.	•	5721
—	Ann A.	1560	—	Asaph B.	5999	1809.	"	5803
—	Ann D.	6825	1759.	Asenath,	5213	1813.	"	5853
1840.	Ann E.	7102	1771.	"	283	—	"	6153
1844.	"	6289	1777.	"	348	1817.	"	1295
1831.	Ann J.	7680	1796.	"	885	1835.	"	7224
1830.	Ann M.	1863	1807.	"	865	1821.	Betsey C.	905
1833.	"	1441	—	"	5961	1890.	Beulah M.	3997
1730.	Anna,	5080	1813.	"	899	1793.	Bliss,	586
1742.	"	5110	1786.	Ashbell,	5340	1767.	Brigham,	400
1778.	"	5298	1809.	"	6020	1809.	"	926
1779.	"	5365	1809.	Asher H.	1282	1846.	Byron R.	8811
1789.	"	464	1893.	Augusta,	3914			
1791.	"	5427	1803.	Augusta A.	5601		C.	
1791.	"	5620	1820.	"	1422	1723.	Caleb,	59
1800.	"	5547	—	Augustus,	812	1798.	"	5581
1801.	Anna L.	5543	1829.	"	1404	1829.	Caleb A.	6621
1803.	Anna N.	448	1830.	Augustus B.	5860	1794.	Calista,	1154
1824.	"	1913	1834.	Augustus P.	6345	1779.	Calvin,	286
1770.	Anne,	544	1842.	Aurelia,	3201	1790.	"	5370
1815.	"	752	1846.	"	3221	1803.	"	714
1810.	Anne V.	1093	1823.	Aurelia L.	1050	1818.	"	6115
1832.	Annette,	6851	1819.	Aurelia R.	6424	—	Camilla C.	516
1848.	Annie C.	3030	—	Austin,	5400	1833.	Candace,	7143
1816.	Anson H.	1374	1805.	"	5784	1876.	Carl E.	3900
1836.	Arad J.	2372	1824.	Austin G.	1430	1880.	"	3982
1848.	Arabella,	1195	1822.	Austin S.	5988	1809.	Carlos C.	772
1816.	Araetus,	1256	1794.	Azel,	5312	1847.	Carlos E.	1742
—	"	2440	—	— Azubah,	410	1833.	Carlos M.	1730
1775.	Aribut,	420				1809.	Caroline,	1111
1807.	Armenia,	5777		B.		1813.	"	1830
1828.	Arodine,	7076	1841.	Balinda,	7902	—	"	5913

INDEX I.

1826. " 779	— " 6910	1791. " 860
1828. " 6672	1798. Charles F. 5441	1791. " 5466
1845. Caroline A. 1751	1844. " 2950	— " 5319
1813. Caroline E. 5595	1829. Charles G. 1622	1808. " 6110
1833. " 1631	1841. " 2200	1817. " 6802
1834. " 6852	1821. Charles H. 1532	1835. " 7682
1839. " 6704	1828. " 5599	1848. " 1868
1848. " 8650	1842. " 2052	1818. Clarissa E. 5986
1854. " 1197	1842. " 7130	1814. Clarissa G. 5890
1844. Caroline H. 6681	1830. Charles L. 1600	1838. Clarissa M. 7116
1847. Caroline J. 8061	1831. " 1540	1811. Clark, 5731
1805. Caroline L. 951	1840. " 1591	1843. Cleone T. 2416
1840. Caroline M. 7352	1848. " 7290	1830. Cleora, 6816
1821. Caroline S. 1328	1875. " 3960	1807. Climena, 1244
1830. Caroline W. 1054	1806. Charles N. 1251	1847. Clinton, 1505
1885. Carrie A. 3901	1846. " 1691	1880. Clyde W. 3970
1715. Catharine, 551	1847. " 1186	1809. Colatinus, 5829
1772(" 346	1821. Charles R. 5724	1901. Colette L. 4080
— " 1365	1811. Charles T. 6336	1890. Cora M. 3944
— " 6181	1779. Charles W. 260	1827. Cordelia, 5880
1825. " 6008	1833. " 1864	1837. " 7351
1819. Catharine A. 653	1833. " 1055	1842. " 6561
1822. " 6426	1781. Charlotte, 406	— Cornelia, 680
1796. Catharine J. 5531	" 5202	— " 6205
1837. Catharine P. 1633	1807. " 6086	1829. " 7891
1844. Celia 1955	1812. " 784	1882. " 7222
1845. Celia C. 1194	1840. " 7895	1818. Cornelia H. 6610
1826. Celinda A. 1903	1847. " 7887	1822. " 7110
— Cerintha, 6204	1817. Charlotte M. 6239	1834. " 6842
1825. Charity, 6418	1818. " 5597	— Cornelia M. 1552
1753. Charles, 5250	1824. Charlotte R. 1714	1839. " 1865
1763. " 5117	1895. Chase L. 4060	1832. Cornelius, 1935
1780. " 5740	1783. Chauncey, 5367	— Corydon C. 6183
1789. " 5194	1824. " 5875	1785. Curtiss, 321
1803. " 5548	1782. Chester, 820	1769. Cynthia, 484
1805. " 5714	1829. " 914	— " 1155
1806. " 1110	1794. Childs, 893	1800. " 674
1811. " 1112	1766. Chloe. 343	1810. " 2350
1814. " 531	1807. " 952	1834. " 1917
1818. " 665	1826. Chloe A. 964	1848. Cynthia L. 3370
1820. " 1034	1847. Chloe E. 7105	1801. Cyrena, 5755
1820. " 5572	— Christiana, 5314	1804. Cyrus, 5776
1829. " 1251	1901. Claire, 4062	1820. " 1812
— " 6190	1911. Clara B. 4030	1841. Cyrus C. 7103
— " 6393	1897. Clare A. 4110	1830. Cyrus S. 2366
1832. " 8280	1879. Clarence A. 3992	
— " 2220	1862. Clarence P. 3951	**D.**
1837. " 7225	1909. Clarence P. Jr	1791. Don, 5663
1842. " 1132	4065	1805. " 5765
1845. " 7322	1844. Clarence S. 2253	1819. Don D. 6811
1847. Charles A. 8060	1801. Clarendon, 6082	1821. " 6804
1821. Charles B. 1360	1832. " 7882	1831. " 6817
1823. Charles C. 1550	1764. Clarissa, 189	1833. Don N. 795
— " 6241	1766. " 5460	— Danforth, 5701
1806. Charles D. 515	1771. " 5280	1709. Daniel, 5016
1836. " 1918	— " 305	— " 5020
1820. Charles E. 1920	1775. " 5263	1746. " 5112
1836. " 1190	— " 5283	1747. " 5089

142 INDEX I.

1740.	"	183	1806.	"	607	1902. Edna M.		4042
1773.	"	5290	1811.	Diana,	991	1759. Edward,		354
	"	5300	1835.	Diana S.	2130	1772.	"	377
1779.	"	462	1836.	Diedrik M.	2131	1786.	"	822
1794.	"	5514	1816.	Diantha,	1420		"	5520
	"	5541		Diodate B.	6203		"	1692
1802.	"	5502	1817.	Ditus,	7071	1834.	"	6680
1807.	"	1082	1864.	Dollabella,	3952	1841.	"	8312
1815.	"	5506		Dorothea,	5933	1842.	"	8313
1816.	"	5827	1814.	Dorothy,	916	1820. Edward B.		730
1821.	"	1095	1904.	"	4130	1839.	"	8194
	"	5923	1895.	Dorothy A.	3945	1878.	"	3955
	"	7272	1814.	Dorothy O.	6165	1912.	"	4143
1808. Daniel I.		6233	1796.	Drusilla B.	1071	1841. Edward C.		3200
1806. Daniel J.		660	1764.	Dudley,	5321	1846. Edward F.		7872
1791. Daniel M.		670	1775.	"	5463	1847. Edward G.		8433
1811. Daniel W.		7050		"	5543	1829. Edward H.		6482
1814.	"	5833		"	5965	1819. Edward L.		6351
1710. David,		5017	1814.	"	6321	1834.	"	1570
1732.	'	144	1825.	"	1036	1835.	"	6622
1749.	"	5090	1840.	"	8311	1843. Edward M.		2680
1758.	"	371	1831.	Dudley M.	2670	1848.	"	8442
1775.	"	5188		Dudley W.	6590	1819. Edward N.		994
1778.	"	5285	1815.	Dwight,	1810	1815. Edward S.		6421
1782.	"	5292	1817.	"	1032	1817. Edward T.		6422
1786.	"	5425		"	1872	1823. Edwin		1930
1797.	"	467		"	6222		"	7843
1800.	"	896	1860.	Dwight R.	1214	1839. Edwin D.		8195
1801.	"	5821				1825. Edwin E.		1860
1844. David B.		6723		E.		1828. Edwin M.		6121
1811. David D.		5977	1676.	Ebeneser,	16	1841.	"	1511
1829. David E.		1102	1777.	"	17	1829. Edwin P.		7057
1848.	"	8314	1694.	"	23	1812. Edwin T.		6238
1880. David M.		1534	1701.	"	50	1809. Elbridge,		942
1806. David N.		724	1728.	'	201		Eleanor,	5284
1804. David S.		5495	1764.	"	542	1820.	"	511
1844.	"	1958		"	5239	1804. Eleanor L.		6161
1699. Deborah,		21	1819.	Ebeneser W.	1833	1741. Eleazer,		163
	"	81	1860.	Edith,	3950	1804.	"	930
1782.	"	5465	1874.	Edith M.	3891	1777. Eleazer M.		404
	"	6152	1879.	"	3922	1773. Electa,		284
1813.	"	6307	1705.	Editha,	5015	1774.	"	573
1813. Deborah A.		6003	1713.	"	56	1788.	"	5205
1800. Della,		5582	1752.	"	5091	1785.	"	850
1818.	"	1033	1803.	Edgar B.	5590	1795.	"	5490
	"	1971	1835.	Edgar F.	6641		"	5315
1824. Della A.		1902	1833.	Edgar G.	1952	1803.	"	6063
1809. Della C.		953	1834.	Edgar M.	2671	1812.	"	1324
1831. Della M.		1180		Edissa,	5276		Electa A.	7842
1849. Dell M.		1212	1767.	Edmund,	227	1761. Eli,		355
	Denison,	6921	1802.	"	605	1768.	"	5217
1821.	"	7073	1803.	"	5718	1781.	"	5191
1807. Dennis C.		782	1817.	"	1421		"	5192
1782. Deodatus,		632	1818.	"	510	1780.	"	852
1863. Dewey,		1215	1831.	"	1432		"	5324
1838. De Witt,		1919	1892.	Edmund A.	3994		"	5540
	Diadema,	5354	1838.	Edmund L.	1443	1813.	"	5549
	"	5405	1885.	Edna,	2730		"	5552

INDEX I. 143

—	"	5561	1826.	"	6360	1831. Emma E.		5617
—	"	5931	1826.	"	6013	1903.	"	4100
—	"	5942	1839.	"	2522	1848. Emma J.		8820
—	"	6500	1840.	"	2004	1736. Enos,		125
1827. Elias,		5565	1842.	"	7320	1833. Epaphro A.		7151
1770. Elihu,		5260	—	"	6754	1772. Epaphroditus,		
—	"	1241	1891.	"	3913			5261
1801.	"	1242	1810. Elizabeth A.		6234	1815.	"	5806
1811.	"	5787	1833.	"	2493	1816.	"	7070
1807. Elihu M.		5628	1845.	"	1781	1741. Ephraim,		5100
1725. Elinor,		60	1845. Elizabeth B.		7732	—	"	5328
1754. Elijah,		152	1807. Elizabeth C.		1092	—	"	5921
1754.	"	492	1825. Elizabeth D.		1122	1815. Erasmus W.		5891
—	"	5106	1823. Elizabeth H.		1329	1773. Erastus,		460
1780.	"	5355	1827.	"	1924	1774.	"	5282
1793.	"	5484	1837.	"	6623	1775.	"	310
1802.	"	6160	1832. Elizabeth M.		7860	1775.	"	5430
1811.	"	933	1847.	"	1701	1777.	"	5364
—	"	6201	1904. Elizabeth S.		4070	1780.	"	5291
1846.	"	6353	1823. Elizur,		778	1787.	"	5193
—	"	8202	1835. Elizur C.		1720	1805.	"	1091
1799. Elijah W.		5442	1844. Ella M.		6651	1808.	"	5830
1840.	"	6271	1829. Ellen,		657	1810.	"	5448
— Eliphalet,		5651	1840.	"	2082	1813.	"	1080
1749. Elisha		5104	1846.	"	2011	1822.	"	6117
1793.	"	5295	1847.	"	9090	1824.	"	5857
—	"	5380	1837. Ellen A.		1619	1836. Erastus S.		6721
—	"	6080	1840.	"	6524	1807. Erastus W.		771
1836. Elisha C.		8193	1826. Ellen C.		1850	1817. Eri H.		5872
1803.	"	5822	1829.	"	1851	1768. Erial,		5259
1804. Eliza,		6303	1833.	"	1953	1835. Erial B.		7152
1806.	"	6085	1847.	"	6375	1733. Esther,		5072
1807.	"	1281	1833. Ellen G.		1953	1734.	"	204
1808.	"	1159	1840. Ellen H.		7730	1740.	"	114
1835.	"	1990	1837. Ellen J.		7230	—	"	972
—	"	1871	1842. Ellen M.		6400	1763.	"	5215
1837. Eliza A.		2002	1842.	"	9130	1810.	"	6111
—	"	7690	1838. Ellen R.		2003	1816.	"	5854
1829. Eliza B.		2410	1848. Ellen S.		6664	1830.	"	7077
1839. Eliza F.		1183	— Elvira,		5951	1828. Esther C.		2483
1823. Eliza J.		6342	1821.	"	5856	— Esther F.		7941
1839.	"	2052	1831. Elvira U.		2662	1846. Esther R.		6543
1804. Eliza M.		5445	1811. Emeline,		5586	1842. Eugene,		7912
1819.	"	6005	1845.	"	7886	1847.	"	1165
1687. Elizabeth,		20	— Emeline A.		5704	1904. Eugene C.		4020
1718.	"	48	— Emerson,		1841	1738. Eunice,		5132
1723.	"	5041	1830.	"	6841	1738.	"	160
—	"	83	1802. Emily,		721	1734.	"	146
1736.	"	122	1806.	"	925	1743.	"	180
1743.	"	164	1819.	"	5855	1775.	"	545
1773.	"	408	1834.	"	7350	1775.	"	5296
1777.	"	1597	1848.	"	7012	1776.	"	290
1798.	"	903	1821. Emily C.		5598	1794.	"	5772
1800.	"	5625	1822. Emily E.		695	1795.	"	360
1816.	"	651	1830. Emily M.		2484	1795.	"	6300
1819.	"	6417	1803. Emma,		1243	—	"	856
1820.	"	644	1848. Emma A.		2142	1796.	"	5710
1821.	"	666	1831. Emma C.		6673	1823.	"	754

INDEX I.

Year	Name	No.
1839.	Eunice A.	1823
1844.	"	7871
1811.	Eunice O.	1341
1837.	Eunice S.	1604
1906.	Eva,	4050
1817.	Eveline,	935
1827.	Eveline M.	1006
1906.	Evelyn M.	4112
1850.	Everett,	1166
1840.	Everett W.	6732
1841.	Ewing W.	2673
——	Experience,	5147
1800.	"	5493
1732.	Ezekiel,	203
1771.	"	553
1811.	"	1246
1845.	"	2420
1730.	Ezra,	5070
1740.	"	5075
1743.	"	5501
1773.	"	5333
1800.	"	5971
1813.	"	5788

F.

Year	Name	No.
1783.	Fanny,	5392
1795.	"	5691
1797.	"	5692
1805.	"	505
1813.	"	5870
1839.	"	6843
1817.	Fayette G.	5892
——	Ferdinand A.	6182
1813.	Fidelia,	5984
1837.	"	7683
1794.	Flavel,	5747
1785.	Flavia,	583
1789.	"	584
1808.	"	990
1808.	"	1353
——	Flavilla,	5940
——	Flora,	5901
1844.	Florena W.	6712
1847.	Florence E.	2562
1800.	Frances,	479
——	"	741
1830.	"	1934
1833.	"	1123
1833.	"	1424
——	"	5911
1838.	"	7310
1836.	Frances A.	——
1847.	"	8812
1847.	Frances B.	6858
——	Frances E.	6330
——	"	6333
1818.	Frances L.	1396
1825.	"	1402

Year	Name	No.
1843.	"	2631
1820.	Frances M.	6168
1832.	Frances P.	1852
1832.	Frances R.	6344
1791.	Francis,	825
1804.	"	705
1817.	"	1801
1845.	"	1594
1828.	Francis A.	1103
1833.	"	1105
1838.	Francis E.	2373
1821.	Francis H.	1356
——	Francis M.	1555
——	"	1562
1810.	Franklin,	6066
1819.	"	1327
1825.	"	1330
——	"	5912
1841.	"	1192
1844.	"	2435
1846.	"	1940
1827.	Franklin H.	1052
1815.	Franklin O.	6792
1766.	Frederic,	483
1786.	"	1150
1803.	"	1320
1815.	"	509
——	"	3860
1840.	"	1211
1821.	Frederic A.	6352
1846	"	8380
1876.	"	3981
1900.	Frederic O.	4111
1844.	Frelinghuysen	9030

G.

Year	Name	No.
1784.	Gad,	293
1793.	"	5664
1843.	Gad C.	7360
1899.	Galen A.	4040
1833.	Gardiner,	6674
1790.	George,	5513
1798.	"	5492
1801.	"	5712
1818.	"	6322
1822.	"	5573
1825.	"	7841
1829.	"	1038
1834.	"	8291
1838.	"	7085
1845.	"	8205
1846.	"	1542
1845.	George A.	7721
1816.	George B.	5506
1837.	George D.	1571
1815.	George E.	760
1847.	"	1711

Year	Name	No.
1848.	"	2704
1832.	George F.	1015
1838.	George M.	2513
1885.	"	3942
1847.	George N.	3260
1844.	George S.	8432
1816.	George W.	6255
1821.	"	1084
1831.	"	1906
1838.	"	2120
——	"	6911
1843.	"	1193
1843.	"	7903
1802.	Gershom B.	6230
1906.	Gertie J.	4101
1837.	Gertrude,	1671
1843.	"	7010
1733.	Gideon,	121
1812.	"	5778
1781.	Gideon B.	287
1748.	Giles,	166
1784.	"	426
——	"	971
1815.	Giles L.	992
1832.	Gilford,	7082
1791.	Gordon,	1262
1736.	Grace,	5073
1780.	"	5464
1811	Guy,	6412
1818.	Guy B.	5451

H.

Year	Name	No.
1875.	Halsey T.	3980
1701.	Hannah,	5031
1733.	"	230
1750.	"	167
——	"	5143
1756.	"	5116
——	"	5152
1769.	"	5331
1774.	"	5187
1777.	"	412
——	"	5382
1784.	"	633
1798.	"	895
1805.	"	5973
1809.	"	7030
1812.	"	943
——	"	5554
1845.	Hannah E.	2160
1840.	Harlan B.	2374
1888.	Harlan H.	3943
1808.	Harlam,	5786
1883.	Harold,	3910
1881.	Harold O.	3993
1913.	Harold E.	4031
1776.	Harriet,	461
1797.	"	478

INDEX I. 145

1799.	"	603	1903.	Helen F.	4081	1841.	"	7731
1799.	"	828	1833.	Helen G.	7120	1808.	Henry N.	661
1802.	"	5764	1896.	"	3995	1836.	"	6703
1806.	"	1391	1842.	Helen L.	9020	1829.	Henry P.	1431
1806.	"	5603	1827.	Helen M.	1403	1836.	"	7100
1808.	"	1245	1834.	"	8192	1805.	Henry R.	5591
1813.	"	1094	1840.	"	6642	1826.	Henry S	1890
1815.	"	1831	1902.	"	4001	1848.	"	1790
1816.	"	1610	1834.	Helen R.	1660	1845.	Herbert L.	7251
1819.	"	1531	1844.	Helen S.	7340	1783.	Hervey,	442
1820.	"	7036	1846.	Helen U.	7932	1837.	Hester A.	2520
1821.	"	654	1755.	Heman,	186	1700.	Hezekiah,	41
1821.	"	786	1793.	"	476	1768.	"	876
1821.	"	6425	1831.	"	6701	—	"	5351
—	"	6600	1804.	Heman E.	1390	—	"	5655
1822.	"	6813	1802.	Henrietta,	5583	1800.	"	911
1840.	"	7741	—	"	6250	1829.	Hinman F.	1014
1841.	"	2488	1839.	Henrietta G.		1797.	Hiram,	6302
1842.	"	1993			1450	1811.	"	5804
1846.	"	8315	1836.	Henrietta L.		1813.	"	5805
1812.	Harriet A.	2351			2111	—	"	5922
1820.	"	5614	1773.	Henry,	450	1706	Hiram S.	672
1823.	"	1101	1779.	"	470	1837.	Hobart,	6730
1827.	"	2402	1788.	"	1151	1844.	Homer L.	2702
1840.	"	1444	—	"	1322	1846.	Homer S.	2053
1844.	"	6550	1812.	"	1293	1754.	Horace	133
1841.	Harriet B.	6254	1817.	"	643	1766.	"	375
1877.	Harriett B.	3991	1818.	"	801	1772.	"	565
1829.	Harriet C.	2491	—	"	811	1782.	"	320
1832.	"	2411	1818.	"	1611	—	"	5523
1836.	"	1172	1820.	"	6006	1795.	"	1270
1837.	"	2413	1828.	"	6815	1796.	"	5524
1847.	"	1202	1832.	"	2250	1816.	"	761
1843.	Harriet E.	6391	1834.	"	1936	1827.	"	2482
1845.	"	7240	1835.	"	1500	1829.	"	5881
1848.	"	2300	—	"	2450	1820.	Horace B.	5893
1836.	Harriet K.	1501	1838.	"	7863	1845.	Horace E.	7450
1821.	Harriet L.	1620	—	"	8201	1819.	Horace G.	6440
1810.	Harriet M.	982	1841.	"	7864	1813.	Horace H.	6413
1839.	"	7303	1839.	Henry A.	1572	1811.	Horace L.	5793
1841.	"	2121	1841.	"	7720	1820.	Horace R.	5987
1840.	Harrison,	1681	1807.	Henry B.	981	1813.	Horace W.	5978
—	"	2690	1823.	"	1361	1845.	"	8441
1829.	Harrison C.	7080	1834.	"	2110	1779.	Horatio,	590
1840.	Harrison V.	2561	1836.	Henry C.	2001	1790.	"	891
1786.	Harry,	5293	1842.	"	8060	1813.	"	1030
1838.	"	2432	1843.	Henry F.	1580	1814.	Horatio E.	715
1841.	"	7304	1804.	Henry J.	6231	1811.	Horatio N.	691
1814.	Harvey,	1255	1833.	"	8191	1770.	Hosea,	405
—	"	5702	1837.	Henry K.	1162	1010.	Howard E.	4002
—	"	7840	1814.	Henry L.	611	1844.	Hubert,	1176
1843.	Helen,	2150	1834.	"	7115	1881.	"	3023
1843.	"	6381	1841.	"	1451	1881.	Hubert K.	3941
1894.	"	3915	1845.	"	7951	1816.	Hudson,	5562
1836.	Helen A.	1210	1847.	"	2102	1833.	Huldah M.	1160
1840.	"	1231	1814.	Henry M.	2352	1796.	Huram,	6301
1907.	"	4140	1828.	"	2365			
1844.	Helen C.	3000	1838.	"	1510			

I.

1767. Ira,	5200
1777. "	5240
1780. "	5265
1781. "	5366
1786. "	5743
1799. "	5667
1804. "	6081
— "	5703
1809. "	5730
1812. "	6112
1818. "	5807
1822. "	6795
1826. "	5735
1830. "	5736
— "	6750
1832. "	7061
1844. "	7896
1845. "	6857
—. Ira F.	2353
1807. Ira R.	5585
1830. Ira S.	6807
1805. Irod,	898
1757. Irene,	5107
1770. "	5360
— "	5924
1795. "	6083
1834. "	7893
1713. Isaac,	5019
1750. "	5114
1782. Isaac C.	623
1788. "	626
1844. "	7930
1808. Isaac H.	5447
—. Isaac N.	678
1826. "	840
1846. Isabel H.	6652
1848. Isabella J.	2008
1739. Israel,	74
1776. Ithamar H.	195

J.

1798. Jabez,	5313
1753. Jacob,	108
1753. "	5115
1779. "	5422
1791. "	444
1827. "	1037
1842. Jacob T.	6856
1733. Jael,	145
1804. Jairus,	722
1780. James,	193
1795. "	862
— "	858
1805. "	864
1807. "	506
1882. "	3971
1828. James A.	1914

1848. "	1234
— James B.	1563
1906. "	4044
— James G.	6913
1835. James H.	1603
1846. "	8001
— "	7270
1812. James I.	520
1827. James P.	6612
1837. "	1854
1842. "	1866
1819. James R.	729
1842. "	1640
1832. James W.	1601
— Jane,	810
— "	6752
1844. "	2010
1847. "	2436
1826. Jane C.	5616
1833. Jane E.	7681
1847. "	7000
1839. Jane L.	2410
1842. Jane M.	6722
1844. Jane O.	1504
1845. Jane S.	7232
1845. Jarvis,	2201
1755. Jedediah,	352
1828, "	841
— "	854
— "	1840
1839. Jefferson D.	7884
1756. Jemima,	281
1816. Jennette,	928
1846. Jennie W.	1233
1737. Jeremiah,	73
— "	241
1810. "	662
1815. "	642
— "	5551
1736. Jerusha,	210
1776, "	574
— "	5153
— "	5301
1806. "	5823
1827. "	7220
1798. Jerusha W.	5782
1748. Jesse,	5078
— "	5930
1730. Joel,	143
1747. "	235
1751. "	350
1759. "	5145
1779. "	622
1789. "	824
— "	970
1801. "	5668
1880. Joel H.	1814
1832. "	2402

— John,	2
1669. "	13
1673. "	15
1677. "	5001
1698. "	40
1701. "	5012
1704. "	5032
1728. "	142
1738. "	5060
1748. "	5113
1762. "	5181
1767. "	344
1774. "	194
1788. "	881
1796. "	5580
1801. "	503
1813. "	1113
1814. "	5571
1815. "	5450
1823. "	802
— "	1974
— "	5681
— "	6031
1823. "	6430
1825. "	6120
— "	6591
1775. John B.	5431
1835. "	6260
1835. John C.	1632
1835. "	2031
1814. John D.	1354
1847. "	8316
1812. John E.	6237
1836. "	6853
1888. "	7302
1795. John F.	446
1835. "	1954
1812. John G.	6088
1813. "	5611
1903. John H.	4043
1832. John I.	1170
1838. "	1174
1826. John M.	2661
1912. John R.	4021
1817. John S.	1530
1808. John W.	6252
1810. "	5831
1829. "	1891
1829. "	1905
1836. "	6710
1846. "	7311
1872. "	3921
1818. Johnson L.	1355
1680. Jonathan,	18
1697. "	24
1712. "	62
1729. "	71
1737. "	232

INDEX I. 147

1772.	"	5218	—— "	6924	1832.	"	1925
1771.	"	621	1843. "	1741	1833.	"	6702
1802.	"	5494	1807. Julia A.	1371	——	"	3862
1817.	"	917	1811. "	609	1845. Laura E.		1201
—— Joseph,		5000	1817. "	693	1835. Laura J.		1182
1699.	"	5007	1821. "	1400	1845. Laura S.		1824
1702.	"	5013	—— "	1551	1822. Lavina,		1423
1703.	"	42	1841. "	7117	1828. Lavinia A.		5859
1731.	"	5071	1845. "	9081	1844. Leander,		9131
——	"	5151	1828. Julia E.	2541	1870. Lee S.		3890
1745.	"	165	1841. "	7330	1823. Leicester,		996
1756.	"	5211	1828. Julia M.	996	1896. Lenox C.		4061
1773.	"	411	1844. "	2060	1827. Leonard,		8283
1777.	"	300	1809. Julia R.	5593	1809. Lester,		707
1790.	"	5521	1829. Julia S.	1630	1765. Levi,		5257
1792.	"	5623	1870. Julian,	3953	1800.	"	5763
1818.	"	1811	.1836. Juliette,	1442	1817.	"	5834
1834.	"	6433	1797. Julius,	602	1808. Levi C.		5766
1838.	"	2050	1823. "	1401	1827. Levi E.		2490
1842.	"	2005	1840. Julius A.	7231	1837.	"	7079
1828. Joseph A.		7113	1813. Julius H.	1393	1830. Levi R.		7150
1844. Joseph C.		1607	1757. Justin,	370	1754. Lewis,		223
—— Joseph D.		8181	1778. "	5336	1787.	"	594
1821. Joseph E.		1880	1780. "	555		"	5272
1832.	"	2370	1781. "	5391	1836.	"	8291
1838. Joseph L.		2112	—— . "	5401	1837.	".	2731
1817. Joseph M.		956	1790. "	882	1838.	"	7900
1818. Joseph S.		5733	1803. "	5960	1812. Lewis A.		1411
1827.	"	1861	1812. "	1254	1775. Liberty,		273
1828.	"	2540	1815. "	6166		"	1561
——	"	2554	1838. "	7684	1884. Lida A.		3925
1835. Josephine F.		1853	1806. Justin E.	5446	1879. Lillian A.		3930
1840. Josephine O.		2113	—— Justus,	101	1886. Lillie P.		3926
1775. Joshua,		5363	—— "	6202	1856. Lillie S.		1177
1809.	"	6067			1778. Linus,		580
1817.	"	6114	**K.**		1803.	"	870
1831.	"	7892	1874. Katherine,	3954	1744. Lois,		5063
1828. Joshua S.		2510	1813. Kellogg,	508	1759.	"	239
1846.	"	6663	1776. Kelsey,	566	1768.	"	5184
1701. Josiah,		31	1784. Keziah,	414	——	"	274
1826.	"	755			——	"	5545
1792 Jube C.		901	**L.**		1796.	"	5761
1814.	"	934	1838. LaMott,	7063	1808.	"	677
1833. Judson,		5575	1781. Laura,	171	1809.	"	690
1804. Judson H.		1370	1794. "	827	1847.	"	1134
1834. Judson R.		2363	1804. "	5720	1834. Lois A.		1433
1783. Julia,		313	1805. "	5785	1792. Lora,		861
1785.	"	5206	1806. "	5496	1811. Lora A.		1283
1801.	"	780	1819. "	1900	1816. Loren,		1285
1814.	"	6801	1822. "	6160	1845.	"	7332
1817.	"	728	1823. "	1012	1816. Lorenzo,		6010
1820.	"	777	—— . "	1221	1816. Lorenzo M.		7053
1822.	"	1035	1825. "	1813	1794. Loring P.		671
1832.	"	8285	1830. "	6370	—— Lorraine,		5964
1834.	"	7062	1831. "	1820	—— Louisa,		740
——	"	6331	1844. "	3230	——	"	1553
1842.	"	1592	1820. Laura A.	957	1820.	"	1910
1842.	"	8294	1826. "	7880	1822.	"	6118

1837.	"	7894	1780. Lucy E.	441	1787. Marcus,	314
1845. Louisa B.	1700	1786. "	443	1822. "	791
1825. Louisa J.	2364	1829. "	1042	1730. Margaret,	202
1810. Louisa M.	783	1848. Lucy W.	6631	1777. "	5085
1820. "	6794	1706. Luke,	52	1758. "	5253
1811. Louisa S.	6253	1761. "	5146	1789. "	5299
1876. Louise D.	3990	1763. "	560	1835. "	2571
1786. Lovina,	634	1764. "	561	—— "	5670
1833. "	1000	1779. "	567	1839. "	1721
1834. "	7083	1805. "	1271	—— "	5025
1844. "	2122	1840. "	8293	1890. "	3912
1752. Lovisa,	237	—— Luman,	1870	1843. Margaret F.	6733
1796. "	5753	1698. Lydia,	5010	1826. Margaret M.	6197
1848. Lucelia,	1760	1706. "	33	1908. Marjory M.	4141
1826. Lucetta,	5858	1732. "	111	1707. Maria,	5428
1742. Lucia,	5270	1744. "	5088	1804. "	606
1792. "	5751	1759. "	188	1839. "	1590
1794. "	5090	1767. "	5258	1848. "	2151
1826. "	7075	1769. "	564	1821. Maria E.	6611
1810. Lucinda,	750	—— "	5189	1825. Maria H.	7056
—— "	2362	1770. "	5185	1841. "	2132
1820. "	5835	1793. "	477	1803. Maria K.	950
1842. Lucinda E.	7353	—— "	5275	1794. Maria L.	5530
1798. Lucius,	921	1801. "	5775	1815. "	1394
1836. "	1937	1805. "	1280	1824. "	1533
1837. "	7010	1808. "	1291	1839. Mariette,	1163
1838. "	6818	1810. "	507	1793. Marinda,	902
1760. Lucretia,	480	1815. "	1010	—— "	1973
1787. "	823	—— "	853	—— "	5941
1808. "	5824	1817. "	753	1837. Marquis,	1938
1814. "	1800	1817. "	1115	—— Marshall,	5956
1846. "	7931	1817. "	5789	1729. Martha,	110
1842. Lucretia A.	3861	—— "	5963	1753. "	215
1737. Lucy,	211	1839. "	2433	—— "	275
1738. "	162	1844. "	1133	1761. "	543
1752. "	5105	1841. Lydia A.	1184	1786. "	5481
1756. "	5252	1839. Lydia C.	1605	1788. "	5426
—— "	361	1838. Lydia M.	2487	1802. "	675
1772. "	5186	1794. Lyman,	5760	1813. "	641
1773. "	5302	1806. "	706	1813. "	5732
1785. "	625	1808. "	1252	1814. "	927
—— "	5404	1811. "	983	1824. "	5725
1791. "	430	1812. "	5737	—— "	6335
1793. "	5771	1844. Lyman M.	7104	1837. "	1822
1794. "	406	1831. Lyman P.	7114	—— "	1972
1796. "	5491	—— Lysander,	5960	1847. "	7306
1803. "	829			—— Martha A.	3863
1805. "	1352	**M.**		1815. "	6235
1812. "	610	1887. Mable,	3911	1824. "	6119
—— "	6922	1752. Mahala,	185	1842. "	8431
1822. "	5836	1757. "	187	1841. Martha C.	7752
1830. "	7060	1797. "	701	1842. Martha E.	1503
1833. "	2570	—— "	1158	1844. Martha M.	3202
1828. Lucy A.	1397	1799. Major,	6063	1833. Martha R.	2000
1828. "	7890	1809. Malvina S.	1372	1847. Martia,	1995
1836. "	1106	1901. Mara E.	4041	1777. Martin,	285
1837. "	2672	1838. Maranda J.	7101	1801. "	720
1834. Lucy C.	7300	1790. Marcia,	5750	1836. Martin N.	1661

INDEX I. 149

1802. Marvin,	5800	1814. "	6791	1840. Merrick E.	2700
— Mary,	4	1823. "	1040	1879. Mildred,	3940
1666, "	12	1823. "	2400	1889. Mildred L.	3902
— "	5003	1833. "	1602	1767. Mills,	249
1690. "	5011	1833. "	2251	1783. "	245
1703. "	32	1837. "	6390	— "	5544
1706. "	43	1840. "	8182	1813. "	363
1711. "	35	1843. "	1200	1848. Milo E.	2141
— "	102	1843. "	1780	1886. Milo F.	3972
1726. "	141	1844. "	1690	1732. Milton,	1617
1726. "	200	1844. "	6562	— Minerva,	5408
1736. "	5133	1844. "	8810	1802. "	6064
1738. "	5074	1845. "	1512	— "	6110
1739. "	233	1846. "	6630	1836. "	7862
1744. "	229	1848. "	1595	1845. Minerva L.	2674
1744. "	5111	1826. Mary F.	656	1773. Minoris,	5281
1746. "	150	1845. "	2123	— "	5287
1759. "	5232	1811. Mary H.	5594	1804. Mirandis,	5700
1765. "	5216	1841. Mary J.	7154	1718. Miriam,	57
1772. "	193	1842. "	7885	— "	86
— "	302	1831. Mary L.	1104	— M. Lauren,	6751
1774. "	347	1842. "	6643	1819. Morris,	961
1774. "	5420	1846. "	1581	1810. Mortimer L.	1392
1780. "	5662	1847. "	7441	1732. Moses,	120
1789. "	5745	1906. "	4082	1763. "	280
1798. "	673	1814. Mary M.	7052	1802. "	704
1801. "	713	1841. "	7751	1826. Moses L.	6620
1805. "	1321	1804. Mary O.	5627	1783. Mun,	502
1806. "	1074	1829. Mary R.	5616	1790. Murray,	323
— "	5553	1842. "	2140	1832. Myron,	6371
1814. "	6089	1805. Mary S.	5504	1834. "	1541
1816. "	6415	1811. "	5570		
1818. "	6416	1814. "	522	**N.**	
1821. "	1257	1821. "	1120	1754. Nancy,	238
1823. "	645	1836. "	2560	— "	304
— "	1220	1839. Mary W.	8041	1787. "	5207
1835. "	7301	1792. Matilda,	5288	— "	5317
1836. "	1991	1836. "	8040	1797. "	5440
1836. "	6372	1844. "	8036	1802. "	1073
— "	6826	1803. Mattoon,	905	1839. Nancy A.	2680
1838. "	6854	1862. Maude,	3870	1806. Nancy B.	5791
— "	6912	1908. Maude L.	4045	1843. Nancy H.	7170
1841. "	1939	1850. May E.	1196	1846. Nancy L.	9030
— "	6592	— Maynard,	5004	1747. Naomi,	214
1847. "	6290	— Mehitable,	5034	1908. Natalie,	4064
1847. "	7980	1808. Melancthon,	6065	1701. Nathan,	26
— "	6755	1833. Mellville A.	1405	1822. "	1613
1848. "	1505	1703. Mercy,	51	1715. Nathaniel,	5033
1746. Mary A.	130	1710. "	61	1737. "	40
1807. "	6251	— "	85	1762. "	373
1811. "	5767	1735. "	231	1769. "	5461
1827. "	6700	1738. "	148	1786. "	880
— "	6180	1760. "	552	1825. "	8282
1843. "	7088	1776. "	554	1745. Nehemiah,	5102
1844. "	1641	1783. "	624	1772. "	5353
1825. Mary C.	2481	1785. "	427	1808. Nelson.	5604
1841. "	1185	1701. "	627	1831. "	7081
1813. Mary E.	727	1801. Mercy M.	5487	— "	7271

1826.	Nelson C.	7112	1792.	"	324	1803.	"	1381
1823.	Nelson L.	2363	1795.	"	5473	1808.	"	608
1812.	Newberry,	874	——	"	5962	——	"	5680
1778.	Newell,	311	1808.	"	5982	——	"	5700
1814.	"	774	1821.	Pamela V.	1921	1831.	Ralph B.	1440
1806.	Newton,	830	1802.	Parma,	923	1825.	Ralph R.	1051
1839.	Nicholas W.	8440	1805.	Pattison,	871	1828.	"	1053
1740.	Noah,	5061	1770.	Patty,	402	1713.	Rebecca,	46
1766.	"	5183	1832.	Paullona,	5877	1761.	"	226
1816.	Noah D.	1326	1816.	Persis,	6810	1829.	Rexy A.	7040
1783.	Noah H.	582	1824.	"	6805	1756.	Rhoda,	5212
1779.	Noble,	243	1839.	"	6540	1759.	"	340
1782.	"	576	1789.	Phebe,	429	1774.	"	5334
1795.	Norman,	628	1789.	"	5471	1794.	"	500
1803.	"	1090	1816.	"	5871	1790.	"	896
1803.	"	504	1847.	"	7323	1830.	"	1915
1821.	"	962	1834.	Phebe C.	1016	1799.	Rhoda M.	502
1830.	"	8031	1832.	Phebe M.	1916	1762.	Richard,	481
1909.	Norman C.	4142	——	Phelps,	1263	——	"	682
——	Norris,	6150	1819.	Philetus,	5873	1904.	Richard F.	4063
			1838.	Philemon R.	1731	1833.	Richard W.	1181
	O.		1847.	Philena,	3231	1824.	Richmond L.	6796
1796.	Obed,	5485	1779.	Philo,	5204	1751.	Robert,	184
1790.	Octavius,	900	1811.	"	773	1764.	"	357
——	"	1970	1812.	"	5610	1785.	"	473
1807.	Oel,	5715	1816.	"	775	1794.	"	711
1814.	Olive,	6022	——	Philura,	6200	1800.	"	863
1844.	"	7321	——	Pierrepont,	5910	1800.	"	904
1844.	"	1770	1782.	Plin,	5338	——	"	1323
1821.	Olive L.	876	1806.	"	5981	1805.	"	5602
1841.	Olive M.	7087	1806.	Plin B.	6000	1828.	"	1862
——	Oliver,	100	1789.	Pliny,	5482	——	"	1971
1761.	"	5109	1749.	Polly,	192	1828.	Robert E.	8030
1783.	"	5266	——	"	380	1845.	"	1710
——	"	5402	——	"	5304	1826.	Robert H.	6671
——	"	6206	1789.	"	5341	1842.	Robert I.	1175
1826.	Olivia,	646	1799.	"	702	1833.	Robert J.	1044
1846.	"	1959	1800.	"	703	1840.	Robert N.	1855
1791.	Oreda,	883	1803.	"	5503	——	Roderic,	5286
1734.	Orpha,	112	1799.	Polly M.	5693	1764.	"	374
——	"	1153	1845.	"	7913	1817.	"	6167
1807.	Orril,	5802	1800.	Polly P.	380	1825.	"	6170
1829.	"	7221	1795.	Porter,	6061	1801.	Rodman G.	5600
1776.	Orrin,	5203	1844.	Prosper R.	2114	1783.	Rodney,	472
——	"	5542	——	Prudence,	5550	1787.	"	1260
1821.	"	5564				1792.	"	892
1822.	"	1911		**Q.**		1826.	Rodney E.	1912
1845.	"	6662	1800.	Quartus,	922	1838.	Roger S.	1502
1844.	Oscar,	1031	1852.	Quincy Dorr,		1842.	"	1740
1827.	"	1932			1213	1843.	Roland G.	1452
1838.	"	1191				1817.	Rollin,	800
1843.	"	7331		**R.**		1812.	Rosanna,	6320
1848.	Osmand A.	7873	1745.	Rachel,	5077	——	Rosina,	5316
1839.	Ozro E.	6560	1761.	"	5255	1752.	Roswell,	222
			1782.	"	5741	1781.	"	424
	P.		1785.	"	5368	1784.	"	5339
1772.	Pamela,	5202	——	"	5236	1804.	"	980
1789.	"	890	1783.	Ralph,	5424	1818.	Roswell M.	1395

INDEX I. 151

1774.	Rowena,	5262	1810.	Samuel D.	725	1814.	Sarah C.	650
1779.	Rowland,	480	1798.	Samuel E.	447	1885.	"	8180
1831.	Rowland H.	1043	1837.	"	1856	1796.	Sarah D.	1070
	Roxanna,	271	1840.	"	1061	1843.	Sarah E.	1232
1780.	"	575	1827.	Samuel F.	1041	1817.	Sarah G.	5613
1791.	"	5770	1826.	"	6024	1830.	Sarah H.	842
1797.	Royal,	5773	1783.	Samuel H.	5510	1835.	"	7750
1829.	Royal N.	7142	1813.	"	692	1824.	Sarah J.	1614
	Ruby,	5400	1840.	Samuel J.	6711	1829.	"	5574
	Russel,	5092	1798.	Samuel M.	325	1831.	"	8190
1756.	"	5093	1807.	Samuel S.	5592	1840.	"	3220
1789.	"	5208	1835.	Sandford,	7084	1845.	"	1867
1789.	"	1261		Sarah,	3	1847.	Sarah L.	6644
1791.	"	5294	1664.	"	11	1800.	Sarah M.	604
1791.	"	5311	1686.	"	5005	1810.	"	6164
1799.	"	5774	1691.	"	22	1832.	"	8032
1813.	"	5832	1708.	"	44	1835.	"	7870
1829.	Russel J.	5894	1709.	"	53	1843.	"	1445
1839.	Russel M.	7153	1720.	"	84	1835.	Sarah P.	6808
1725	Ruth,	199	1731.	"	5131	1820.	Sarah T.	6240
1781.	"	312	1736.	"	147	1791.	Sebra,	596
1804.	"	781	1742.	"	5062	1794.	"	597
1807.	"	872	1742.	"	234	1826.	Sebra W.	1013
			1742.	"	75	1788.	Selah,	5369
	S.		1748.	"	220	1795.	Selden,	5780
1803.	Sabrina,	897	1755.	"	5251	1815.	"	1284
1819.	"	7072	1759.	"	5108	1785.	Seth,	593
1809.	Saburna,	5976	1760.	"	5180	1823.	Seth R.	1922
1797.	Sally,	5970		"	5322	1897.	Seward P.	3916
1813.	Sally L.	5794	1770.	"	345	1800.	Sharly G.	5716
1809.	Sally S.	5792	1771.	"	5332	1806.	Sherman,	640
	"	1839		"	5406	1808.	Sherubiah,	6001
	Salmon,	5326	1778.	"	422	1838.	"	7740
	"	5957	1778.	"	451		Sidney,	381
1809.	Samantha,	873	1778.	"	474		Silas,	5403
1671.	Samuel,	14	1780.	"	631	1812.	Silas B.	6800
1698.	"	30	1781.	"	244	1728.	Silence,	80
1704.	"	27	1782.	"	425	1736,	" .	161
1720.	"	5040	1784.	"	5511	1787.	"	851
	"	82	1789.	"	5744	1799.	"	910
	"	105	1799.	"	5820	1738.	Simeon,	5140
1743.	"	115	1802.	"	887	1758.	"	5144
	"	5150	1815.	"	1114	1785.	"	5470
1753.	"	5230	1815.	"	6414		"	6332
1764.	"	270	1817.	"	1011	1759.	Simon,	216
1774.	"	5462	1823.	"	667	1768.	"	563
	"	5650	1820.	"	8284	1769.	Sodema,	5201
1808.	"	913	1837.	"	1130		Solomon,	5234
1809.	"	6002	1843.	"	7305	1776.	"	421
1809.	"	6410	1806.	Sarah A.	728	1780.	"	423
1810.	"	6306	1811.	"	954	1790.	"	595
1813.	"	7082	1818.	"	6340		"	5653
1818.	"	6011	1820.	"	694	1824.	Solon T.	1375
	"	6310	1821.	"	7055		Sophia,	5190
1845.	"	1672	1830.	"	1650	1771.	"	571
1845.	"	1994	1839.	"	1992	1784.	"	821
1834.	Samuel C.	1618	1823.	Sarah B.	2600		"	5318
1838.	"	8292	1842.	"	2701	1787.	"	822

1791.	"	5342	1827.	"	1950	**V.**		
	"	5423	1842.	Sylvia S.	1732	1845.	Virginia A.	7361
1796.	"	894				1837.	Virginia P.	1680
	"	1264	**T.**			1809.	Volney,	1340
1807.	"	931	1737.	Tabitha,	113	1821.	"	5874
1816.	"	7034	1774.	Talitha,	5219			
1820.	"	790	1796.	"	5623	**W.**		
	"	5950	1727.	Tamar,	70			
1834.	Sophia A.	1171	1798.	Temperance,	5754	1834.	Wallis,	7223
1816.	Sophia D.	5085	1822.	"	7074	1793.	Walter,	6060
	Sophia E.	517	1822.	Thaddeus,	1933	1912.	Walter B.	4003
1838.	Sophia H.	6650	1815.	Thaddeus D.	1081	1835.	Walter De F.	
1802.	Sophronia,	5783	1711.	Thankful,	54			6660
1804.	"	924	1721.	"	49	1790.	Wareham,	315
1825.	Sophronia M.	2401	1740.	"	5142	1787.	Warren,	5310
1837.	"	1017	1751.	"	151	1796.	"	5781
1846.	Sparrow W.	6281	1756.	"	224	1840.	"	7440
1788.	Spaulding,	5661	1761.	"	341		"	5932
1792.	Spencer,	5472	1823.	Theodosia E.	2480	1848.	Warren E.	8370
1820.	"	1612		Thomas,	1	1826.	Warren H.	6840
1792.	Squire,	636	1662.	"	10	1834.	Warren W.	2430
1765.	Standish,	5235		"	5002	1806.	Wealthy,	6304
1799.	"	5711	1689.	"	21	1818.	"	5563
1792.	Stanley,	316	1699.	"	5030	1841.	"	6541
1829.	"	704	1708.	"	34	1824.	Wealthy F.	963
1846.	Stephen,	5064	1728.	"	5130	1827.	"	1615
1766.	"	562	1769.	"	5148	1826.	Wealthy M.	1357
1815.	"	5612	1772.	"	572	1826.	Wheaton,	6427
1808.	Stephen B.	5629	1777.	"	242	1810.	Wheeler,	1292
1843.	"	2574	1816.	"	664	1838.	Wilbur F.	6346
1812.	Stephen M.	7051		"	6212	1817.	Willard,	993
1777.	Stephen O.	5390	1824.	"	792		Willet,	5555
1806	"	6162	1830.	"	2511	1692.	William,	5006
1843.	"	8042	1834.	Thomas B.	2512	1715.	"	47
1743.	Submit,	207	1820.	Thomas D.	524		"	5042
1745.	"	208	1837.	Thomas F.	7883	1730.	"	190
1806.	Sullivan,	940	1825.	Thomas H.	6670	1748.	"	131
1820.	Sullivan M.	936	1799.	Thomas L.	5500	1764.	"	482
1842.	Sumner B.	1164	1817.	Thomas M.	652	1780.	"	490
1809.	Sumner W.	4000	1751.	Thomas S.	132	1784.	"	301
	Susan,	491	1805.	"	770	1784.	"	5480
1834.	"	6720	1805.	"	1290	1786.	"	5512
1839.	"	6373	1814.	"	6420	1787.	"	197
1840.	Susan A.	6855	1822.	Thompson H.			"	1152
1843.	Susan F.	1856			6257	1796.	"	501
1755.	Susanna,	5210	1714.	Timothy,	55	1800.	"	326
1756.	"	135	1720.	"	58	1801.	"	1157
1791.	"	5746	1750.	"	221	1804.	"	5584
1798.	"	5624	1791	"	585	1809.	"	5505
1824.	Sybil,	997	1753.	Tryphena,	351	1809.	"	5850
1770.	Sylvester,	5238	1788.	"	635		"	6150
1779.	"	413		"	875	1810.	"	6411
1807.	"	041	1817.	"	1832	1814.	"	523
1810.	"	1253				1819.	"	2360
1813.	"	5718	**U.**					6220
	"	6920				1824.	"	8281
	Sylvia,	5407	1810.	Urial,	5851	1827.	"	793
	"	5952	1821.	Ursula A.	2361	1840.	"	8430

INDEX I. 153

1848.	"	7362	1840.	"	8035	1834.	"	6380
1806.	William A.	6232	1841.	"	2500	1840.	"	7901
1835.	"	1161	1842.	"	6374	— Winston,		272
—	"	8200	1844.	"	1593	**Z.**		
1911.	"	4010	1845.	"	7121			
1831.	William B.	999	— William I.		7940	— Zachariah,		5381
1812.	William C.	5852	1748. William J.		191	1757. Zebulon,		170
1825.	"	1923	1834. William L.		2371	1769.	"	401
1819.	William F.	6256	1846. William P.		2007	1787.	"	428
1821.	"	1100	1848.	"	2070	1820. Zebediah D.		6812
1837.	"	1060	1831. William S.		6640	1791. Zelotus,		5483
1812.	William H.	1020	1863.	"	3871	1825.	"	6343
1814.	"	955	1812. William T.		726	1757. Zervia,		353
—	"	6334	1803. William W.		5972	1863.	"	356
1817.	"	6350	1816.	"	6090	1802. Zilpha,		912
1840.	"	2573	1825.	"	7850			

INDEX II

NAMES OF THOSE WHO HAVE MARRIED INTO THE FAMILY.

[Look *generally* for the names of *females*, as *parents*. The names of *males* will be found under the head of *children*.]

Abbey.
— Sarah C. 2352

Ackley.
— Sarah, 5100

Adams.
1771. Azuba. 165
— David, 81
1825. Eliza, 5621

Aikin.
1836. Nancy J. 447
— Samuel C. 5582
—   "   5583

Albright.
1843. Mary, 1240

Allard.
1825. Hiram, 5775
1833. Isaac, 5777

Allen.
1842. Elizabeth W.
  5584
— James, 1257
1882. Asa A. 3950
. Harold
  Alfred
  Richard
  Arthur
  Edgar
  Donald
  Dorothy
  Hugh
  Eleanor
1910. Maude, 3890

Alvord.
1830. Jerusha, 5981
1784. Samuel, 541
1787. "   851
—   "   5842
1792. Thirza, 5353

Ameaman.
— Jane, 691

Anderson.
1846. James, 7141

Andrews.
1843. Calvin, 935

Andrus.
— Elizabeth, 5056

Armitage.
1836. Sarah E. 520

Arnold.
1829. William E. 5824

Ashley.
— Aaron, 44
1830. Daniel, 607
— Hannah, 5040
1825. James, 51
1789. Joseph, 551
1799. Moses, 550
1827. Norman, 1821

Atchinson.
1776. Lucy, 222

Atkins.
1844. Almira, 780
1802. Phebe, 359

Atwater.
1817. Eliza, 5483
— Joshua, 5594
— Lucy, 5200

Austin.
1835. Ann E. 506
1846. Camilla, 510
1840. James, 511
  Arthur
1903. Jessie S. 3955

Avery.
— Miles, 6416

Ayer.
1876. Latham H. 1200
  Ernest
  Latham
  Faith

Babcock.
1833. Allen, 1250
1834. Mabel, 1253

Bacon.
1866. Henry C. 1183
  Julia
  Louis
  Laura

Bagg.
1724. Abigail, 40
1826. Justus, 604
1806. Lovisa, 472

1783. Oliver, 351
1787. Sophia, 562

Baillie.
1834. Annie, 5442

Baker.
1816. Clarissa, 5780

Baldwin.
— Abel, 5186
1819. Chauncey, 5762
1821. Joel, 5746

Bancroft.
— Willey, 673

Barnes.
1827. Celestia, 6084
1886. J. Alton, 1177
  Ralph E.
1722. Sarah, 21

Barrett.
1874. Fannie M. 1213
1817. Stephen, 5761

Bartlett.
1841. Elizabeth, 6067

Bates.
1842. Ann S. 705

Beach.
1819. Moses Y. 1073
1800. Sarah, 501

Beardsley.
1848. Caroline V. 5857
1824. Salome, 5786

Bedortha.
1808. Eunice, 350
1796. Jonathan, 546
1750. Joseph, 111

Beebe.
1763. Asa, 5088
—   5087
— Asa, 5322
— Dudley, 5319
1828. Ezra H. 5755
— Lucinda, 5323
. Paphyrus, 5404

Bellowes.
— Mary, 5712

Benton.
— Ozias, 5251

INDEX II.

Zadoc, 5258
Benjamin.
1832. Elizabeth, 6230
Bestar.
1801. Nancy, 5261
Bigelow.
1729. David, 5015
— James, 5182
Bingham.
— Flavel W. 5586
Birge.
1757. Experience, 5033
Blackman.
1825. Daniel, 5785
Blaisdell.
1847. Mary F. 1860
Bliss.
— Caleb, 56
1731. Elizabeth, 31
1775. Eunice, 123
1817. Gad, 290
1732. Hannah, 62
1847. Isaac G. 754
Booth.
— — 856
Bostwick.
— — 5311
Botsford.
— Benjamin, 5187
Bowler.
— Clara L. 3960
Boyden.
1848. John, 1050
Bracket.
1800. Patty, 5336
Bradley.
1791. Jacob, 403
Brainard.
1826. Ansel, 5820
1834. Clarissa, 5629
— John, 5822
— Stephen, 5077
1754. Susanna, 5073
— Sylvia, 5825
1792. William, 5105
Brewster.
— — 5462
Briggs.
— Abby, 1254
Brinsmade.
1845. James E. 6810
Brisbane.
— Nancy, 1393
Brockway.
1843. Harriet, 5872
Brooks.
1794. Anna, 5361

Brower.
1835. Angelica, 725
Brown.
— John P. 521
1870. Mary E. 1174
1910. Marie L. 3910
Buel.
1829. David C. 5627
1833. Elizabeth J. 5628
— Hiram, 6180
Bulkley.
1801. Abigail, 5422
1846. Annie W. 1621
1798. Gershom, 5420
1761. Joshua, 5063
Bullard.
— John, 5143
Bullen.
1867. Henry L. 1201
Laura D.
Henry W.
Bunnell.
1829. Salmon, 990
1904. Frank S. 3954
Richard D.
Catherine S.
Burchard.
1842. Caroline, 1612
Burrell.
1832. Augusta, 501
1858. Arora J. 1210
Rose D.
Royal O.
Burt.
1839. Adelia, 715
1683. John, 11
1845. Mary S. 1833
1709. Mercy, 18
Bush.
— Hezekiah, 721
— Milton, 1159
Butts.
1805. Deborah, 5338
1802. Hannah, 5337
— Mason, 1831
Cadwell.
1764. Ebenezer, 113
Cady.
1807. Clara, 5366
— Joseph, 1328
Calkins.
1812. John, 5751
1815. Lydia, 5752
Camp.
1838. Mary G. 5991
1835. Sophia A. 5590
Campbell.
1816. Levi, 5745

1814. William, 5744
Card.
1833. Lorinda, 1392
1910. Osmon, 3911
Everett D.
Carew.
1793. Polly, 280
Carrier.
1795. Ebenezer, 5283
1789. Joseph, 5184
Casey.
— Dennis, 5613
Carter.
— Asa, 5764
1842. Emily, 5731
1833. Hiram, 1243
1820. Isaac, 556
1872. Mary, 1165
— William, 741
Chambers.
1878. Annie L. 1176
Chamberlin.
1792. Abiah, 5257
— Benjamin, 5252
1772. Elizabeth, 5089
— John, 84
1808. Nancy, 5293
Chandler.
— Orrin, 5427
Chapin.
1813. Charles, 5335
1797. Climena, 553
1788. Esther, 372
1792. George, 548
1819. Harriet, 712
1826. Harriet, 1271
1831. John M. 5082
1775. Mercy, 235
1758. Rhoda, 142
1804. William, 625
Chapman.
— Anna, 5093
Chase.
1838. Cyrene, 5661
1894. Ida O. 3915
1822. Luther, 5783
— Sarah, 1270
Childs.
1788. Asenath, 371
Christianson.
1906. Clare D. 3982
Church.
1835. Harvey, 1300
Clapp.
— Alonzo, 6111
— — 5232
1831. Nathan, 931

Clark.
— Catharine, 5821
— Josiah, 5316
1823. Love, 5773
— Mariba, 460
1831. Mary, 593
— Silas, 5317
1841. Stacy B. 790
1838. Susan L. 1370
— Thankful, 272
1690. William, 5003
Clemans.
1835. Frances, 706
Clesson.
1737. Thankful, 5033
Cloud.
— S. G. 532
Cobb.
1836. George W. 6791
Coburn.
1775. Seth S. 122
Coffin.
1838. Winnifred G. 611
Colton.
1809. Rufus, 823
Conkling.
1904. Eleanor C. 3970
Cook.
— Charles, 953
1815. Chloe, 595
— Samuel, 5511
Cooley.
1786. Alexander, 564
1802. Elizabeth, 462
1843. Harrison, 786
— John, 164
1830. Sherman, 991
Cooper.
1826. James, 5975
1659. Sarah, 1
Corbit.
— — 912
Corey.
1825. Jane E. 5486
Cother.
— Susanna, 191
Cowles.
1903. Ida L. 3900
1815. Chloe, 5482
Crandall.
1822. Amos, 5772
Cripe.
1905. Eva, 3923
Crosby.
1834. Archibald, 915
Cross.
1844. Esther, 6116
1827. Luther, 5693

Curtis.
— Gideon, 5274
— Sally, 197
Cushman.
1842. Marcia H. 5778
1842. Nelson, 7140
Cutler.
1808. Hannah, 426
Damon.
1841. Lyman, 916
De Forest.
1833. Catharine H. 5592
Dennison.
1906. Clara, 3993
Deming.
1810. Peny, 594
Dewey.
1792. Laura, 195
1776. Mercy, 52
1814. Persis, 5663
1802. Polly, 576
Disbrow.
1875. Hiram A. 1163
Greta
Ruth
Albert
Louise
Doty.
1804. Amelia, 310
Downs.
1808. David, 75
Drake.
1829. Maria, 603
1847. Mary Ann 605
Dumbleton.
1697. Mary, 14
Duncan.
1762. Elizabeth, 121
Dunham.
1827. Eliza, 5800
Durand.
1867. Cyrus Y. 1194
G. Harrison
E. Dana
Walter Y.
Albert C.
Alice May
Dutton.
1817. George, 1070
Dwight.
1820. Frances, 475
1791. Henry, 188
1722. Sarah, 182
Dyer.
— — 5880
Eastman.
— Benjamin, 146

Edwards.
1842. Cleora, 5666
Ellsworth.
1825. Benjamin, 1154
Ensign.
1837. Sally J. 5974
Ely.
1810. Anne, 292
1790. Asenath, 358
1828. Aurelia, 1090
— Chloe, 824
1788. David, 570
1813. John D. 406
1749. Joseph, 141
1808. Jube, 361
1837. Lois, 186
1825. Lucius, 828
1804. Lucy, 592
1794. Mary, 450
1787. Moses, 343
1825. Moses, 427
1811. Nancy, 440
— Oliver, 402
1791. Polly, 282
1828. Russel, 829
1759. Samuel, 162
1796. Solomon, 574
1799. Solomon, 575
— Theodosia, 565
Fairfield.
— Joseph, 5142
Farnam.
1783. Elisha, 224
1824. Jeduthan, 1380
1836. John F. 7052
1820. Mary, 467
— Polly, 286
Fasset.
1810. Sarah, 5661
Faxon.
— Daniel, 5428
Fellowes.
1814. Eldula, 5339
Felton.
1849. Silas, 1813
Fenwick.
— Mary J. 5983
Fergeson.
— J. G. 5314
Ferguson.
1781. Mary, 133
Field.
1739. Amos, 5034
1829. Harriet, 5585
Fitch.
1860. Henry M. 1184
Willard
Laura E.

Foot.
1740. Anna, 5019
1740. Irene, 5018
1729. Margaret, 5014
Foster
1825. Cyrus, 781
1844. Emily L. 5805
— Harriet, 5573
Fox.
1757. John, 231
Franklin.
1844. Jonathan F. 6418
Freeman.
1819. Cynthia, 5665
1884. Sidney, 1177
Frink.
1817. Ruba, 413
Frost.
1845. Norton, 5870
Fuller.
1878. Linda, 1192
1896. Mabel A. 3981
Gale.
—. Augusta, 5713
Gates.
1838. Ursula M. 6163
Gaylord.
1762. Catharine, 203
1826. Margaret, 468
1770. Nathaniel, 214
Gardiner.
1800. Emma E. 5204
1810. Harriet, 5208
Geldmacher.
1911. Silver H. 3942
Gilbert.
1813. Ashley, 5201
1834. Lucy A. 770
Gillett.
1833. Catharine, 726
1750. Jonathan, 70
1808. Linus, 584
Gilson.
1826. Abel, 910
Goddard.
— Hilpah, 424
Goff.
1847. Emily H. 5712
1786. Phebe, 5144
Goldthwait.
1819. Ebenezer S. 6064
Goodrich.
— Alfred, 861
Goodyear.
1824. Lois, 602
Goss.
1829. Caroline, 707

Gould.
1813. Eleanor, 5310
Granger.
1788. Abi, 183
Graves.
— Milliscent, 5188
Gray.
1837. Eliza, 5562
Green.
— —— 5471
Griffith.
1820. Mary Ann, 5521
Groesbeck.
— Nicholas, 430
Gunn.
— Charles, 927
Guy.
— Johanna, 6081
Hale.
1778. Eunice, 221
Hall.
1824. Abigail, 5666
— Lyman, 5205
— —— 48
— Martha, 5472
1802. Mary B. 5203
Hamlin.
1803. Jerusha, 566
Hancock.
1908. Ethel B. 3941
— Moses, 5953
Hanford.
1839. Julia B. 5978
Hart.
— Almira, 314
1840. Sarah E. 800
1843. Sarah J. 729
Harton.
— John, 5547
Haskell.
1839. Emily, 6000
Hastings.
1911. Ada Elizabeth, 3962
Haswell.
— Oliver P. 5614
Hawes.
1814. Solomon, 5771
Herroun.
— —— 5650
Higby.
— Minerva, 1410
Hildreth.
1844. Abel F. 6005
1818. Milliscent, 5524
Hills.
— Mercy, 820

Hillyer.
1834. Clarissa, 6002
Hinman.
1811. Hannah, 196
1802. Hannah, 500
Hitchcock.
1812. Amanda, 442
1794. Bede, 227
1836. Emeline C. 5505
Hoadley.
— Lucretia, 315
Hoag.
1823. Cornelia W. 5600
1833. Eliza, 5602
1832. Mary, 5600
1840. Warren, 7054
Hodges.
1821. Betsey, 5971
Hogh.
1840. —— 801
Holyoke.
1658. Elizur, page 10
Holden.
1903. Bertha, 3902
Holmes.
1801. Daniel, 620
1816. Daniel, 627
1869. Lida A. 1173
Hooker.
1828. Julia, 5765
1835. Mary, 6166
Hopkins.
— Eunice, 5205
Horsford.
— Daniel, 5116
Horsley.
1825. John, 865
Horton.
1827. Mary H. 5972
Hoskins.
1843. John, 784
Hotchkiss.
1881. Amaranda, 5495
Hovey.
— Sarah, 273
Hubbard.
1830. Laura O. 5494
— Lavinia, 5294
Hubbell.
— Rhoda, 47
Humiston.
— —— 5473
Hungerford.
1833. Ansel, 6161
1729. Esther, 5013
1827. Rebecca E. 6160
Hunt.
1786. George, 484

INDEX II.   159

Huntington.
1837. Cinderilla, 5787
Hurlbert.
1784. Eleanor, 5144
Ingals.
1841. Mary L. 508
Ingersoll.
1844. Ebenezer L. 777
— Eunice, 47
Ingraham.
1748. Hannah, 31
1758. Martha, 201
Isham.
1774. Martha, 5112
Ives.
1795. Abraham, 360
— Lois, 131
Jackson.
1769. Irene, 5103
Jewell.
1844. James, 776
Jones.
1898. Asaph, 3891
— Ernest
   Sumner
   R. Orlando
1845. Brooksanna, 5564
1792. Catharine, 5181
1834. Charlotte P. 5626
— Ebenezer, 140
1805. Elizabeth, 248
1752. Isaac, 80
1787. Ithamar, 341
1754. Joel, 5085
1744. Mary, 59
1811. Olivia, 241
Johnson.
1878. David, 1212
1820. Dyer C. 5782
1833. Eliza L. 724
Johnston.
— John C. 5205
1902. Sarah E. 3980
Judd.
— Lydia, 355
— Salithan, 5360
— Simeon, 853
Kellogg.
1834. Brainard D. 6165
1776. Elisha, 5210
1775. Hannah, 5017
1889. Jared C. 6168
1791. John, 5216
1828. Jonathan D. 5403
— Samuel, 5531
Kelsey.
1762. Lydia, 212

Kelso.
1827. Joseph, 6110
Kelton.
— Caleb, 5253
Kendall.
1767. Hannah, 5101
1765. William, 148
Kent.
1743. Hannah, 15
Keyes.
1906. Daniel J. 3952
— Vincent D.
— Malcolm W.
— Charlotte E.
Kilborn.
1766. Dimmis, 5102
1761. Jonathan, 110
King.
1832. Elizabeth A. 640
— Eunice, 5236
1808. Eunice, 5740
1794. Hannah, 5260
1831. Susan, 5492
Kingsley.
1841. Henry C. 6610
Kinney.
1840. Kendrick K. 507
— Kellogg
— Myron
Kneeland.
1835. Edward, 873
1821. Lydia, 6060
Knowlton.
— Nathaniel, 5754
Know.
1867. Sue M. 1164
Lassals.
— Sally, 420
Laughlin.
1832. Polly, 1381
Laurence.
1846. Clarence, 6360
Layton.
1841. Jane, 6166
Lee.
1812. Marion, 5193
1800. Polly, 5188
Leet.
1828. Amanda M. 671
L'Hommedieu.
1839. George, 6417
Leonard.
1778. Abigail, 168
1817. Cyrus, 601
1814. John, 443
1814. John, 5362
1746. Jonathan, 60
1730. Josiah, 58

1771. Oliver, 167
— Polly, 152
— Reuben, 57
— Rowley, 860
— William, 6303
Leslie.
— James, 674
Lewis.
— Jane, 5548
Lincoln.
— Sophia, 692
Loomis.
1759. Ann, 5060
1817. Orrin, 600
1725. Sarah, 5012
1753. Sarah, 5082
Long.
1846. Jenette, 5827
Lord.
1849. Phebe L. 6003
Lyman.
1874. Helen S. 1186
1820. Horace, 5490
1788. Lois, 165
— Lucretia, 5581
Lyon.
1830. Barbara, 515
Mandeville.
1824. Maletha, 6063
Marble.
1836. Jane L. 661
Marcy.
1823. Samuel, 5600
Markham.
— Dorothy A. 1255
Marsh.
1714. Elizabeth, 5004
Marshall.
1461. Adah, 5140
Martin.
1821. Matilda, 593
Marvin.
1790. Anna, 5214
1802. Elizabeth, 5264
1817. Lucy, 2747
Mason.
— David, 151
1810. Peter, 597
Mather.
1810. Susanna, 5743
Mattoon.
— Elizabeth, 42
May.
— Esther, 420
1811. Samuel, 5464
Maynard.
— John, page 9
— Sarah, 2

INDEX II.

McCleave.
— Eunice, 5200
McClelland.
1880. Rev. Thomas, 1202
Harry
Kellogg D.
Cochran B.
Ruth M.
McGilfrey.
1841. Polly, 6091
McIntire.
1786. Lucretia, 482
McKean.
1832. Henrietta, 704
McKinstry.
— Henry, 5200
Mead.
— William F. 5704
Merrick.
1818. Daniel, 827
1685. Elizabeth, 10
1687. John, 12
— Lois 115
Mershom.
1834. John, 5871
Miller.
1814. Aurelia, 822
— Henry, 928
1782. Hepziba C. 352
— — 5426
— — 6153
Mills.
— Sarah, 73
Moody.
1825. Julia, 5980
— Sylvester, 5334
Moore.
1730. John, 61
Morgan.
1785. Abigail 370
— Anna, 5290
1742. Eunice, 45
1757. Isaac, 211
— Julius, 410
1774. Justin, 215
1830. Laura, 830
1785. Miles, 33
1759. Nathan, 200
— Rachel, 50
1802. Sarah, 411
Morley.
1814. Silvanus G. 464
Morse.
1818. Henry, 1071
Morton.
1810. Joseph, 5481

Mott.
1848. Emily, 1880
Mun.
1747. Sarah, 58
Munro.
1842. Almira E. 801
Munsell.
1836. Guy C. 751
Munson.
1841. John S. 6704
1741. Sybil, 37
1831. William B. 6790
Murray.
1783. Martha, 5145
Narramore.
1824. Amos, 5487
Newcomb.
— Daniel, 5315
Newell.
— Charles, 5263
1774. Ruth, 132
Nichols.
1841. Minerva P. 785
— Ruth, 5463
Noble.
— Abiah, 5113
1848. Curtis, 5597
1793. Daniel A. 5420
1767. Johanna, 213
1801. Lydia, 555
1799. Polly, 285
1826. Reville, 894
Nogle.
1895. Sidney G. 3920
Augusta
Clair
Earl
Lennie
Vivian
Cecil
Kenneth
Norto
1881. Jennie M. 1166
Northam.
1784. Hannah, 5231
1722. Jonathan, 5011
1779. Samuel, 5108
Oaks.
1843. Amelia H. 769
Olmsted.
1776. Dorothy, 5106
Ormsby.
— Ira, 5970
Osborn.
1772. Abigail, 73
1817. Horace, 465
Otis.
1766. David, 5111

1873. Theron P. 1182
— Norman D.
Oldfield.
1910. Gertie A. 3980
Palmer.
1829. Frederick, 1092
Parker.
1836. Annis, 6088
— Jason, 271
1844. Jonathan, 7074
— Sarah, 270
Parkhurst.
1836. Mary, 5831
1794. Rachel, 5238
Parkman.
1837. Edward, 5976
Parmelee.
1818. Leonard, 603
Parsons.
— Elisha, 1832
— Eliza, 5484
Patterill.
1792. Esther, 374
Pease.
— Charity, 5150
— Flavius, 5284
Peck.
1832. Lucius B. 5732
— Peter, 5522
Pendleton.
1834. Lavira, 6066
1826. Miletus, 923
Pepoon.
— — 5080
Perkins.
1844. Eli, 7035
— Joseph, 1074
Peters.
— Joseph, 5189
Pettibone.
1841. Giles, 899
Philips.
1841. Emma, 5852
— Ira, 675
1801. Mary, 5192
1794. Prudence, 5146
1810. Sally, 5194
Pierce.
1788. Eunice, 5236
1785. Priscilla, 5235
Pierrepont.
1828. Flora, 5312
Pigg.
1898. Maggie, 3871
Pitt.
1796. Silence, 400
Pixley.
— — 302

1840.	John,	887		*Rogers.*		—	William S.	5662
1808.	Mary,	5512	1813.	Alice,	5520		*Sherman.*	
	Plummer.		1788.	Henry,	226	—	James,	5423
—	Jeremiah,	1824		*Root.*		1805.	Martha	241
	Pomeroy.		1831.	Ezekiel,	5828		*Sickles.*	
—	— —	346	1800.	Henry,	198	1819.	Rachel,	5510
1823.	Adaline,	868	1830.	Julia A.	504		*Silstry.*	
1862.	Elizabeth C.	1162	1839.	Mary A.	5891	—	William,	5570
	Pond.		—	Phebe,	446		*Skinner.*	
—	Levi,	6304	1834.	William H.	505	1734.	Jerusha,	52
	Porter.			Orville		1762.	Joseph,	5110
1810.	Ezekiel,	554		William		—	Joseph,	6250
	Powers.			Walter		—	Louisa,	5430
—	James,	5207		*Rose.*		1842.	Sherman,	995
1817.	Mary,	5580	— —	Peter,	281	1843.	Sherman,	997
	Preston.			*Rugg.*		1848.	Thomas H.	1120
1820.	Maria,	5760	1832.	Heman,	5767	1810.	Warren A.	5620
	Pringle.			*Russel.*			*Smedley.*	
1848.	Lucy C.	6090	1790.	Eunice,	5259	1840.	Jane E.	5506
	Proctor.			*Sabin.*			*Smith.*	
—	Elisa,	1811	—	Darius,	5262	1755.	Aaron,	210
	Proser.			*Sackett.*		—	Anna,	5421
—	James,	850	1831.	Cornelia A.	503	1848.	Caroline,	1890
	Punderson.		1759.	Lucretia,	190	1833.	Catharine,	5830
—	Thomas,	5209	1835.	Mary A.	509	1859.	Catharine,	1181
	Putnam.			*Samson.*		—	Charles H.	5985
1842.	John P.	654	1842.	Edward,	6113	1841.	Charlotte,	5832
	Ramsdale.		1819.	Olive,	815	1788.	David,	189
—	Fidelia,	6112		*Sampson.*		—	David,	202
	Randall.		1834.	Harriet,	6001	—	John,	952
1799.	Jessie,	5465		*Sawyer.*		—	Justin,	5826
—	Polly,	423	—	—	5325	1810.	Lydia,	5200
	Ransom.			*Schuyler.*		1847.	Margaret,	6007
1766.	Dimmis,	5064	—	—	5273	1697.	Mary,	15
1835.	Eliza M.	5446		*Scott.*		1724.	Mary,	50
	Reed.		1837.	Achsah,	5806	— .	William,	6303
—	John,	1291		*Scoville.*			*Snow.*	
—	William,	1040	1835.	Mary A.	774	— —	Josiah,	6152
	Rhoades.			*Scranton.*		1796.	Lydia,	5259
1840.	William B.	6813	1830.	Maria M.	1390	1705.	Martha,	163
	Rice.			*Searl.*		1789.	Temperance,	5256
1814.	Roxanna,	293	1827.	Phirilla,	1320		*Spangenberg.*	
—	—	6234		*Searls.*		1843.	Hannah,	791
	Richardson.		—	Gaius,	284		*Spaulding.*	
1844.	Mary,	5893		*Seeley.*		1844.	Harriet A.	1020
	Richmond.		1846.	Samuel S.	666		*Spear.*	
1812.	Mary,	5660		*Seymour.*		—	David C.	1156
	Rider.		1827.	Catharine,	714		*Spears.*	
—	—	5834	1841.	Nathan P.	651	1820.	Mary,	444
	Rising.			*Sheldon.*			*Spencer.*	
1835.	Susan,	476	—	Lucy,	45	1842.	Cornelia F.	5592
	Roberts.			*Sheldon.*		1708.	Garrett,	5005
1822.	Chloe,	920	1835.	Erastus,	5622	1696.	Grace,	5001
1840.	Moseley G.	6425		*Shepard.*		1830.	Matilda,	782
	Robinson.		—	Charles,	445	1815.	Sarah,	710
1801.	Polly,	5239	1847.	Sarah,	802	1845.	Sarah S.	6163
				Shepherd.		—	—	5300
			—	Mather,	461			

INDEX II.

Sperry.
1833. Olive, 5851
Sprague.
1824. Merceline, 864
Stanley.
1745. Susanna, 37
Staples.
— John, 5212
Stanton.
1812. Joshua, 5770
Stebbins.
1828. Anna M. 5756
1724. Benjamin, 43
1733. Benjamin, 46
1754. Ebenezer, 230
— Edith, page 7
1728. Martha, 30
1785. Solomon, 187
1694. Thomas, 4
Steele
1868. George W. 1180
1861. Mary F. 1161
1786. Rhoda, 5151
1777. Tryphena, 236
Stevens.
1816. Nancy, 670
Stewart.
1807. Lucretia, 5340
Stewlock.
1832. Mary A. 1350
Stiles.
1839. Delina, 1282
1806. John, 544
Stillwell.
1803. Phebe, 567
Strong.
1792. Achsah, 5461
1798. Betsey, 5148
— Elihu, 5468
1816. Eliza, 5484
1831. Lorenzo K. 1831
— Oliver, 5143
— Ralph, 5190
Sturtevant.
1791. Deborah, 5235
Swan.
1845. Richard W. 6008
Swift.
1828. Ann, 5483
Taft.
1822. Abraham, 6086
1816. Asa, 6080
1837. Eliza, 6087
1834. Isaac, 6089
1822. John W. 6083
Taylor.
1897. Alice Edith, 3921

— Amos, 5341
1840. Charles M. 7072
1742. Eldad, 49
1754. Eldad, 204
1746. Joseph, 199
— Thomas, 466
Terry.
1843. N. H. 7110
Thacher.
1846. Thomas A. 644
Thayer.
— 484
Thomas.
— Erastus, 425
Thompson.
1815. Anna, 316
— Ann M. 1290
Thurston.
1909. Ida M. 3970
1829. Sally, 6231
Tilotson.
— Oliver, 780
Titus.
1833. Sophia, 5801
Toles.
1831. Indiana, 771
Topliff.
— Alfred, 713
Torrey.
1828. Elizabeth, 5667
1838. — 925
Tower.
1873. Emma M. 1211
Towns.
1838. Johanna, 1810
Townsend.
1883. Nettle, 1214
Tracy.
1826. William E. 5625
Treat.
— Lester H. 740
Trowbridge.
1840. Ezekiel H. 6340
Tucker.
1842. Amelia S. 6113
Tuttle.
1792. Lydia, 5330
1849. Sylvester, 6342
Vandercater.
— Elizabeth, 1203
Vanhorne.
1773. Anna, 183
Vinton.
— Ablathar, 5332
Waite.
1838. Charlotte, 5569
1812. Hannah, 852

Wakefield.
1840. Martha, 1390
Wallis.
— Matilda, 6065
Ward.
1782. Rebecca, 59
1778. Sebra, 223
Warriner
1703. Samuel, 19
Watson.
— Catharine, 5571
Webb.
1834. Adaline, 5977
Weller.
1827. Almira, 720
Wells.
1727. Mary, 21
1746. Mary, 101
West.
1846. Maranda M. 5448
1821. Warren. 5623
Wharton.
1902. Charles, 3930
Mildred D.
Edith M.
Irene E.
Wheeler.
1828. Rebecca, 5668
White.
1830. Daniel G. 478
— Eldad, 5331
1770. Elijah, 180
— Julius, 477
— Phinehas, 5994
1880. Sally, 5500
1801. Samuel, 342
Whitmore.
— Susanna, 5807
Whitney.
1822. Dexter, 6085
1847. L. D. 5856
Wickham.
1796. Elizabeth, 376
Willard.
1809. Daniel, 5741
1804. John, 5742
— Lucy, 5291
Willey.
1834. Mary P. 6162
Williams.
— Augustus, 5392
1780. Daniel, 5213
— Elijah, 5091
1840. Joseph S. 6423
1842. Sarah E. 5447
1771. Sybil, 5104
Williston.
1788. Israel, 571

INDEX II. 163

Wilson.
— Elizabeth, 5286
1696. Hannah, 5002
1832. Hiram, 903
— Orrin, 5794
Wolcott.
— Mehitable, 854
— William, 6307
Wood.
1770. Lucy, 73
Woodbridge.
1736. Timothy, 86

Woodford.
1837. George, 783
— Roger, 313
Woodruff.
1820. Ava, 895
1834. Lavilla, 772
Worthington.
1796. Anna, 5117
1830. John J. 6164
Wright.
1862. G. Frederick, 1160
Augusta
Etta M.

Fred B.
Helen M.
— Joel, 5318
— Nancy, 311
— Obed, 5750
Yeomans.
1774. Daniel, 5107
— Sophronia, 608
Young.
— Eunice, 5081
Younglove.
1840. M. C. 6611

www.ingramcontent.com/pod-product-compliance
Lightning Source LLC
Chambersburg PA
CBHW070551160426
43199CB00014B/2463